SOMERSET
with Bath and Bristol

Shirley Toulson, who now lives in Oxfordshire,
 .....g Mendip
and the Somerset landscape generally. This resulted
in two books: *The Moors of the South West: 1* and
 Her other topographical books
 nion Guide to Devon as well as
 in Wales, East Anglia, Derby-
 England and Scotland.
 cape and local history, her main
 folklore, mythology, poetry,
 novels. Before becoming a full-
 ked as an education journalist,
 ation from 1970 to 1974 and
 Times Education Supplement
 rdian.

Pimlico County History Guides
(General editor: Christopher Hibbert)

Already published:

Bedfordshire by Simon Houfe
Dorset by Richard Ollard
Norfolk by Tom Pocock
Suffolk by Miles Jebb
Sussex by Desmond Seward

Forthcoming:

Cambridgeshire by Ross Clark
Lincolnshire by Henry Thorold
Oxfordshire by John Steane

SOMERSET

with Bath and Bristol

───

SHIRLEY TOULSON

with a Foreword by Christopher Hibbert

A PIMLICO COUNTY HISTORY GUIDE

For Richard Raynsford
with grateful thanks for many Somerset walks

PIMLICO

An imprint of Random House
20 Vauxhall Bridge Road, London SW1V 2SA

Random House Australia (Pty) Ltd
20 Alfred Street, Milsons Point, Sydney
New South Wales 2061, Australia

Random House New Zealand Ltd
18 Poland Road, Glenfield
Auckland 10, New Zealand

Random House South Africa (Pty) Ltd
PO Box 337, Bergvlei, South Africa

Random House UK Ltd Reg. No. 954009

First published by Pimlico 1995

1 3 5 7 9 10 8 6 4 2

Papers used by Random House UK Limited are natural,
recyclable products made from wood grown in sustainable
forests. The manufacturing processes conform to the
environmental regulations of the country of origin

Typeset by Deltatype Ltd, Ellesmere Port, Cheshire
Printed and bound in Great Britain by
Mackays of Chatham plc, Chatham, Kent

ISBN 0-7126-9887-6

Contents

	Acknowledgements	*vii*
	Foreword by Christopher Hibbert	*ix*
	Introduction	1
I	From Stone to Iron	6
II	The Romans: Roads, Villas and Temples	29
III	Christ and Arthur	46
IV	The Saxons in Somerset	57
V	From the Conquest to the Reformation	72
VI	Tudor Somerset	90
VII	Wars and Rebellions	99
VIII	An Age of Reason and Romance, Squalor and Elegance	112
IX	Industry, Agriculture and Victorian Values	129
X	In Peace and War: 1900–1960	146
XI	The Nuclear Age	161
XII	Bath	171
XIII	Bristol	185
	Bibliography	201
	Index	205

Acknowledgements

It is sadly impossible to list all my many Somerset friends, who, wittingly or not, have made such valuable contributions to the making of this book; but I should like to mention those people whose help I sought in their professional capacities and who gave me such generous assistance: Mary Gruyspeardt and Ann Heely of the Abbey Barn Museum in Glastonbury; Dr R. Charles-Chillcott and Mrs P. Rowe of the Radstock and Midsomer Norton Museum Society; David Bromwich of the County Local History Library in Taunton, and Jane Swinard of Wells Public Library.

My thanks also go to the Field Studies Council and the staff at Nettlecombe Court for providing me with a base for my explorations of Exmoor and leading me to places which I might not have discovered for myself. I am also very grateful to Ronald Hutton, Roy Lewis, Richard Raynsford and John Steane who patiently read chapters of the book in draft form. Any errors which remain are, of course, entirely my responsibility.

Finally, I should like to record my gratitude for the memory of two writers on Somerset, whom I was particularly fortunate to have known: Kathleen Young, who adopted the county to which she was evacuated during the war, when she married a Charterhouse farmer; and Robin Atthill, native and historian of Mendip, with whom I was lucky enough to walk the hills and visit the churches.

Foreword

The author of the book on Bedfordshire in this series has drawn attention to the diversity of landscapes in that county. The claim of variety is well justified; but even more so is it in the case of Somerset. For here there is the sea coast along the Bristol Channel, the high lands of the Mendip Hills, stretching from the north-west to the south-east of the county above Shepton Mallet and the cathedral city of Wells, and of the Quantock Hills rising above Taunton then falling towards Bridgwater Bay. There is high ground on Exmoor, too, and on the Brendon Hills; there are combes and gorges, orchard-filled valleys, wet lands and lakes, flats and sandy beaches. In the north the stone is of that pale yellow colour which distinguishes the crescents and terraces by Bath's great architect, John Wood. From Doulting in the south-eastern foothills of the Mendips comes the silvery-grey stone of which so many buildings in and around Wells are constructed; in the west red sandstone is to be found; and in the Polden Hills between Bridgwater and Somerton the blue limestone known as lias.

Of such materials Somerset's fine medieval churches were built, the blue lias of the villages of West Pennard and Long Sutton contrasting with the red sandstone of Bishops Lydeard.

Most of the churches in Somerset and Avon are in the Perpendicular style, and either built or reconstructed in the fifteenth century. They can be found all over Somerset and Avon, from Dunster in the west to the equally charming village of Mells in the east, from Yatton in the north, where St Mary's is one of the most imposing of them all, to Martock in the south, where the tie-beam roof of the nave is one of the finest of its kind in England. Their towers are splendid, 'the great glory of the county', in the words of a West Country antiquarian, quoted by John Betjeman, who himself singled out for special praise four in the south not far from Taunton, all dedicated to St Mary: those of North Petherton, Huish Episcopi, Isle Abbots and Bishops Lydeard; one to the north in Avon between Bristol and Weston-super-Mare, that of All Saints, Wrington; and two south of the Mendip Hills, St Cuthbert, Wells and St John the Baptist, Glastonbury.

The church of St John the Baptist is largely Perpendicular but centuries before it was built there were other churches at Glastonbury and an immense and ancient abbey founded, according to the *Anglo-Saxon Chronicle*, by Ine, King of Wessex from 685; and long before that, as history merges into myth, Glastonbury had been a place of Christian pilgrimage, the focal point of what was to become Somerset, the disputed borderland between the Celts and the invaders from the continental shores. Here, it was said, St Patrick was buried, having returned from Ireland in his old age in order to die in his homeland; here, so tradition also had it, St Brigid came to live; here St Joseph of Arimathea, having brought to Glastonbury the chalice used at the Last Supper, built a primitive church of wood and wattle on what was then an island, the waters of the Bristol Channel having reached deep into the Somerset levels, covering great stretches with shallow tidal water. It was to this island, the Isle of Avalon, that the heroic early sixth-century cavalry leader, known as King Arthur, was borne for the healing of his grievous wound, after the fateful battle of Camlann against the Saxon invaders. And, twelve miles south-east of Glastonbury, in the heart of a quiet countryside, there rises suddenly and sharply five hundred feet above the little village of South Cadbury, a yellow limestone hill. It is a hollow hill, so old men who have lived all their lives in its shadow will still tell you; and if on St John's Eve you could find the golden gates that lead inside it, there you would discover King Arthur sitting in the middle of his court at Camelot.

Certainly at Cadbury Castle in recent years there have been discovered fragments of pottery similar to those unearthed at Tintagel in Cornwall – where King Arthur is supposed to have been born – and splinters of glass of a type imported from the continent in the sixth century as well as the outlines of a large feasting hall of the same date.

Disentangling the intertwined threads of legend and history, Shirley Toulson has provided a valuable introduction to this absorbing county. Throughout Somerset, as in Dorset, there are constant reminders and recurring echoes of a distant past; and she tells us about them with the assurance of one who has known the county and its neighbour, Avon, for many years. She takes trouble to write about the unexpected as well as the familiar, about medieval hillocks known as pillow mounds which were constructed for rabbits, a prized delicacy, to breed in their burrows and which can still be seen on Exmoor and Brean Down, and the terraces created by twelfth-century farmers on the hillsides at Westbury-sub-Mendip, as well as the numerous neolithic barrows between Weston-super-Mare and Frome and the mysterious circles of stones at Stanton Drew south of Bristol.

As we approach nearer to our own day buildings take shape and men and women become personalities. At the end of the twelfth century, masons start work on Wells Cathedral whose west façade, with its three hundred statues and sculptural details by local craftsmen, stands comparison with that of Reims. About the same time Cistercian monks begin to build Cleeve Abbey where a timber-roofed refectory is one of the finest of its kind. Three centuries later Bishop Oliver King, a man much given to listening to wizards and soothsayers, according to Sir John Harrington, who lived nearby at Kelston on the estate of his rich wife, decides to rebuild the Abbey Church at Bath after a dream in which a voice has commanded him, 'Let an Oliver establish the crown and a King restore the church.'

By the time of Oliver King's death, wealth created by the industries of Somerset had helped not only to reconstruct, restore and beautify many of its churches but also to create the first of those splendid houses which, after the Reformation, were to grace the country's landscape. Poundisford Park near Pitminster was set in the former deer park of Taunton

Castle. Combe Sydenham, in the Brendon Hills near Stogumber, standing on land once owned by Cleeve Abbey, was built in the 1580s and became the home of Elizabeth Sydenham, the wife of Sir Francis Drake. A decade later work began on the magnificent Montacute House, built of honey-coloured Ham Hill stone for Sir Edward Phelips, who was to become Speaker of the House of Commons; and, as Shirley Toulson says, 'No one who visits Montacute can forget the entrance to the Great Hall . . . the wall at the further end of the hall covered by a plaster frieze showing an early version of the practice of a Skimmity Ride, immortalised by Thomas Hardy . . . In this instance, the hen-pecked husband, who tried to sneak a little beer, is being paraded round the village by his dominant wife.'

Her book is full of stories of such Somerset and Avon people as well as of the counties' celebrated worthies. We read of a poor milkmaid forced to take refuge on a little island with mice and shrews and other wild creatures when the sea sweeps in all around the coast by Combwich; and of the old woman hanged as a witch at Wincanton after having been caught walking backwards round the parish church; and of the men held prisoner in Westonzoyland church after the massacre of the Duke of Monmouth's troops at Sedgemoor, some of them killed in trying to escape, some sent to work on the plantations of the West Indies, many sentenced to death by the notorious Judge Jeffreys who presided over his court in the Great Hall of Taunton Castle where the County Museum is now housed.

It was around the Castle at Taunton that one of Somerset's most celebrated sons, Robert Blake, defied the Royalist troops in the Civil War, protesting that he would rather eat his boots than surrender, cutting the thatch from the town's roofs to feed his hungry horses, and at last having the satisfaction of seeing his enemies retreat. John Pym, 'King Pym', the great Parliamentary statesman, was also a Somerset man, born at Brymore, near Blake's birthplace at Bridgwater.

A few miles east of Bridgwater stands the small village of Nether Stowey and it was in a cottage here that Samuel Taylor Coleridge came to live with his newly married wife, the sister of Robert Southey whom he had met at Bristol; here it was that he enjoyed the intimate friendship of William and Dorothy Wordsworth; and here, or at a farmhouse in the woods above Culbone, on the Exmoor-Devon border, that, when writing *Kubla Khan*, he was interrupted by the 'person on business from Porlock'.

Somerset has always had an attraction for poets from the time of Alexander Pope, who, on one of his visits to the county, had a man shoot down the 'sparry concretions' from the roof of a cave at Wookey Hole to adorn the grotto in the garden of his villa at Twickenham, to that of T.S. Eliot who claimed descent from the Eliots of East Coker, the scene of the second of his *Four Quartets*, where his ashes are buried in the parish church of St Michael. No poet, however, has caught the atmosphere of the Somerset landscape so well as Coleridge:

> Therefore all seasons shall be sweet to thee,
> Whether the summer clothe the general earth
> With greenness, or the redbreast sit and sing
> Betwixt the tufts of snow on the bare branch
> Of mossy apple-tree, while the nigh thatch
> Smokes in the sun-thaw; whether the eave-drops fall
> Heard only in the trances of the blast,
> Or if the secret ministry of frost
> Shall hang them up in silent icicles,
> Quietly shining to the quiet moon.

CHRISTOPHER HIBBERT

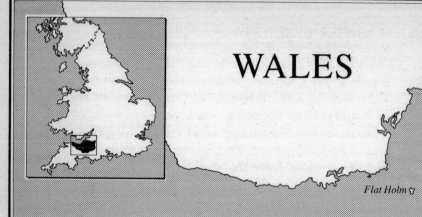

WALES

Flat Holm ⌂

Steep Holm ⊃

Brean Dow

Culbone
Oare
Porlock
Minehead
Luccombe
Blue
Anchor
Watchet
Lilstock
Dunster
Wilton
Stogursey
Timberscombe
Old Cleeve
Washford
Dodington
Exe
Wheddon
Cross
Cleeve
Abbey
Nether Stowey
Canningto
Simonsbath
Exford
Luxborough
Nettlecombe
Stogumber
Crowcombe
Withypool
Winsford
Brompton
Regis
Elworthy
W. Bagborough
Hawkridge
Clatworthy
Brompton
Ralph
Cothelstone
Kingst
Dulverton
Chipstable
Wiveliscombe
Bishop's
Lydeard
West
Monk
Brushford
Milverton
Tone
Bradford
TAUNTON
Ashbrittle
Stoke St Ma
Wellington
Co
Sampford Arundel
Staple Fitzpa
Castle Neroch
Churchingford

DEVON

SOMERSET

Introduction

The wide expanse of Somerset is a borderland, standing between the extreme south-west of the country and the rest of England. Like most such borderlands, its own borders have frequently been in dispute: in the west, Devon nibbles into Somerset's Exmoor, while a little further to the south the bound between the two counties runs waveringly and uneasily through the mysterious tangled lanes and deep valleys of the Blackdown Hills.

To the east, where Somerset meets the chalk downs of Wiltshire, and to the south, where it joins Dorset, the boundaries should logically follow the watersheds, but they have been constantly re-drawn through the centuries, as parcels of land changed hands. The most recent and drastic alteration to Somerset's bounds occurred in the north-east of the county with the creation of the transient county of Avon. Although, even here, we cannot ignore the fact that the stone wall running along part of the Mendip ridge and now forming the boundary between Somerset and Avon actually follows the course of a Saxon bound. For the purposes of this book, I have largely ignored Avon and treated Somerset as its original whole, a practice adopted by the county's Archaeology and Natural History Society. The cities of Bristol and Bath, which have long been granted independent status – dating back, in the case of Bristol, to the reign of King John – obviously have played an important part in Somerset's history and so I have included them, but treated them separately, as it were, in chapters XII and XIII at the end of the book.

Only in the north, where the high tides of the Bristol Channel put the matter out of dispute, can we be absolutely clear where Somerset ends. Yet even here, the coastline has fluctuated and been controlled by the hand of man, as the swampy inland sea, which once covered north Somerset from Mendip to the Quantocks, gradually submitted to progressively more and more effective drainage systems.

Within these shakily drawn perimeters, the county presents its different faces, separated and defined by its hills and rivers and connected by road systems, which for the most part still follow the routes of prehistoric tracks and Roman highways. The routes of the roads have proved more long-lasting than the communications of canal and railway, which have now largely become happy hunting grounds for the industrial archaeologists and tourist play areas.

With one notable exception, the main rivers that have shaped this county rise in the high lands of Mendip to the north-east and in the expanse of Exmoor to the west. From earliest times these waterways have naturally affected Somerset's industrial and political history. Many of them were navigable far inland, until the draining of the shallow sea that once stretched from Bridgwater Bay as far south as Glastonbury.

The river that has had the greatest impact on Somerset's history is the Parret. It rises in the south of the county near Yeovil, flows north through Langport, and is joined by the easterly-flowing Tone. To the east of this river, the withy fields and peat-lands of the Somerset moors stretch to the feet of Mendip. Naturally, the rivers of that area have been most drastically affected by the wet land drainage as their courses were canalised out of recognition. The River Brue is the prime example. Its course, from its head waters at the county's Wiltshire border, near Bruton, has a history of turbulent flooding so that it has now to be controlled by extensive underground flood-control measures. Although these are fairly recent, the canalising of the river to the north-west, around Glastonbury, dates from some of the earliest attempts at the drainage of the moors. Here, despite the naming of a road bridge as Pomparles (Pons Perilous), the imagination refuses to conceive that these are the waters which finally received Arthur's Excalibur.

The rivers of Mendip remain largely a mystery. Emerging from the limestone hills, their courses through the subterranean caverns have still not been fully charted. Yet when they emerge from the rock, it is with such force that they once empowered many mills, and to such an extent that Somerset's cloth industry once rivalled Yorkshire's and paper-mills were common in the area. Two notable ones remain, both making use of the waters of the Axe, as that river emerges from the caves of Wookey Hole. One of these mills still produces fine hand-made paper and its operation is part of the Wookey Hole tourist complex. The other is part of the international Inveresk Group and so involved in large scale commercial undertakings.

At Chewton Mendip, on the main road between Wells and Bristol, another Mendip river, the Chew, springs dramatically out of the rock behind the cottages to the east of the road climbing up to the Mendip plateau. This river's main function now is as a feeder to the reservoir of the man-made Chew Valley lake, which provides a main resource for Bristol. However, the river which brought trade to that city, and indeed is largely responsible for its situation, is the Avon. Rising in Wiltshire, and flowing into the mouth of the Severn at Avonmouth, this waterway once formed the natural boundary between Somerset and Gloucestershire.

To the west of the Parret, the Exe flows into Devon. It rises on the north-eastern heights of Exmoor, where a plate of impermeable tin, extending along a high ridge, causes a bog, locally known as The Chains, which is as formidable as the notorious wet lands of Dartmoor. By the time it reaches the county border to the south of Dulverton, the Exe is a fast-flowing moorland river, running through wide open spaces and ancient woodlands.

Tracks and roads are the most obvious man-made features of any landscape. It is the narrow pathway running straight across open country or twisting through woods, the stony track ascending a steep hillside, or the ancient ridgeway route that give a place a human dimension and lead the walker into history. Somerset has plenty of such ancient highways, prehistoric trading routes covering long distances and local hollow-ways carved deep into the sides of the hills. The Roman Fosse Way, running diagonally across England as it joins Lincoln and Exeter, passes through the county, sometimes reduced to a barely discernable footpath, sometimes covered by a major highway.

Modern road building, in particular the M5 in the north and the A303 merging with the M3 in the south, has had its own effect on the county's history. Whereas, at one time, anyone travelling through the south-west peninsula to Cornwall would usually break the journey in Somerset, you can now rush through the county, barely registering its existence or noticing anything beyond the fenced-off verges.

I shall hope to show what a serious loss this is. Somerset is a county worthy of a patient exploration, best done on foot. Traces of her more recent past can be found along the banks of her almost-vanished canals. They are a reminder that this was once a mining county. Coal was brought with great difficulty, out of the narrow twisted veins to be found in the coal measures at the south-eastern tip of Mendip's limestone. That industry continued until the mid-1970s and the pyramids of coal batches, as the slag heaps are locally termed, still bear witness to it. In the west of the county, nineteenth-century entrepreneurs exploited the mineral wealth of Exmoor and the Brendon Hills, though now these are all matters for the industrial archaeologists and the historians.

The mines may be closed, but the Somerset hills are now being torn apart in an even more ruthless manner. I refer to the roadstone quarries. There was a time when Somerset stone, from the conglomerate of Mendip's limestone rock to the honey-coloured blocks cut out of Ham Hill near Yeovil, was used for Somerset's building. Elaborate, tall-towered churches; mansions; farmhouses; cottages and barns, built through the centuries, seem to grow out of the landscape. Many of these buildings took their stone from small quarries dug in the hillsides for that purpose and now grassed in. The story is quite different today, as the hills are rapidly being levelled to provide roadstone for the whole of southern

England. This large-scale destructive quarrying is changing the face of the county even more rapidly and irreversibly than the new roads it services. It is sadly ironic that it is Somerset stone that is now being used to blot out Somerset's rich pastures.

Such desecration is not peculiar to Somerset, but that is where I have most closely observed it. When I studied the county and saw what is being so irretrievably lost, I wanted to look more closely at this landscape's making. So, in writing this contribution to the Pimlico County History Guides, I have started with the evidence left by Somerset's prehistoric settlers and then tried to trace the way that human history has marked the landscape of the county from the time of the earliest Stone Age settlers to the turbulent years of the twentieth-century wars and beyond.

I must confess to being something of a foreign observer. I am not Somerset-born. I believe that most people have their native river and mine is the Thames; but for fourteen years, my views were shaped by waters flowing out of Mendip rock. It is primarily in gratitude for that time that this book was written.

I

From Stone to Iron

Somerset is a county of variety, contrast and paradox. Nowhere is this more apparent than in its coastline, bordering on the most extensive tidefall in Europe as the combined forces of the Rivers Severn and Wye flow into the Bristol Channel. This creates an inter-tidal stretch composed of a wide band of mud, sand and stratified rock from Aust Cliff by the Severn Bridge to the west of Bridgwater Bay. Past Minehead the scene changes. Here the graded pebbles of Porlock Bay form a high shelf, that looks at first glance like a man-made barrier. West again, wooded cliffs border Exmoor to the mouth of the Lyn River in Devon.

The paradox stems from the changing sea levels. At times, most of northern Somerset was an inland sea; at others, especially in the west, forests now totally submerged, extended well to the north of Porlock; and in 1827, an inmate of Williton workhouse, who was digging gravel on the beach at Doniford, discovered a large, serrated object that proved to be a mammoth's tooth. It was on this beach that latter day archaeologists were to find hoards of mesolithic flints.

In the pre-Roman Iron Age, the Bristol Channel was much narrower than it is now. I have gone at low tide, walking across the mud about a quarter of a mile from Goldcliffe in South Glamorgan to see excavations of an Iron Age dwelling there. These remains stand now at the very edge of the water, and have been preserved by their twice daily tidal drownings. Around them are traces of trackways across the lias beneath the mud, and the whole complex lies just to the west of some further mesolithic finds.

This reference to Wales at the start of a book on Somerset is strictly relevant, for even now with the Bristol Channel at its present width, Wales is close by and generally visible from the north of the county, and from the high ground of Mendip, the Polden Ridge, the Quantocks and Exmoor. Throughout Somerset's history trading links with Wales have been important, and they will be among the constant threads that guide these wanderings through time and place.

The earliest record of human habitation in Somerset and indeed in Europe lies in the discovery of the bones and flint implements of a man who lived in the limestone caves above Westbury-sub-Mendip on the southern escarpment of the hill. Mendip's limestone continues under the waters of the Channel to culminate in the coal measures of South Wales. This very early man, living well before the last Ice Age, must have been aware of the Welsh hills as he hunted and no doubt climbed the trees on the wooded heights of Mendip. His view must have been shared by his remote descendants, the hunter-gatherers of our own inter-glacial age, who lived in the rock shelters around Wookey Hole and Ebbor Gorge.

The ice cap that formed over Europe some twelve thousand years ago did not extend south of Wales, so it is not surprising that we should find traces of very early habitation in Somerset. Twenty-six caves and rock shelters have been found in the wooded hills around Wookey Hole and Ebbor Gorge alone, and some of these, inhabited from the earliest Stone Age, had been dwellings up to the Roman period and later. The Gorge is now a national nature reserve, managed by English Nature who have it on lease from the National Trust to whom it was presented in 1967 as a memorial to Sir Winston Churchill. This means that the public are free to visit, but are asked to keep to the footpaths, an important injunction as banks of scree could easily be dislodged by walkers. One of the many rock shelters in the gorge is, fortunately, fairly easily reached and access is permitted from the stony path that climbs up through a narrow passage to the cliff at the top of the gorge.

In the rock's face, on the left-hand side as you climb, you will find a precipitous path going along a ledge of the hill. It leads to the wide open mouth of a shallow cave protected by over-hanging rock. When you return to the path and climb up the rough, natural rocky steps through the narrow pass to the top of the hill, you will find that one of the stones forming the steps seems to have been placed in such a way as to cover another stone, in which a basin appears to have been hollowed out for the collection of rain water.

So far the chief areas of mesolithic finds besides those along the coast around Williton, have been at Middlezoy – an island outcrop on Sedgemoor – and on Mendip. It was in the latter area, in 1977, at Lower Pitts Farm, between Wookey Hole and Priddy, that traces of a dwelling of this period were discovered. The family that lived there inhabited the hut it had fashioned sometime between seven thousand and three thousand BC.

It was not until people began farming that they settled long enough to make any sort of lasting monuments to their dead and to attempt, as we still do, to transcend mortality by some funerary ritual. We can only guess at the form the early rituals may have taken from the burial places that are left. One such neolithic, or new Stone Age, barrow stands in a large field on a high spur of land above Wellow, some five miles south of Bath at Stoney Littleton Farm. As recently as the early 1980s it was possible to get a key from the farm in order to unlock the gate in the fence surrounding the barrow, and so crawl into the chambered interior. Now, sadly, owing to the wear on the structure, open access has proved unfeasible, and visitors must content themselves with walking round the outside of the barrow; noting its orientations; enjoying the view of the meandering Wellow Brook; and then pondering its three pairs of interior chambers, well displayed, in the model in Bristol Museum. It is a poor substitute for the sensation of awe that came as you crawled through the barrow's four-foot high south-east entrance into the corbelled passage and its adjacent chambers, where the remains of the early farmers of this valley were honoured.

It so happens that we do know just a little of two of the people who were buried here: a middle-aged man and an elderly woman. Their bones were discovered in May 1816 by the Revd John Skinner of Camerton, an amateur archaeologist, who carried out work for Sir Richard Colt Hoare of Stourhead in Wiltshire. We shall meet him again.

In 1858 T.R. Joliffe, then lord of the hundred, paid 16 shillings for the restoration of the barrow 'injured by the lapse of time – or the carelessness of former proprietors' as one is informed by the legend on a stone slab set up by the entrance. Mr Joliffe was also at pains to inform the visitor, somewhat inaccurately, that this barrow was declared to be 'the most perfect specimen of Celtic antiquity still existing in Great Britain'. However, archaeologists affirm that although his notion of prehistoric eras may have been awry, his restoration was fairly accurate, and we must thank him for saving the barrow from farmers who could use such places as a stone quarry. We must be especially thankful that he saved the door jamb adorned with an ammonite cast; a stone was probably specially selected for that prominent place by the original builders of the tomb. In 1884, Lord Hylton of Kilmersdon, a descendant of T.R. Joliffe, placed the monument in the hands of the Commissioners of Works, who protected it under the provisions of the first Ancient Monuments Act, which had been passed two years previously.

The builders of such a monument as the Stoney Littleton long barrow must have had a sophistication and intelligent ability that gave purpose to their lives beyond the day to day collecting of food. We know something of them through the flint tools that they used, most of which must have been brought into this area from some distance, for there is neither flint nor chert in the Mendip limestone.

It is thought that most of the tools used here were fashioned out of flints that came from the chalk uplands of Wiltshire. R.D. Vranch who found a hoard of Stone Age flint implements near the village of Mells to the west of Frome, claimed that the area, now totally disturbed by quarrying, probably lay on an important transport route. As Mr Vranch also discovered many waste flints among the completed artefacts, he also suggested that this was possibly a manufacturing site, where the imported flints were shaped before being carried further into Somerset. If that was so, then the Stone

Age hoard marks the start of a tradition of agricultural tool manfacture in the Mells area, which was to reach its climax with the nineteenth-century edge tool workings.

Apart from Stoney Littleton, there are only nine other long barrows recorded in the county; but the most casual drive across Mendip to Exmoor will take you past many of the high, round barrows, where people who had learnt the skills of working in copper and bronze interred their tribal leaders; for we have to believe that only notable leaders were given ritual inhumation. Even so, there must have been many of them. In 1939, L.V. Grinsell reported to the Somerset Archaeological and Natural History Society that there were 320 round barrows between Weston-super-Mare and Frome, and the rough estimate now is that there are ten round barrows to the square mile on Mendip alone.

Allowing for the fact that some must have been flattened by ploughing and by the taking of the stones from the cairns that once covered them, there must have been as many on Exmoor. Some Somerset barrows have suffered also from having had stones added to them, so that like Exmoor's Dunkery Beacon the original shape is completely lost. The process still goes on, as walkers seem compelled to add a stone to an existing cairn in much the same way as it seems almost instinctive to throw votive coins into water.

The worst depradation of the barrows, however, has come about through the attentions of enthusiastic amateur archae-ologists of whom John Skinner was one. He often employed unsupervised labour for the task of barrow-opening. L.V. Grinsell (SANHS Vol 85. 1939) quotes an 1814 entry from Skinner's papers, in which he recorded that when he was examining a barrow to the north-west of Priddy, he was approached by a person who told him that some twenty years ago when 'he and another labourer were taking stone from a high hillock, called Beacon Barrow he found in a stone cist, a number of brazen spearheads and weapons . . . there were twelve to twenty of them, all in good preservation'. So he sold them to a person at Westbury, a Farmer Bull, for two gallons of cider.

Fortunately, many of the finds from successive, later excavations have found their way into the museums. Among them is the beaker, now in the Castle Museum at Taunton, found in the cist at Yenworthy near Culbone. Many such grave goods make it possible to give a rough date to the interment; and in fact, whole generations have been fixed as 'the Beaker people' because of the shape of their pots. In most of these burials the dead man is curled in a foetal position in order to enter the womb of the earth. For his journey from there to another world he was provided with drink in earthen jars, a few weapons, and some food, often in the form of a joint of pork. At Pool Farm near West Harptree, on the northern slopes of Mendip, a stone beside the burial mound was curiously marked with mysterious cup-shaped indentations and with the imprints or carvings of six disconnected feet with widely splayed toes. This slab is now in Bristol City Museum and you can see a moulded copy of it in the museum at Wells. No one has yet ventured an explanation of its significance.

The only testimony we have of the religious beliefs of the people who built the barrows lies in the remaining monuments that are not specifically or entirely connected with burials. In Somerset we have the magnificent triad of stone circles at Stanton Drew by the River Chew; the three mysterious henges that form the Priddy circles; the ritual henge of Gorsey Bigbury on the Mendip plateau, which Kathleen Young, the wife of the farmer of that land, described as being shaped like 'a soup plate with an upturned saucer in the middle'; and the various stone rows and circles of Exmoor.

L.V. Grinsell believed that the three Stanton Drew circles, some six miles south of the centre of Bristol, are almost as important as the monuments at Avebury and Stonehenge. These circles are best reached from the B3130 between Chew Magna and Pensford. Two of them have stone avenues (as at Avebury) extending towards the east. A single fallen stone, associated with the monument, lies in a farm hedge by the main road on the further side of the River Chew from the stones. It is known as Hautville's Quoit, and is associated in folklore with a semi-legendary Norman overlord of that name. There is also a 'cove', consisting of one fallen and two standing stones associated with the circles. It is in Stanton Drew village behind the Druid Arms Inn, and may at one time have been the forecourt of a much earlier long barrow.

The three circles, made up of rose-hued sandstone, are on farmland now, and used solely as pasture. Walking across the grass, it is easy to be so absorbed in the patterns and colourings of the individual stones as well as the grace and strength of the configurations, that you do as I once did, and walk straight into the electric fence designed to regulate the grazing. Beware, the resultant shock can bring you to your knees, appropriate enough in such a sacred place, but unpleasant. The 'sensitives' with whom I was walking on that occasion swore that they felt vibrations from the stones; perhaps anybody as agnostic as I needed such a rude awakening.

In the seventeenth century, this was arable land, so John Aubrey had no such cattle-related problems when he visited the site in 1664; but as the barley crop was then standing high, he couldn't see the stones either. Two years later, the anonymous author of the curiously titled *A Fool's Bolt Soon Shott at Stonage* found the remains of a human skeleton here. Beside it there was 'a round bell, like a horse bell, with a skrew as the stemme of it'. There is no other trace of a burial here, and that one may not have taken place when the stones were set up.

Strachey's 1736 map of Somerset marks the Stanton Drew circles as the Weddings. That name comes from the general tradition in Christian folklore, which explains the puzzling standing stones and circles as representing the petrified forms of dancers or revellers who violated the Sabbath. In this case, because there are so many stones, a whole wedding party was envisaged, all turned to stone for desecrating the Sabbath by continuing their frolics from Saturday night into Sunday.

The three mysterious henges at Priddy stand some 900 feet above sea level, north of a spectacular group of barrows, with which they must surely have been in some way connected. These barrows are best approached from the field gate, to the west of the Miners' Arms. There are two groups of barrows here. Eight of them form a wide shallow arc near the gate, one of which (the fourth from the west) is thought to have been a bell barrow, indicating the burial place of an important tribal leader.

A little further south, and on slightly higher ground, a group of nine barrows was formed. Seven of them flank the slope of North Hill, while another pair stand slightly to the north-east of the main group. Each barrow is about nine feet in height with a diameter of some forty-five yards. Such an obvious landmark as this group of barrows was used to mark a parish boundary between Priddy and Chewton Mendip. So we will come back this way when we look at medieval perambulations and surveys.

In the west of the county, the stone rows and circles of Exmoor need some hunting out, for unlike the clear granite rows of Dartmoor, the Exmoor stones are mostly insignificant in themselves. Much of our recent knowledge of them comes from the patient hard work of Hazel Eardley-Wilmot. Her most significant re-discovery came in 1975 when she located the 161 stones comprising the row known as the White Ladder and marked as such on the 1819 enclosure map. These stones stand just beneath the ridge above Kinsford Water, which marks the county boundary. Protruding only a few inches above the turf they are not easily found, even though sixty-one of them by Miss Eardley-Wilmot's count are of a shining white quartz.

More easily located, and equally mysterious, are the Whitestones on the heather moor of Porlock Common, to the south of the A39. Just under six feet in height, these two stones lean to the east. Miss Eardley-Wilmot thinks they once formed a pair of male and female, long and broad stones, such as are found in the Avebury avenues. Other archaeologists through the ages have suggested that they were once part of a lost stone circle. Certainly their proximity to many other Bronze Age monuments indicate that this coastal section of Exmoor was a well-populated and important place in that era.

To the south of the Whitestones on Porlock Common, beside the lane that goes to Exford, you can just make out a stone circle. It is made up of about ten remaining small standing stones of green micaceous sandstone. To the north-west, on Culbone Hill, there is a stone row. This was discovered in 1981 by the Ordnance Survey archaeologist, Norman Quinnel. This row runs through thick woodland undergrowth and is made up of some twenty-four earth-coloured stones which run east from the barrow in the woods above Twitchen Plain.

The best known, if not the most spectacular, of the Exmoor round barrows is the solitary mound by the roadside some three miles to the north-west of Exford, on the open moor between Lucott Cross and Wellshead. It is generally known as Alderman's barrow and has become a favourite meeting place for walkers. From the thirteenth century, it was used to mark the boundary of the Royal Hunting Forest of Exmoor.

Most of the Somerset stone circles and rows must have been erected about the same time that the great stones of Avebury and Stonehenge were being placed in Wiltshire. L.V. Grinsell has a marvellous image of the people on the north Somerset coast watching as ships took the Blue Stones from Pembroke-shire's Preseli Ridge up the Bristol Channel to the mouth of the Avon. Even if the current theory is correct and the Stonehenge Blue Stones were in fact glacial erratics found in north Wiltshire; there is no doubt that there was always considerable trade through south-west Wales to the mouth of the rivers flowing into the channel. It could have happened.

Further inland, in Langridge woods, on the southern slope of the Brendon Hills, about a mile and a half to the north of Treborough church, a most unusual stone-lined grave of the Bronze Age period was found in 1820 by workmen taking stone from the covering cairn in order to make a rough road for hauling timber. The grave, which is still there by the forest path, is seven feet long, two and a half feet wide and three feet deep. Here the body of a man was laid to his full length, and the workmen, showing more reverence than archaeologists can usually afford, reburied the man in a corner of Treborough churchyard. Perhaps it is fortunate that the grave is unmarked and nobody seems now to know where he lies. I hope it may be beneath the rowan to the north-west.

The valley in which that grave was discovered was marked as Drucombe on the Ordnance Survey map of 1809, but in succeeding maps, and indeed on the current one, it is presented as Druids Combe. The amateur archaeologists of the nineteenth century were apt to follow the practice of their forebears and refer to all ancient monuments as Druidical. We now know that the Druids who are associated with the Celtic tribes did not come to Britain until sometime towards the end of the first millennium BC, and although they may have made use of the Bronze Age ritual sites, they did not erect any megalithic monuments of their own.

The Celtic incomers worked with iron, and it is to them that most of the hill forts are attributed, although many of these probably had their beginnings in the Bronze Age or earlier, and were used as corrals, where domesticated animals could be kept safe from wolves and wild beasts. With the coming of the warring Celtic tribes, greedy to extend their territory and plunder travellers making their way along valley routes, these hilltop enclosures were fortified with earth banks and ditches, and protected by massive pallisades and stone walls. It is ironic that such warlike structures now give so much pleasure to country walkers. Their commanding positions, ensuring wide views over the surrounding landscape, make them an interesting and delightful goal, especially as they are usually reached by ancient ridgeway tracks or by river paths through the valleys beneath the forts' escarpments.

In Somerset, the hill fort on Ham Hill near Yeovil has become a country park, which in this case is not nearly as tame a matter as the phrase suggests. In fact, it is fitting that the hill which has been quarried for centuries to provide the rich, mellow, golden stone of which so many of the local houses are built, should now be available for everyone to enjoy the magnificent views over the south of the county from the fort's remaining high earthen banks. This was the only hill fort in England, so I am told, to feature a public house; but even though the Prince of Wales pub was popular, it went out of business in 1993. Although a road runs across the hill, the fort is still a good place to visit. There are two ways to reach it. You can either drive up the lane from Stoke sub Hamdon, which lies beneath the northern slope; or you can walk along the wooded ridge from the pointed mound that gave Montacute its name.

If you walk round the ramparts of the fort, you will find that this extensive enclosure, covering some 85 hectares, is roughly L-shaped, the rectangular southern part being supplemented by a long northern spur, whose high western banks give you the best views of the surrounding country. To the west of this northern spur, the protection afforded by the bank and deep ditch is enhanced by an escarpment which falls sharply into a strip of woodland.

As this site has been extensively quarried from the medieval period, it is not always easy to discern the pattern of the original defences, set up it is believed, some time in the third or fourth centuries BC. The hill was occupied long before that, for some of the pottery finds may date from the seventh century BC, and archaeologists believe that neolithic farmers lived here.

On the north side of Mendip, on the wooded hill above Congresbury, Cadbury fort (locally referred to as Cadkong to distinguish it from the more famous Cadbury in the south of the county) guards the River Yeo, now running from Blagdon Reservoir to the Bristol Channel through a plain of drained moors, and once a substantial waterway. Being so near the spreading Bristol conurbation and the still slightly genteel town of Clevedon, the footpaths around this camp are popular with weekend walkers making their way on to the hills after lunch at the Plough by the river. Their paths climb up through hazel, elder and blackthorn thickets, with the occasional blush of spindle-berry in autumn, to the eight acres of open pasture that form the enclosure of the hill fort.

Although this hill is only 500 feet above sea level, because of the low-lying nature of the surrounding country, there are panoramic views, extending on clear days to the coast of Wales. Steep slopes protect the fort to the north, west and south, and the footpath across the enclosure takes you up to the entrance through the extensive ramparts to the east. This was most probably the site of the original gateway. A small part of the northern section of the enclosure has been excavated, and the finds, including two fine brooches, are now in Taunton museum.

West of Congresbury, in the coastal woods above Weston-super-Mare, there is another hill fort, which serves as a dog exercising/jogging route, and a place for pleasant weekend strolls. Worlebury is also one of the best hill forts in Somerset for the amateur archaeologist to indulge his speculations. Banks of loose stones, probably derived from the rocky surface of the hill itself, make up the original stone walls; and it is still possible to discern the sites of the storage pits at the eastern end of the ten acre enclosure.

Overlooking the mouth of the Severn, this fort is partly defended by the steep fall of the land into Sand Bay. As you climb up to the fort from the coastal road by Weston's Birnbeck Pier, you come quickly to the massive rampart and the deep wide ditch of the outer defences. There are further fortifications lying on the further side of a thirteen-foot wide entrance. Besides being so close to the fort at Congresbury, Worlebury, is only eight miles from the Welsh coast and seven and a half from the fortification on the summit of Brent Knoll (see page 18).

To the east, on the height of Mendip, where the underlying old red sandstone erupts through the limestone of the hills, the impressive hill fort of Dolebury stands on a spur of high ground above Burrington Combe. You can reach this fort by climbing up from the combe to Blackdown and walking west along the ridge above the conifers of Rowberrow, or by taking a shorter, steeper way up the hill from Rowberrow church, just off the A38. This is a place for more serious walkers than either of the hill forts we have visited so far.

The inner rampart of this twenty-acre enclosure is clearly defined, surrounded by a massive barricade some eighteen to twenty feet high. From the original entrance at the western end, you can see how this fort defended the crossing point of two natural lines of communication, where the valley road now covered by the A38 meets the A368 running along Mendip's northern contour.

As it crosses Mendip to the west, the M5 to Exeter runs past the green, flat, triangular hilltop, clearly defined by the earthworks that form the fort of Brent Knoll; an indication that the motorway's route follows a natural line of communication to the south-west, and one that needed guarding. The heights of Brent Knoll also provided a good place from which to watch out for any unknown ships coming into Bridgwater Bay.

Footpaths lead up to this height from East Brent to the north and Brent Knoll village to the south, the latter providing the shorter but steeper climb. This hill fort, standing on lias sandstone, is now in the care of the National Trust. It was once a prominent island rising out of the swampy sea that covered most of north Somerset until methodical drainage works began some thousand years ago.

To the west of Bridgwater, above Nether Stowey on the eastern edge of the Quantocks, Dowsborough Camp provides another look-out point over Bridgwater Bay, although it is now so heavily wooded that in summer you cannot see the coast from the top of the hill fort. You reach this fortification by taking the lane that runs off the A39 to the west of Nether Stowey and then following the footpath that runs north through the woods, just before the lane makes a sharp turn to the south.

Although this hill fort is also frequently known as Danesborough, it is most unlikely that it played any significant role in the Danish invasions of the eighth and ninth centuries. The name probably comes from the Welsh word *Dinas*, a fort; another reminder both of the proximity to Wales and the fact that although these heights were occupied from the time of the Bronze Age, it was the Celtic tribes who built the great fortifications.

To the south of Dowsborough, just by the car park on the height of the Quantock ridge, an earthwork extends south through scrubby heath to the forest plantation. It consists of a six foot high rampart with a fairly deep ditch to the west. Further traces of it have been found south of the exposed section. At one time it was thought that it might be part of the

Civil War defences, but it is now generally believed to be closely associated with the adjoining hill fort, and could mark an Iron Age tribal boundary. No one knows how its name of Dead Woman's Ditch came about. It is shown as such on Day & Masters Somerset map of 1782, some seven years before the tragic murder, recorded by Coleridge, with which it is generally associated.

It is worth approaching the dramatic and beautifully sited hill forts of Exmoor by the lane running west from the B3188, which links Williton and Wiveliscombe. This lane crosses the ridge of the Brendon Hills and runs past the mis-named Elworthy Barrows. These earthworks are not barrows at all, but the half-formed ramparts of an unfinished hill fort. You can see them clearly from a field gate on the south side of the lane. Why these extensive earthworks were not completed is one of the mysteries of pre-history, a conundrum that is entangled by the presence of the numerous barrows along the ridge running west to Wheddon Cross. There is no other hill fort protecting this vital trade route and vantage point.

The nearest Iron Age camp from here lies to the south, on a wooded hill at the eastern edge of what is now Clatworthy Reservoir. The Water Board has allowed a nature trail, starting at the north of the dam and working its way up to the precipitous ditch and earth bank enclosing the fourteen acres of Clatworthy Castle, which overlooks the valley of the Tone, part of which has been flooded to form the reservoir.

This fort, like others we shall look at on Exmoor, was probably inhabited by the Dumnonii, 'the people of the land'. Writing about them in the third century AD, Solinius tells us that they refused to use coins, making their transactions entirely by barter. If he was correct, and the absence of any coins found during excavations would seem to prove that he was, then the inhabitants of Iron Age West Somerset shared a bartering form of economy with the Silures of South Wales, with whom they frequently traded.

Above the channel on Minehead's North Hill are the ramparts of Bury Castle reached from the village of Selworthy; and Furzebury Brake near the cliffs to east. On the south side of that fort there are traces of field terraces, indicating that as late as the first century BC these enclosures were used as agricultural settlements as well as defensive positions.

To the south-east, Black Ball camp in Dunster Park on the summit of Gallox Hill is approached through woods; and the ramparts, enclosing some three hectares, are covered in bracken, heather and scrubby bushes. About a quarter of a mile to the south, on the highest point of the hill, there is another fortification. In this case, two stone ramparts divided by a ditch supplementing the outer ditch defend a circular enclosure of about one hectare. This hill fort is one of several which have associated outer defences. About 125 yards to the south there is a single rampart, 180 yards long taking a zig-zag course along the hill-side. Originally thought to have been yet another defensive position from the Civil War, it is now believed to date from the Iron Age and to have served something of the same defensive purpose in relation to the neighbouring hill fort as the mysterious Dead Woman's Ditch on the Quantocks performed for Dowsborough Castle.

My favourite walks to the Exmoor hill forts are further to the south and west. They involve walks by the Barle, a river that is a constant source of delight and unexpected enchantments. There are three hill forts to the north-west of Dulverton. Oldberry Castle stands on the spur of land above the town, and the twin fortifications of Brewers Castle and Mounsey Castle defend a bend in the river on the Devon border, some three miles further west. These two Iron Age forts are named for the Norman lords who owned the surrounding land. The oddly named Cow Castle, further up river near Simonsbath, is derived directly from the Celtic *caer*, meaning a fortification or castle.

This shapely hill fort can best be reached by a two and a half mile walk along the Barle, going south-east from Simonsbath. In wet weather the riverside footpath can be very marshy, and then you may find it wiser to approach the site by going over the hill from Winstitchen Farm. A slightly longer walk to Cow Castle starts just north of Landacre Bridge, and follows the contours of the hills to the north-west.

Cow Castle stands on a sandstone hill above the confluence of the Barle and Whitewater. Its ramparts reach in some places to eight feet, and they enclose a most unusual inner ditch, a feature that nearly always indicates a ritual rather than a defensive site; however, in this instance it may simply represent some internal quarrying at an unknown date.

Turning east from Exmoor towards Taunton, we come to one of the few Somerset hill forts that have been recently excavated and studied. The camp at Norton Fitzwarren, which was the subject of a community archaeological exploration in 1992, has been studied and carefully excavated at various dates during this century. The early work and that carried out in the 1960s and 70s showed that this site, a few miles to the north-west of Taunton was occupied by Stone Age farmers before two Bronze Age ramparts were erected on either side of an eight foot ditch at the end of the second millennium BC. The later and more extensive Iron Age ramparts and associated defensive ditch enclose just over five hectares. This site was so important that it seems to have been refurbished at the time of the Roman occupation.

The importance and antiquity of Norton Fitzwarren were to become proverbial, for although there were no tales told, as they were of Cow Castle, about the place having originally been built by the fairies to escape the malice of the elemental earth spirits, it was boasted that 'When Taunton was a furzy down/Norton was a walled town'. That, despite the fact that there are no traces of any occupation of this enclosure after the first century AD, proves that the ramparts of this hill fort, now badly eroded and indiscernible in many places, must once have been a spectacular landmark.

Somerset's most famous hill fort, South Cadbury, lies between Wincanton and Ilchester to the south of the A303. It also was occupied from neolithic times. Popularly believed to be the site of Arthur's Camelot, it was extensively excavated by Leslie Alcock between 1966 and 1970. A fairly steep walk up a muddy lane to the south of South Cadbury church brings you up to the north-eastern entrance of the fort, taking you through the fourfold ramparts constructed round an enclosure of some seven hectares in 500 BC. The main entrance appears to have been in the south-west corner.

Excavations on this site disclosed traces of several circular huts, a smithy and a temple, as well as large storage pits. It was occupied until AD 70, when the Romans attacked the fort burning down the south-west entrance and leaving evidence of a wholesale massacre of the inhabitants and their children; all of them were, no doubt, members of the Durotriges tribe, whose coins have been found at Ilchester and South Petherton. In the Dark Ages a new timber rampart was built at South Cadbury and a rectangular timber hall was erected in the enclosure. It was this that led to the site being associated with King Arthur, and I shall return to it in chapter III.

Hill forts, which are common enough right through Britain, are not the only Iron Age settlements in Somerset, a county renowned for its pallisaded lake villages. I recall being told about them in a Home Counties dame school in the early 1930s. Set up in the third millennium BC on man-made islands in the reedy swamps that once covered the moors that lie between the Quantock Hills and the mouth of the Severn, these settlements were rediscovered by a Midsomer Norton doctor.

Arthur Bulleid made the claim that he was 'brought up in archaeological surroundings' and furthermore that he had been 'fortunate in having parents who fostered antiquarian pursuits'. In 1888, having read Ferdinand Keller's study of Swiss lake dwellings, Bulleid became convinced that similar villages must have existed in the Somerset swamps. So he spent the next four years looking for possible sites among the peat cuttings on the moors to the east of the Polden ridge. Eventually he was able to record: 'on a Wednesday afternoon in March 1892, when driving across the moor from Glaston-bury to Godney, a field was noticed to be covered with small mounds, an unusual feature in a neighbourhood where the conformation of the land is for miles at a dead level'.

The following Sunday, he made a more thorough investigation of the site and was delighted to find among the loose soil of the mole hills, numerous pottery fragments, together with a whetstone and some pieces of bone and charcoal. They were remnants from some twenty families who, it is believed, lived in the lake village from about 200 BC to the third or fourth century AD.

In September 1895, a farmer from Westhay in the parish of Meare, approached Arthur Bulleid with some fragments of Iron Age pottery, found when he was digging post-holes in order to put up a fence round his haystack. So as soon as the Glastonbury excavations were completed to Bulleid's satisfaction, he turned his attention to Meare, and in 1908 he began to excavate a second village.

There is nothing to see on the ground now but a field by the roadside on the moor between Glastonbury and Godney, whose gate carries an inscription informing you that this was the site of a Lake Village. Ridges and mounds in the pasture give evidence as to where the excavations took place and that is all. However, if you go to the Tribunal Museum in Glastonbury High Street, you will find evidence of how the people of that village lived. They must have been fairly sophisticated, judging by the engraved spindle whorls, combs, brooches, decorated pottery, a dice box, and the famous, bronze-riveted Glastonbury bowl. For transport, these people had wheeled vehicles, for sophisticated hubs and spokes are among the finds. Two of their boats are on view to the public; one here and one, discovered at Shapwick beneath the Polden Ridge, at the Castle Museum, Taunton. Each boat is made from a single oak tree.

In the very first year of the excavations at Glastonbury, the Wincanton Field Club took a train trip to view the site; and the lake village excavation continued to attract visitors to the 1930s, when John Masefield, then Poet Laureate, was one of the many visitors to the corrugated iron hut from which Arthur Bulleid conducted his researches.

In 1992, as a way of celebrating Bulleid's discoveries a hundred years previously, his hut was renovated and re-erected in West Hay, at the Somerset Levels Museum. There, archaeologists supervised the construction of a thatched, Iron Age round house and a pole lathe such as was used for shaping tools. As I write, the land around this hut is being put under cultivation, and crops of grain and beans such as were grown round the lake villages will be harvested here. In a nearby compound surrounded by hazel hurdles, a Soay ram and two ewes (a breed of sheep that was certainly familiar to Iron Age people) are afforded shelter in a turf-roofed shed.

The lake village shepherds practised transhumence; that is, they took their sheep up to summer pasture on the Polden Ridge or on to the heights of Mendip. Those who took the latter course probably lived alongside the flocks during the summer months in the enclosure of Maesbury hill fort some eight miles to the north of the site of the Glastonbury village. The actual routes these herdsmen took have never been fully charted, although we do know something of the trackways they must have used, some of which were laid down thousands of years before the lake villages were constructed. Many of the routes they followed are still in use, but the original road-making is now well-buried under layers of tarmac and crushed Mendip stone. Others must still lie buried in the peat which started to build up about six thousand BC, when the sea level rose and the forests of birch and pine that then covered the mid-Somerset lowlands decayed into a swampy salt marsh.

Several of the tracks have been excavated and carefully described. They are now internationally renowned. The most notable is the Sweet Track, which dates from the end of the fourth millennium BC, making it the oldest recorded trackway in the world. It was discovered in the winter of 1970 by Ray Sweet, a peat cutter, who came across its timbers together with a flint arrowhead, while he was clearing a ditch. Fortunately, he had the curiosity and good sense to explore and report his find. Although an archaeologist has been employed since the late 1970s to supervise large scale commercial peat takings, much of the history of the Somerset moors must have been lost as machines took the place of men in digging the peat.

When the course of the Sweet Track was followed, it was found to run between Shapwick and Westhay, and it must have been built across the reedy swamps less than a thousand years after the sea had finally retreated from the moors. It was an astonishingly sophisticated construction, being made of oaken planks supported by hazel and alder spokes driven into the ground at an angle of forty-five degrees. The walkway so formed was secured at the sides and at each end by small locking pegs.

Although the Sweet Track is of such great antiquity, it is thought to lie on the route of an even earlier trackway, known to archaeologists as the Post Track, and made out of long planks of ash and lime supported by hazel posts, some of which were incorporated into the later construction. A reconstructed section of the Sweet Track runs through land managed by English Nature on Shapwick Heath, to the south of the Somerset Levels Museum, where there is a further reconstruction at the Peat Moors Visitors' Centre.

As the climate became drier, hummocks of sphagnum moss, cotton grass and even heathers started to grow on the swampy ground. With a slightly firmer base, the numbers of trackways must have multiplied. These later ones were usually made of hazel hurdles reinforced with brushwood. At least one such hurdle road has been discovered that had its panels secured firmly enough to give it the strength to enable animals to be driven along it from the Polden ridge to the village of Meare. A reconstruction of part of this trackway, which was found at Walton Heath is now on display at the Castle Museum in Taunton.

Another track is generally known as the Abbots' Way, because of a false assumption made when it was discovered in 1835 that it had been used by monks from the medieval monastery at Burtle. An excavated section of the peat through which it ran has recently been purchased by Somerset County Council from the firm which works this ground. At one time a surface reconstruction a few yards long was laid over the course of the trackway and made available for the public to walk along; unfortunately, as I write, that is no longer possible.

The original surface of the Abbots' Way, constructed in the middle of the third millennium BC, was made up of split alder planks, in-filled with branches and held in place by long vertical poles, which also marked out the route in times of flood. From the middle of the second millennium BC, many hurdle tracks appear to have been laid across the raised peat bogs around Meare. One of them, named the Eclipse track, running for some 1,000 metres has been dated at 1800 BC. Other finds extend from that date to one on Godney Moor laid down in 400 BC.

In the 1930s, Arthur Bulleid discovered a trackway across Meare Heath dating from 1400 BC. It was finally recorded and fully excavated in the 1970s by Bryony Cole, then Field Archaeologist for the Somerset Levels Project. This is the most sophisticated of the trackways across the moors, being constructed above a course of brushwood. The 'roadway' itself was made of oak timbers supported by cross beams, rather in the manner of railway sleepers, held in place by oak stakes.

Reconstructions of that, and of the other types of trackways across the levels have been reconstructed across a cutting at the Peat Moors Visitors' Centre, enabling you actually to walk back through history.

The discovery of various objects beneath many of the trackways shows that the people who used them exchanged goods over long distances. The flints that were found near the Sweet Track, like those discovered at Mells, probably came from Wiltshire; and the green jadeite axe-head also found by this trackway and now in the museum at Taunton, must at some time have come from the continent. It is a lovely, shapely thing.

Sometime around 3000 BC, a wooden platform (now known as the Baker platform) was built to the west of the island on which Westhay now stands. This marsh platform was joined to the dry land by a walk way, and at least two trackways converged on it from across the bogs. At times of flood, the platform could be approached by boat, for a slipway has been discovered as well as the vestiges of what might well be a mooring post. Under one of the trackways a little wooden figure was discovered. You can see the cast of it in the Castle Museum: a hermaphrodite figure, labelled the god-dolly by puzzled archaeologists, and celebrated in 'From the Somerset

Levels', a poem by Elma Mitchell, a Scottish-born poet, who has lived in Somerset since the 1960s:

> Little wet god,
> Wood-one,
> I was buried
> Out there, in the sticks,
> In the swamps,
> Face-down, in the sodden causeway.
> Floating in time, in peat,
> I held
> Everything up.

For most of the other ancient trade routes in Somerset we must look, as elsewhere, at the ridgeways and river crossings. One of the most spectacular prehistoric ridgeway routes runs along the western edge of Exmoor from Sandyway Cross to the rocky outcrop known as Mole's Chamber, from the name of the river which runs from it. This ridge is still used to mark the county boundary with Devon. It is a way defined by Bronze Age barrows on both sides of the metalled lane that follows the ridge, with one curve to the west through Devon's Bray Common. The old wall marking the county boundary knows no such deviation; in fact it goes right through Setta Barrow, one of the major tumuli of the moor.

The other major Somerset ridgeways take you along the Quantocks from the Triscombe Stone to the sea; above the moors along the Polden Hills; and following the West Mendip Way by the old boundary wall from Winscombe to Crook Peak, which was recently used to define Somerset's division from Avon.

As for river crossings, the most dramatic must be the ancient crossing of the Parret at Combwich, north of Bridgwater. Now a painfully tidy suburban estate, Combwich still has its Old Ship and Anchor inns to remind you of its maritime past. The wide river mouth was regularly crossed here from the Bronze Age or earlier until the eighteenth century, when Thomas de Quincey, author of *Confessions of an Opium Eater*, came this way.

Most of the prehistoric finds show us what was brought into

the county, but Somerset had at least one vital export. The lead mines of Mendip were to have the most immediate significance in the history of the county and indeed of the whole country. Greed for the wealth of Mendip lead was as great a pull as greed for oil is now, and it was to be one of the main reasons why the Romans ventured into this cold and horrible island beyond the limits of the civilised world.

The Mendip lead mines were worked for so long that unfortunately the Iron Age, Celtic workings have been completely overlaid by those of later centuries. It is only possible to say that the Celts must have had a hand in shaping the grassed-over pits and mounds of the old mines, the gruffy or 'groovey' ground, which is now such a characteristic feature of the Mendip plateau.

II

The Romans: Roads, Villas and Temples

Roman lead mining on Mendip was concentrated at Charterhouse, a community of scattered farms whose name comes from the time when the land was owned by monks from the Cistercian Abbey at Hinton Charterhouse near Bath. The lead that was mined there until the late nineteenth century was rich in silver, which the Romans soon sent to their mints in Rome and Lyon.

In less than five years after the conquest of Britain, the Roman lead mines on Mendip were fully established, and large ingots, or pigs, of the ore were transported to the Bristol Channel ports located at the modern Sea Mills and Uphill; and more extensively south-east towards Southampton and the sea-route to the continent. Some of these pigs of lead must have been lost in transit, for they have been discovered from time to time in recent years. One such lost pig of lead, now in the British Museum, is inscribed with the name of Britannicus, son of the emperor Claudius, who was murdered by Nero in AD 55. The dating of this particular pig of lead is further defined by the additional names of Veranius and Pompeis, consuls in Rome in AD 49. That piece of evidence was found near Blagdon in 1853, on the route, as we shall see, between Charterhouse and Uphill. Four other pigs, unearthed more recently at Green Ore, south-east of the Charterhouse, are now in the museum in Wells. They are inscribed with the name of the Emperor Vespasian (AD 69–79) and the farm on which they were discovered now bears his name. Roman pigs of lead were being discovered long before the nineteenth century. In 1544 one was discovered near Wookey Hole, also dating from AD 49, its inscription relates to the ninth year of the Tribunician power of Claudius.

In contrast to these durable reminders of Roman lead mining we only have shadows on the grass on the hillsides to remind us of the Roman presence at Charterhouse. There was a substantial township here before the Romans left, and in the early years it was controlled by a military fort, a garrison of the legionnaires who supervised the work of Celtic slaves in the mines. If you look north-west from the sandy path running through the Elizabethan and nineteenth-century workings, you can see the outline of the amphitheatre on the slope of Blackdown, across the lane that runs from the B3134 past Charterhouse church. Excavations in the early 1920s revealed that this modest amphitheatre was constructed of earth and timber, and it now shows up as a dark, circular patch in a field to the left of the farm track running up to the radio mast on the top of Blackdown.

In his *Natural History*, the Elder Pliny had something to say about the extraction of vertical veins of lead such as are found in the Mendip limestone. He contrasts the convenience of the British lead, lying so near the surface with that in Spain and Gaul, which had to be mined 'with great toil'. Some of the trenches used by the men working the Roman mines are still discernible at Charterhouse, interspersed with deep pits from which lower levels of the mineral were extracted.

Mendip lead was to be used to line the baths at Bath, and it can still be seen in the pipes that form part of the drainage and heating systems. Like the silver that was extracted from it, most of the lead went much further afield, however. In 1883, a pig of it was discovered south of Boulogne, its inscription dating it to the reign of Nero (AD 54–68). Now on show at the museum of St Germain-en-Laye to the west of Paris, it also informs us that this British lead was produced by the Second Legion, evidence that at any rate in the first century, the military were in control of the mines.

Other pigs of lead record the names of the mining officials working on Mendip and elsewhere in Britain. One such official, Gaius Nipius Ascanius, in charge of the lead-silver works on Mendip in AD 60 went on to manage mines in Flintshire. Some sort of privatisation of the mines seems to have taken place at a later date, for there are records of a company trading as NOVAEC, which appears to have been granted a lease of the Mendip mines. Pigs of lead stamped with that company's name and those of its officials have been found in Gloucestershire and near Southampton, where it was presumably being sent for export.

We do not know what the Romans called Charterhouse. All the pigs of lead that I have mentioned have the source of origin as Britain on their inscriptions, and several extend to read BRIT EX ARG VEB, which has been taken to stand for 'From the British lead-silver works at Veb', that being understood as an abbreviation of the Roman name for the area we know as Charterhouse.

We do know, however, that Charterhouse was certainly not the only source of Roman lead on Mendip. There were other mines at Priddy, Green Ore, where the pigs now in Wells were discovered, and Camerton near Radstock. That latter site is near the Fosse Way, and I will look at it further when I follow the course of that highway. First, I want to trace the course of the lesser roads along which the Mendip lead was carried to the ports.

In the late eighteenth century, Sir Richard Colt Hoare of Stourhead in Wiltshire, postulated the course of the roads linking Charterhouse north-west with the lost port of Uphill, near Weston-super-Mare, and to the Wiltshire border in the south-east. The first of these roads is pleasant to follow. It goes along the course of an ancient ridgeway route for much of the way, taking you above the marshy land, which the Romans started to drain.

This route leaves Charterhouse by the lane that goes west past the church to Tynings' farm. When the lane makes a sharp turn to the south-west, the old track goes straight on as a footpath (now part of the West Mendip Way) taking you through the conifers that cover Rowberrow Warren beneath Dolebury Hill Fort. This path will bring you into the village of Shipham by a lane that continues north-west towards the hill fort above Banwell. On the way, it crosses the A38 at Star, a small cluster of houses on the southern slope of the valley watered by Towermead Brook. This is a beautifully sheltered place. Bronze Age people must have been responsible for the Wimblestone, a massive block of dolomitic limestone, almost six feet square, which leans tipsily among the elder, hazel and hawthorn bushes that go to make up a field hedge on the south bank of the stream. It looks like a capstone from a lost cairn, but no burial has been found near it. Its strange name derives from folklore, and comes from *wimble* (to move lightly) showing that in common with many other standing stones it was thought to possess powers of dancing.

There was a Roman villa in this sheltered valley. Its inhabitants might well have taken the lane running west, which turns into a field path before joining the present A371, running beneath Banwell's wooded hill fort. As the main road turns to the west, the Roman road from Charterhouse to the Bristol Channel runs north of another wooded hill, site of the caves in which a mass of bones belonging to creatures of remote prehistory have been found. If you take the lanes round the western slopes of that hill, you will find a footbridge to take you over the M5, and then if you follow the road west to Upper Canada you will come to the lane that runs along the ridge of Bleadon Hill to the estuary of the Axe. That is a narrow channel now, carving its way through extensive low-tide mud flats. At certain times of the year a ferry will take you across this apology for a river, but it has no distance at all to go, and you will find that it is more a floating bridge than a boat. Up to the Middle Ages, the Axe was navigable as far as Cheddar; and Uphill, which now boasts a few sailing boats moored in a disused, flooded quarry, was an important port. South of Uphill, between the headland of Brean Down and the resort of Burnham-on-Sea, the Romans are thought to have built a sand wall, in an attempt to drain the inland marshes by holding back the tide. In the middle of the third century, a layer of clay was added to the banks, which represented the initial attempt to turn the reedy sea to pasture.

The road from Charterhouse to the south-east is much more straightforward. There are patches of the Roman aggar to be discerned along the footpath going past Ubley Warren farm to

Hayden Grange. You can follow the road that far from the Charterhouse mines, then its course runs over private land, passing the northern-most henge of the three Priddy circles and crossing the B3134 just to the south of the Castle of Comfort inn.

On this part of its course, the Roman road runs close by the Priddy mines which lie to the west of the conifers that cover Stockhill, and goes on towards Green Ore, another source of Roman lead. Here part of the B3135 covers the route of the Roman road to Whitnell Corner, where it crosses the old road from Wells to Bath. In this area the course the Romans took follows a prehistoric thoroughfare, marked out by high barrows.

A footpath covers a short stretch of the Roman road to the south-east of Whitnell Corner, where the B road kinks to the south. The two roads converge again to the north of Maesbury hill fort. Here, further traces of the Roman road are temporarily lost, but if you walk over the grassy earthwork, and follow the lane going south-east past a golf course, you will be back on the Roman route as you climb up to Beacon Hill, the highest point on Mendip. It is here that the lead route crosses the Fosse Way, so it is a place to which we shall return.

As you follow the road towards Frome you will now be on the course of the Roman lead road as far as Long Cross. From there it goes through private land to East Cranmore. From that village, traces of the Roman road have been found, showing that it headed to the south-east from the north of Witham Friary, by Walk farm to the site of the isolated church of Gare Hill on the county boundary.

At Beacon Hill there must have been much traffic between the men carrying the lead from the Mendip mines and the travellers along the Fosse Way, running diagonally across the country from Lincoln to Exeter. That great road enters Somerset through Bath, going over Mendip near the source of the lead at Camerton, where the mineral was mixed with Cornish tin to produce pewter vessels. On this part of the route the A637, which runs from Bath to Radstock through Peasdown St John, follows the course of the Fosse Way very closely. The main road wavers slightly as it crosses the valley of the Cam Brook near Dunkerton, whereas the Fosse Way – now passable, with difficulty, as a footpath coming out by the Prince of Wales Inn – takes the more direct and steeper slope.

Another footpath takes you from Clandown to the west of Radstock to follow the Fosse Way again as it goes directly south-west to join the A367 at the top of the hill across the River Somer. From here to Stratton on the Fosse, you are never allowed to forget that you are on the Fosse Way, what with the Centurion Hotel and the White Post Inn, which has a Roman soldier for its sign.

Once again the main road takes a winding route across a valley and here, to the north of Oakhill, the Fosse Way parts company with it, choosing the steeper, more direct route. If you would follow it to the next clear section of the Way, you must take the footpath that starts from a bend in the main road to the south of the village of Oakhill. From here you climb south-east to join the track that runs up to Beacon Hill, a bit of very rough road way that, for years, has been home to caravan people.

Across the lead road, now the old way from Wells to Frome, you will see the beeches of Beacon Hill, on whose height a steep earthwork and a tall boundary stone, together with a group of barrows, remind you that this has been an important thoroughfare for thousands of years. A very steep path takes you down from this height to join the track that follows the Fosse Way straight as an arrow to Charlton, just to the east of Shepton Mallet. From there it coincides with the route of the road to a hilltop junction, where five ways meet. This is Cannard's Grave, which gets its lugubrious name from its function as the site where felons were publicly executed. There is a pub, a garden centre and a garage here now, but although the inn has changed its name from Cannard's Grave to Cannard's Well, it is still a heavy, foreboding place, the noise of heavy trucks replacing the tramp of the legions' boots.

South of Cannard's Grave, the Roman road coincides with the A37, going through Street on the Fosse and up Pylle Hill. Like the present main road, it seems to have made a rare concession to Ditcheat Hill and to have taken the more gentle ground to the west. At Wraxall, the Fosse Way and A37 head to the south-west together past Lydford on Fosse to Ilchester, the Roman town of Lendinis, one of the most important Roman settlements in the whole of the south-west.

Just to the south of Ilchester, the Fosse Way cuts across to a Roman road running from the Bristol Channel towards Dorchester. The north-west section of this road is clear from Ilchester to Street, near Glastonbury. North-west from there it is thought to have followed the course of the ancient ridgeway route along the crest of the Polden Hills towards the salt works around Bridgwater Bay and the port of Combwich on the mouth of the Parret. There is also a Roman road, engineered from the ancient trackway which ran from Dover via Old Sarum past Cadbury Castle to the east of Yeovil. It joins Ilchester in the northern part of the present town.

From Ilchester, the Fosse Way continues towards the south-west, and as far as South Petherton its route is covered by the A303. At South Petherton, where the main road goes more directly to the west, the lane to Over Stratton follows the route of the Fosse Way. A footpath from that village continues to follow its course, and a further lane takes up the route between Lopen and Dinnington. South of Dinnington, there is no trace of the Fosse Way, but you can pick it up again on White Down at the western edge of the ridge of Windwhistle Hill, and follow its course along the B3167 to another Street (a place name always associated with a Roman road) and then to Perry Street, south-east of Chard. From there the Fosse Way heads towards Axminster, and we leave it at the county boundary, where the B road joins the A358. We have to remember that nearly all the Roman roads in Somerset formed part of a national grid system, and that it can be confusing to look at them in isolation.

The three major Roman towns on the Somerset Fosse Way were at Shepton Mallet, Ilchester and Bath. The settlement at Shepton Mallet was the least significant, but for a few weeks in the summer of 1990 it caused a stir in archaeological history, as substantial Roman remains were discovered along the known Fosse Way route, on a site designed for a new warehouse to meet the needs of the industrial complex that has swallowed up Showerings, renowned for Babycham.

Because of the nature of its water, Shepton Mallet has long been associated with the manufacture of drinks in one form or another; and it was in 1864, when the Anglo-Bavarian Brewery Company set up its massive headquarters on the western outskirts of the town that Roman pottery kilns were discovered on the site. It was common knowledge too that traces of a Roman building of some importance were destroyed when the railway was built. However, despite such finds – the continual collection of Roman coins and ornaments in the fields bordering the route of the Fosse Way, and even the discovery in 1988 of a lead coffin lying in a grave cut out of the rock south of the old Somerset and Dorset railway line to the west of Bullimore Farm – the full extent of the Roman settlement here was not established until the bulldozers started to clear the ground for the great new warehouse in 1990.

When the archaeologists were called in and excavations began in the February of that year, it was clear that the lead coffin was part of a cemetery burial, and even more interestingly, that many Roman buildings and enclosures lay further to the east, and so closer to the route of the Fosse Way. We must remember that it was the Roman custom that all adult burials should be sited away from the settlements of the living.

In May 1990, a full team of archaeologists was given three months in which to complete the excavations of the site before the developers took over. They used the time to collect objects and to record their observations of the Roman walls and foundations that now lie, buried again but carefully plotted, under the service areas surrounding the new warehouse. The outlines of some of the Roman buildings have at least been clearly marked out on the surface.

The fact there is such an extensive Roman settlement on this section of the Fosse Way is hardly surprising, for Shepton Mallet lies about half-way between the more important towns of Bath (Aquae Sulis) to the north and Ilchester (Lendiniae) to the south. It is possible that during the first century there may have been a military installation here, but there have been no finds to suggest a barracks; and in his record of the excavations, Peter Leach states his belief that the main purpose of this Roman settlement was to establish a presence in an area in which the native British were politically powerful.

For some three hundred years, the Romans lived on this southern slope of Mendip, looking north towards Beacon Hill. By the end of the second century their occupation must have been fully established, for among the objects of that date which the archaeologists discovered there were bronze dress fasteners of elaborate designs as well as pottery from Southern Gaul and amphorae in which wine must have been imported from Spain and North Africa.

A typical Shepton Mallet Roman house would have had two or three rooms, often with an added store room and a cobbled surround forming a yard or passageway. One of the buildings excavated showed evidence of the equivalent of a chip-fire. The southern end of the house, thought to be the kitchen, was the scene of such a terrible blaze in the second century that the wooden doorsills were reduced to charcoal, while molten lead from the roof shattered pottery vessels.

By the end of the fourth century, a substantial town had evolved here, its inhabitants all dependent on the Fosse Way for communications with the outside world. Unlike most other Roman towns in Britain, these houses with their adjacent fields seem to have been built haphazardly as the occasion demanded, in an area bounded by the River Sheppy to the north and Cannard's Grave to the south. There was obviously no attempt at a regular street grid, nor have any traces of outer defences been found. Moreover, it seems very likely that although the inhabitants of these houses lived firmly within the Roman administration, many of them were native-born Britons.

This does not appear to have been so much the case at Ilchester, a fortified town garrisoning a thousand men in an area contained by the present town boundaries and formerly the tribal headquarters of the Durotriges. It is generally believed that the Romans called the place Lendinis, the little marsh, because of a tendency for the Yeo to overflow its banks. Nevertheless, it is still the centre of rich agricultural land, as it was in Roman times when it served the legions as the chief market town for the whole of the area now defined by South Somerset and North Dorset.

Indeed, until the nineteenth century, Ilchester was the capital of the county and second only to Bath as Somerset's main town. In AD 60, at the time of the revolt of the Iceni under Boudicca in the east of the country, the Durotriges on Cadbury hill fort harassed the Roman army penetrating west. Their opposition lead to a wholesale massacre of the Celtic people dwelling within the earthworks of Cadbury; but gradually the remainder of the local Britons came to make their homes near the Roman town. Marks of two of their round houses have been discovered near the banks of the Yeo, close to Ilchester.

At least one human story emerges from the daily life of Lendinis. You find evidence for it in Taunton museum where bones from one of the graves from the cemetery by that section of the Fosse Way are displayed. One grave contained the bones of a man and a dog. It is quite clear that this Romano-Briton had a great affection for the animal, for its hind leg shows a healed break, a veterinary success that must have demanded great care and patience.

Because of its hot healing springs, Bath, in the extreme north of that part of Somerset now bureaucratically designated as Avon, became the major town on the Fosse Way. At least three roads converged here in the swamps of the Avon Valley. The Fosse Way set out from here on its way to the south-west by climbing the steeply banked road, still known by its generic name of Holloway, which leads up to Bear Flats and the Wellsway. Another two went north, out of our area: one headed to Cirencester; the other, running south-east from the port of Sea Mills on the Severn estuary, went through Bath towards Silchester and London.

So it was here, at the Roman Aquae Sulis where the hot springs brought water from the depths of the Mendip lime-stone, that the great baths were sunk, housed in buildings of honey-coloured oolite, a stone now known by the name of the city. Part temple, these baths were consecrated to the Roman Minerva and the Celtic Sulis, whose altars were served by priests of both races. Here the omens were cast and animals were sacrificed as a propitiation for human follies. The sacred fires appeared to have been fuelled with Somerset coal, possibly from a seam mined near Camerton. John Haddon points out in his *Portrait of Bath* (Hale 1982) that the third-century Solinus reported that the perpetual fire in the temple of Minerva 'never whitens into ash but as the flame fades, turns into rocky lumps'.

Everyone who visits these baths today is made instantly aware that this was a sacred site as well as a meeting place for healing and recreation. Parts of the temple remain, although the main altar has long gone; some stones from it now being several miles away on the outer wall of the church of Compton Dando near Keynsham.

About the middle of the second century, an earthen rampart was built around Bath. It enclosed an area of some twenty-three acres, so that this town, which must have been home to all the officials and workers connected with the baths could not have measured more than a quarter of a mile from side to side. The regular attenders at the baths came from the large villas, built for wealthy Roman settlers to the south of the city. In later years, many of the privileged people who visited the baths were not native Italians, and did not even come from the continent. They were Celts, born in Britain, who had adopted a Roman way of life. They probably spoke to each other in Latin, the language used on all formal occasions, but they used a tongue somewhat resembling modern Welsh to address their servants and farm workers. Linguistically they behaved in much the same way as the eleventh-century Saxons who speedily adopted the language of their conquerors for all formal procedures. For a more detailed description of the remains of Aquae Sulis, one of the major spas in the whole of the Roman Empire, please see Chapter XII.

Historians have long ceased to believe that the Romans only met barbaric tribes when they came to Britain. By the early

years of the first century, Somerset was already being extensively farmed; and the number of villas discovered in the county
reflects a community more concerned with agriculture than
with military matters. Many of these villa farms were naturally
concentrated along the Fosse Way, and many of them were
within a few miles of Ilchester.

The figured mosaics from these villas illustrate the wealth
and taste of the people who farmed this land, for they are some
of the most elegant in the country. At Pitney, between
Somerton and Ilchester, the mosaic was found to have an
octagonal design with the figure of a deity in each segment. A
more modest floor covering was given up to the symbols of the
four seasons.

Pitney's wealth appears to have come from grain crops and
pigs. A buttressed granary tower was discovered there as well
as an overhead grain store. Two pig sties were also uncovered
and it is generally thought that much of the Pitney grain was
used for animal feed. Cattle as well as pigs were fattened on the
exceptionally fertile lowland pastures of this part of the
country. Where the Friesians graze today, small Celtic shorthorns mingled with a few specimens of a much larger breed in
the fields around the Roman villas.

At Catsgore, two and a quarter miles to the south-east of
Somerton, by the road that ran through Street to link with the
Fosse Way at Ilchester, three or four farms seem to have
flourished until the end of the fourth century. They were
managed from an adjacent villa, first charted in 1950. Twenty
years later, a two-year period of thorough excavations revealed
a Romano-British settlement extending over ten acres. Its
earliest buildings dated from AD 80 and most of them were
substantially rebuilt and extended towards the end of the third
century.

As well as granaries, the farm buildings contained at least
two corn driers, and an outhouse that obviously served as
either a byre or a stable. It is not at all improbable that it was
the latter, for we know from the discovery of a smithy at Low
Ham that horses were much used in this corner of Roman
Britain.

The farm settlements at Low Ham appear to have been worked until well into the fifth century, but many of the neighbouring villas appear to have been abandoned around 367, when the Roman administration started to collapse. The Low Ham villa has provided us with an example of the elaborate delicacy of Roman mosaics in Britain. Now on display in the county museum at Taunton, it is worth visiting for the pleasure of its design and colour. Illustrating the story of Dido and Aeneas, it shows that the occupants of the villas had become familiar with classical literature and enjoyed the stories of the heroes.

That mosaic must have been fashioned some time towards the end of the fourth century, for the plunge bath over which it was laid has been dated to around 330. This suggests that here, as in other parts of the West Country, a sophisticated and civilised way of life continued despite the impending collapse of Rome. It was to persist long after the withdrawal of the legions. However evidence for concern about that collapse comes from a trove of Roman coins of the late fourth century which was discovered in the area; one of many in the country apparently hoarded away at a time of great uncertainty.

Although there is not much evidence that Roman settlements were established to the west of the Quantocks, F. J. Snell in his *Book of Exmoor*, published in 1903, claims that Roman coins were picked up around Exe Head, in the swampy area known as The Chains, near a well-marked prehistoric and medieval trade route. At Simonsbath he was told of 'a tradition that the Romans worked a white iron mine at Barkham (Burcombe on the current Ordnance Survey maps) on the road to South Molton'. But he could find no trustworthy historical evidence of it. We do know, however, that there was a Roman fortlet near Wiveliscombe.

There has long been proof of the Roman settlements in other parts of the county. In 1753, a mosaic was discovered at the site of a Roman villa in East Coker near Yeovil. It shows the outcome of a successful hunt, with two hunters carrying the body of the deer. In the north of the county, a further mosaic was unearthed in 1837 above Whatley Combe, near Mells, an area now much disturbed by quarrying; and in March 1884, in the part of the old county of Somerset now known as Avon, a villa was unearthed at Wemberham. It had been built in marshy country near the Yeo estuary.

This villa was located when, in the course of laying pipes to drain a field, a labourer discovered that he had cut into an area of tessellated pavement. Excavations lasting two months were then undertaken, directed by Mr Smyth-Pigget, who came across vestiges of an elaborate ten-room villa. He also unearthed signs of a Roman wall, external to the villa, and taken to be evidence of an early attempt to drain the marshes and reedy swamps of north-western Somerset.

Mr Smyth-Pigget gave an account of his findings to a meeting of the Somerset Archaeological and Natural History Society at Weston-super-Mare in the September of 1885. Enthusiastically the members took the train from Weston to Yatton where they were met by carriages who took them to the site of the villa. There they were able to admire the floor mosaic, composed of white, blue and red tiles fashioned from local materials and carefully protected by a hastily constructed roof of corrugated iron.

The Whatley Combe mosaic was also protected for a time and the owner of the land on which it stood, a Mr Shore, built a covering shed over it. Unfortunately, the weather in the Mendips, sight-seers and, above all, souvenir hunters proved too much for it. However, a drawing, showing Orpheus with his lyre taming the wild beasts, was made of it, and we have records of a pavement to compare with the mosaic at Low Ham.

There must be many more lost or undiscovered mosaics that once adorned the rich villas in the county.

Yet it is wrong to think that all Romano-Britons lived in or around elaborate dwellings with under-floor central heating systems, plunge baths and sophisticated, decorative mosaics. In the Mendip hills there is plenty of evidence to show that many people still lived in the limestone caves until well into the fourth century. The vast Wookey Hole cave system through which the underground Axe flows was inhabited by them; and as this cave is now open to the public you can go there at any time and see the extent of the living accommodation these great caves could offer. I would advise you to try to make your visit during the winter months when the crowds have gone. Then you may be able to have the cave to yourself apart from the accompanying guide. The jokes will never change. The unfortunate guides have to submit to the script supplied by the managers.

This advice also applies to another show cave, Gough's cave in Cheddar Gorge, named after its discoverer. Here in 1870, several Roman artefacts were discovered including another hoard of late fourth-century coins. At Burrington Combe, nearby, you can only peer into Aveline's Hole, which afforded a more modest Romano-British home; and if you walk along the top of Blackdown to Dolebury hill fort you will pass the entrance to Read's cavern, an overhanging shelf of limestone, beneath which is the entrance to a spacious cavern which was inhabited by several generations.

At Wookey Hole, the cave dwellers were close neighbours of the more fortunate people who lived on the hillside to the east of the caves. A villa was excavated here in 1956, and its uncovering proved that material comfort is not the whole of happiness. We cannot say what tragedy caused the deaths of the seven babies whose skeletons were found in an inner chamber. Possibly they died as a result of an epidemic whose adult victims would, according to Roman custom, have been interred well away from the settlement.

For solace and for protection against the vicissitudes of life, the Romano-British turned to the gods, combining the classical deities with the Celtic spirits. We have seen evidence of this in the dedication of the temple at Bath to Sulis Minerva which links the Celtic goddess Sul to the Roman Minerva, but the tendency is also evident in lesser sanctuaries. Minerva was by no means the only Roman deity to be associated with Bath. If you drive some four miles west out of the city on the A39, and then take the turn to Compton Dando, you will find Roman figures built into the buttress at the north-east corner of the church. The statues, supposed to represent Hercules and

Apollo, are very worn and have been enclosed in glass to prevent further deterioration. When the Revd John Skinner of Camerton came here in the summer of 1820, he noted that it was quite easy to make out the palm branch of Hercules and the lyre associated with Apollo.

There is little doubt, however, that in most instances the Roman gods took precedence. In the octagonal temple discovered at Pagan Hill, near Chew Stoke, the figures of Hercules, Minerva and Mercury were discovered. On the headland of Brean Down, another temple was excavated in 1957. The finds dated it between 340–367 and showed that it had walls of dressed limestone as well as an impressive entrance porch flanked by Tuscan columns of Bath stone. Its central tower with round headed windows was possibly partly constructed to serve as a landmark for sailors negotiating their way through the narrow channels to the port of Uphill.

In 1958, a more extensive Romano-British temple was excavated on Lamyatt Beacon to the north of Ilchester. Originally called Creech Hill, from the Celtic word *cruc* for a hill or mound, Lamyatt rises as a solitary eminence from the South Somerset plain near Bruton, and is not part of the surrounding escarpments. This means that although it can only boast a height of 729 feet it appears to be much higher.

Further excavations in 1973 confirmed that this temple must have been built at the beginning of the fourth century and the votive offerings that were found here indicate that travellers along the Fosse Way would climb up to this temple to pray for protection, and possibly to buy the wheel emblem, a talisman which served the same function as a Christian St Christopher medal. Some of the votive offerings left by the travellers can be seen now in the small museum under the town hall at Castle Carey.

By the time the Romans left Britain there is evidence that some of the cemeteries contained Christian burials. In this context one of the most significant finds was made during the 1990 excavations at Shepton Mallet. One of the three cemeteries adjacent to that Fosse Way settlement contained seventeen graves, all aligned east to west in the Christian

44

manner (the Romans customarily layed their coffins north to south). In one of these graves a circular, silver amulet was discovered with the Chi-Rho symbol pricked out on it, a Christian version of the wheel emblems found at Lamyatt.

After Constantine's acceptance of the new religion by the Edict of Milan in 313, it seems most probable that many of the Roman temples in this country would be given Christian dedications, although I have come across no records of such a change. There is plenty of evidence, however, to prove that in Somerset, as elsewhere, Christian burials existed close to known Roman settlements. In Ilchester, for example, it was estimated that about 1,500 early Christian burials took place to the north of the settlement. They were unearthed when the site of the old gaol was excavated. Yet it is well to remember that it was not only the legions who brought Christianity to Somerset. I will look at the alternative source in the next chapter.

III
Christ and Arthur

In the woods on Culbone Hill, to the west of Porlock and some five miles to the east of the county boundary, there is a standing stone inscribed with a wheeled cross. It was discovered in 1940, and although it stands in private land, you can see it if you take the lane running towards the coast from the A39 at the top of Porlock Hill. The permitted footpath is signed on your left, just after you cross a cattle-grid. From there it is a short walk through larches to the stone, which epitomises the two theories as to how Christianity reached Somerset.

If, as some people believe, knowledge of the Gospels reached the area solely through the Roman legions, then it can be argued that this stone stands close by the route along the north Exmoor coast, leading to the nearby Roman fortlet at Countisbury in Devon. On the other hand, it was far more usual for the Romanised Christians to use the Chi-Rho symbol, as we saw in the Shepton Mallet excavation; and in any case one might well look for a Latin inscription on the stone. There is none.

Those who believe that Christianity actually came to this coast from a church that grew up in Ireland and Wales, and was inspired by teachings brought by early traders from North Africa rather than from the other side of the Mediterranean, will observe that the carving on the Culbone stone is in essence a Celtic Christian symbol. As the Welsh coast is so close by, and as Porlock Bay was a natural harbour, it can be argued that this standing stone (possibly a Bronze Age monument) was inscribed for a Christian community led by a Welsh monk. Certainly, the two nearby churches are dedicated to saints of the Celtic tradition.

You can only reach Culbone church, claimed as the smallest in England, by walking through the woods from Porlock weir to the east or from Silcombe Farm to the west. Although this area was originally known as Kytnor, the place of the kites, its present name derives from one or other of the dedications that are claimed for this tiny medieval building. Some say Culbone derives from Columbanus, a missionary saint to whom the fourteenth-century chapel near the vanished Saxon palace at Cheddar is also dedicated. He was an Irish monk of the late sixth century, who may well have traversed the south-west peninsula on his way to Gaul. Another less likely tradition would have Culbone originate from *Kil Beuno*, the settlement of Beuno, an abbot, also of the sixth century, and connected primarily with North Wales, although he is said to have been born and reared in Herefordshire.

The other nearby Celtic dedication is in Porlock itself, where the church is dedicated to another Herefordshire saint, Dyfrig. He worked mainly in South Wales, but his missionary activities were to spread throughout the South-West. The twelfth-century Geoffrey of Monmouth, whose history is liberally mixed with legend, claims that Dyfrig crowned Arthur as King of Britain, in the Roman city of Silchester, and that he took a leading part in that monarch's wars against the Saxons.

Inland, on the heights of Exmoor's Winsford Hill, whose ridgeway is taken to have been a route used by the Romans, there is another inscribed stone. This one is somewhat more sophisticated and seems to be purely secular. It stands on the open moor and since 1906 it has been protected by a shelter built on the instruction of Sir Thomas Acland, whose family owned the land. This has no doubt helped to preserve the inscription, for the stone is carved with the name of Caracci Nepus, and the deduction is that this was probably a fifth- or sixth-century boundary stone, set up by somebody claiming descent from Caractacus, king of the Silures of South Wales, another proof of the close links between the Celts on either side of the Severn Sea. Excavations around the stone in 1937 have found no trace of a grave.

The Caractacus stone, as it is called, reminds us that not all Dark Age Celtic memorials in Somerset are necessarily Christian; but at Glastonbury one can easily fall into the trap of reckoning all ancient Christian sites to be Celtic, linked with the great legendary Celtic Christian figure of Arthur. The present-day myths of Glastonbury, for the most part a rather ugly little red-brick town, derive from two sources: the desperate need of its abbey, after a disastrous fire in the twelfth century, to attract pilgrims to the site and so restore its wealth and thus its prestige among competing ecclesiastical institutions; and the musings of various late nineteenth-century clerics with mystical leanings. The facts that the Church of England, now in urgent need of funds to maintain the remains of the abbey, ruined at the Reformation, has set up a shop and visitors' centre reminiscent of any tourist theme park; and that the town has been captured for New Age travellers and claimed for the cult of the goddess form only part of my present considerations in so far as both factors remind us of the extraordinary magnetism of Glastonbury Tor. This shapely outcrop of white lias, rising out of the flat surrounding moorland, only latterly known as the Somerset Levels, attracts pilgrims and tourists as constantly now as it has done through the centuries. Heavily wooded in the period we are now dealing with, it must nevertheless have made a remarkable landmark, even without the tower of a vanished thirteenth-century church, which now crowns its summit, and which was built to replace an earlier edifice destroyed by an earthquake in 1275.

The spiritual history of Glastonbury was much influenced by the claims of the twelfth-century monks to restore their abbey's prestige. In 1125, they must have been delighted to read William of Malmesbury's affirmation that St Patrick was buried there, having returned from Ireland in his old age in order to die in his homeland. He is said to have landed at the mouth of the River Hayle in Cornwall and then to have journeyed east through the south-west peninsula until he came to Glastonbury's wattle church. That building was the greatest loss in the twelfth-century fire, for it was said to rank with St

Ninian's Candida Casa in Galloway as the earliest church building in Britain.

According to William of Malmesbury's account, Patrick was followed to Glastonbury by Indract, son of an Irish king, who is actually recorded as living three centuries later. He and seven of his companions were to be murdered by pagan, Saxon brigands, so it is fitting, that as Geoffrey tells us, the seventh-century Ine, king of the West Saxons, should have been inspired by a vision to place Indract's body in a pyramid of stone to the left of the altar in that lost church.

It seems odd that Ine should have been completely unaware that he was honouring Indract by giving him a tomb near the place where latter-day monks were to find the tomb of Arthur and Guinevere. It was the announcement of that discovery in 1190 that was to do more than anything else to restore the wealth and prestige of the abbey, after the terrible fire that destroyed most of the monastery buildings as well as the ancient wattle church.

Patrick and Indract were not the only Irish saints who were said to have made their way to Glastonbury. There is also a tradition that Brigid came here and lived nearby on a small eminence, still known as Beckery, the island of Brigid, and where, in the eigth century a small chapel was built in her honour. It is all lost now under the town's industrial estate.

There is a more lively dedication to Brigid in the thirteenth-century church near Brean Down, for it has been suggested that although the abbess of Kildare probably never came here in person, she may well have sent missionary sisters across the Severn Sea and they would have landed at Uphill. All along the north Somerset coast, in fact, there are places in which it seems likely that Brigid was venerated. Although it is fanciful to claim that Bristol was originally Brigidstowe, it has been argued that many place names such as Axbridge and Bridgwater are not named after river bridges but after the Irish nun. More authentic, to my mind, is the St Bride's field near Cannington. True, it may only be so called because of a lease falling due at Candlemas (St Brigid's feast is February 1), but it remains as witness to the importance which this saint had for the people of north Somerset.

As Susan Pearce and H.M. Porter have both pointed out, there are numerous dedications to Celtic saints all along the Somerset coast and throughout Exmoor. The church in the village of Timberscombe, by the River Avill, just off the A396 to the south-west of Dunster, is dedicated to the Cornish Petroc, the hermit of Bodmin Moor. This saint is honoured in the liturgy of Wells cathedral, and although he probably never left Cornwall, he may well have sent his disciples eastwards.

Further to the east, the headland church at Watchet, believed to be the landfall sighted by Coleridge's Ancient Mariner, is dedicated to the seventh-century Decuman, whose name, as H.M. Porter reminds us, suggests (with its echo of 'one tenth') that he, or more likely one of his ancestors, was a Romano-British tax collector. A medieval life of the saint, written by a canon of Wells, tells us that Decuman crossed from West Wales to Dunster, from whence he journeyed east to establish his hermitage at the place where Watchet church stands now.

Like Indract, Decuman was attacked by pagan brigands, not necessarily Saxons however, for they killed him in the Celtic manner by cutting off his head. Thereupon the saint, in an allegorical tradition perpetuated in many medieval hagiographies of the early Celtic saints, picked up his head and carried it into a nearby dell, from where a spring gushed forth in whose waters he could wash away the blood. After that, as a matter of course, the spring possessed healing powers. At one time, Decuman's well, a few yards to the west of the church, lay in a tangle of undergrowth, which gave the latter-day pilgrims who sought it out a sense of exploration and discovery. Nowadays the path to the well has been manicured and a tidy garden set on each side of it. To offset the loss of wilderness and romance, we may remind ourselves that this sort of care and attention may well have been provided by the medieval monks from the nearby Cistercian abbey at Cleeve, who would have tended this shrine.

These monks must also have been familiar with the

settlement at Carhampton just to the west of their abbey. The much restored red sandstone church of this village is now dedicated to John the Baptist, but it stands on the site where the sixteenth-century John Leland noted a chapel dedicated to Carantoc. That Welsh monk is supposed to have founded an oratory here before continuing his missionary journey by crossing the sea to Brittany.

Carantoc is another Celtic saint who plays a part in Arthurian legend. A local tradition records that as a young man the king held court in a palace which stood on the site later to be occupied by a medieval hall. That hall crowned Conygar Hill, near Dunster, and was destroyed in the wars between Stephen and Matilda. It has now been replaced by an eighteenth-century folly. In Arthur's time the surrounding countryside was being menaced by a sea dragon – a metaphor probably for pagan pirates. Whether Carantoc was destined to confront a horde of wild men or a single savage beast is a matter of interpretation; the story makes it definitely clear, however, that at Arthur's bidding he did not hesitate to call the monster out of the sea and so tamed it (or converted them) that he was able to lead a docile creature by a silken thread to the king's court, where it posed no threat to the people who flocked to see it.

In the ninth century, Asser, adviser to King Alfred, wrote that Congresbury [in the north-east] was originally the burial place of Congar, another saint of the Celtic church. The monastery that he founded was derelict by the time that Alfred decided to set up his religious foundation here, but the suggestion has been made that the traces of a large circular building, discovered when the hill fort at Cadbury Congresbury was excavated, was part of Congar's monastery.

Like other missionaries of the Celtic tradition, Congar probably crossed the channel from South Wales, but folklore gives him more romantic origins. It suggests that he was either the son of an emperor of Constantinople, travelling to Britain on a trading excursion connected with Mendip lead; or that he was the son of Geraint, a king of Dumnonia, who fought with Arthur against Saxon and Irish pirates in Bridgwater Bay.

Keynsham, which lies between Bath and Bristol, and which was known to the sixteenth-century Thomas Gerard as Caynsford, claims to have been settled by another Celtic saint. Following the lead of the Elizabethan antiquary, Camden, Gerard tells us that the place gets its name from 'Keyna or Caine, a devout British saint, a Virgin'. He may, however, have got it wrong, for it has been suggested that Keynsham was simply named after Caega – a Saxon land-owner. Certainly, when an abbey was founded here in 1170 by William, Earl of Gloucester, there was no mention of a native saint. The dedication was made to the Blessed Virgin Mary, and no cult of Keyn has been recorded in the area, although a saint of that name is honoured in Cornwall. Nevertheless, a passage in the fourteenth-century, Latin, life of Keyne by John of Tynemouth seems to have struck a chord with the local people. In a translation of that life by Canon G.H. Doble, an enthusiastic and meticulous student of the lives of the saints of the West Country, writing in the 1920s and 30s, we read that when Keyne crossed the Severn Sea, she asked the local tribal chief to give her some land in which she might serve God:

> He answered that he would gladly give it, but that the place was filled with such a multitude of serpents that neither man nor beast might live there. The virgin however replied with steadfast courage that she trusted in the help of the Most High and in His Name was willing and able to drive out all that poisonous multitude. The place was therefore given to the Virgin, and, after prostrating herself in prayer, as she was wont, she quickly changed all that offspring of vipers into hard stones. For the stones in the fields and villages there even to this day bear the forms of serpents, as if they had been carved by the sculptor's art.

That passage could certainly apply to Keynsham, where the local limestone is full of the fossilised imprints of ammonites, many of which have been used to embellish the buildings.

Fascinating as all the legends of the Celtic saints may be, to my mind Somerset's links with the Celtic church are most strongly realised in the person of that church's contemporary scourge, the monk Gildas, whose footsteps, they say, can still be heard by the site of the vanished priory on the island of Steep Holm, some five miles into the Bristol Channel from

Weston-super-Mare. Gildas would have known the place by its Celtic name of Ronech, and it is there that he built a cell and an oratory dedicated to the Holy Trinity and settled down in solitude to write his great work, *De Excidio Britanniae*. According to his twelfth-century biographer, the Welsh Caradoc of Llancarfan, he spent the nights sleeping on a steep cliff, possibly the place from which you can now watch the cormorants fishing in some of the swiftest and most dangerous currents around the English coast.

Viking pirates sweeping south from the Orkneys finally drove Gildas from his island retreat, and forced him to return to the monastery at Glastonbury. Ironically his *De Excidio Britanniae*, which was completed around 540, declared that the victories of the Anglo-Saxon invaders were just retribution for the way in which the secular and clerical hierarchies of Britain had fallen away from the high ideals of the early church.

There are two conflicting accounts of Gildas's old age. According to one of them, he was to end his days in Brittany, but not before he had stamped his imprint on the mainland of Somerset as well as on the county's one off-shore island. The other, endorsed by the twelfth-century William of Malmesbury, has Gildas dying at Glastonbury in 512 (a discrepancy here with the date of the completion of his major work) and buried there in the old wattle church.

Whatever the truth of his end may be, I think we can take it that the first historian of the British church really did live and work at the old abbey in Glastonbury, and that in the tradition of most Celtic monks and abbots he left the community from time to time to live in more solitary contemplation. When the remote fastness of Ranech became untenable he went across the marshes of the River Brue, now neatly canalised into a drainage ditch, and made his hermitage on a small island, rising out of the reedy swamps at a place where the parish church of Street was to be built.

As Gildas belongs to Brittany and Wales as well as Somerset, so the Christian King Arthur, that mystical Celtic leader, has left traces in those places, and in Scotland and the north of

England as well. Somerset claims him for Glastonbury and both Cadburys, and perhaps there was an Arthur here distinct from the others. For there are those who argue that the name Arthur does not connote any particular individual, rather it indicates a high totemic rank: Arthur, the Son of the Bear.

Be that as it may, it is certainly an individual king of high romance that Somerset honours in much of the country's folklore. Like Gildas, Arthur haunts by the sound of his footsteps and that of his horses' hooves, as once a month, he and his knights ride round the grassy ramparts of the hill fort of South Cadbury. It is said that on Christmas Eve the whole cavalcade comes down off the hill to drink the waters of the spring by the church at Sutton Montis, a building which still retains its Norman chancel arch. Naturally, the other Cadbury, by Congresbury, has put in its claim to be Arthur's real Camelot; and since both Cadburys were occupied until well into the fifth century, they no doubt both provided a base from which strong Celtic tribal leaders held the Saxons at bay. One of them might indeed have supported an Arthur.

If we take the discovery of Arthur's grave at Glastonbury to be a pious fraud inaugurated by monks desperate to find money enough to rebuild the church they had lost by fire – and this is the view of most serious historians – then we still have to ask why, in the twelfth century, they should think that the announcement of such a discovery should be so efficacious, as indeed it was.

Once again, the answer to that question lies in Wales. Some of the Welsh, who sailed their coracles across the dividing sea, brought the legends of Arthur with them to Somerset. The ninth-century *Black Book of Carmarthen* has a section of verses on the graves of heroes, in which the place of Arthur's burial is described as 'an eternal mystery', meaning presumably that although there was a mass of Arthurian legends circulating in Wales at that time, many of which name actual places, not one ventured to mention where the great king was buried. Here was an opportunity that the Glastonbury monks could exploit to the full, especially as the flourishing cult of Arthur was at its height by the twelfth century.

Another mystery of location is propounded by the authentically historic battle of Mons Badonis, in which the Celts had so great a victory over the Saxons that it was a hundred years before the latter seriously penetrated the West Country again. Historians date this battle to sometime during the final decade of the fifth century, but no one has been able to give it a precise location. There are several contenders for the site, the most generally approved being somewhere on the hills around Bath. Geoffrey of Monmouth had no doubt that the battle was fought out there. In a translation of his *History of the Kings of Britain* made by Lewis Thorpe we read that Arthur, having been engaged in battle with the Saxons in the north of England, on hearing that the Saxons were attacking Bath 'finally reached the county of Somerset and approached the siege'. There he called on his men to attack the Saxons 'whose very name is an insult to heaven and detested by all men'.

The King's call to battle was echoed by Dubricius, who

> climbed to the top of a hill and cried out in a loud voice: 'You who have been marked with the cross of the Christian faith, be mindful of the loyalty you owe to your fatherland and to your fellow-countrymen! If they are slaughtered as a result of this treacherous behaviour by the pagans they will be an everlasting reproach to you, unless in the meanwhile you do your utmost to defend them!'

The result of that hard-won but overwhelming Celtic victory, whether you attribute it to Arthur or to an allied force of tribal leaders, was that by the time the Saxons successfully infiltrated Somerset, they had adopted the Christian faith. Although there were several minor skirmishes such as the one led by the Saxon Cerdic and fought out at Cerdic's Ford, a place generally thought to be Chard, it was not until 577 and the great battle of Deorham, to the north of Bath, that the Saxons had their first decisive victory in the west. It resulted in an infiltration which took well over a century to consolidate, although right through the seventh century there was a definite Saxon presence in Somerset. After a Saxon victory in 658 at Penselwood, now on the Wiltshire borders of the county and then at the western edge of Selwood, a vast ocean of trees that covered most of southern England, the Saxon Cenwalh came to Glastonbury where the Celtic Bregored was abbot. Cenwalh seems to have been in a position to confirm that appointment, and, after Bregored's death around 670, to grant lands around Meare to the abbey. It was to hold them for almost a millennium. The gift was a fitting one, for it was here that Beon, an Irish monk, who came to Glastonbury in about 460, built the hermitage where he died.

The ultimate Saxon victory in the west occurred in the year 710, when, as the *Anglo-Saxon Chronicle* records, 'Ine and Nun his kinsman fought against Geraint, king of the West Welsh'. Ine was the Saxon king of Wessex, crowned in 688, and the West Welsh were the Celts of the south-west peninsula, the Dumnonia, in fact. The site of Geraint's ultimate defeat was on the Somerset/Devon border, either at Buckland St Mary to the south-east of Taunton or, more likely, at Forches Corner on the heights of the Blackdown ridge, which is now graced by the bayonet-shaped memorial to the Duke of Wellington and which provides a dramatic backdrop to the view to the south of the motorway going west towards Exeter.

IV
The Saxons in Somerset

The story of the Saxon rule of Somerset begins with Ine, king of Wessex for thirty-seven years from 688; although it was not until 710 that the Saxons finally mastered the Celts in Somerset. It was in that year, as the *Anglo-Saxon Chronicle* informs us that 'Ine also and Nun, his kinsman fought with Geraint, King of the Welsh'. That battle which culminated in a decisive Saxon victory, is believed to have taken place at Forches Corner, where Somerset now meets Devon on the heights of the Blackdown ridge. Nun is said to have been killed in the fighting and his burial may be nearby. There is certainly a Nun's barrow marked on the 1881 map of the area. Because Ine's reign was chronicled by monks, we know of him mostly in connection with the churches he was said to have founded and the lands that he gave to the monasteries. The Anglo-Saxon Chronicle relates that it was he who built the first monastery at Glastonbury, founding a church there dedicated to St Peter and St Paul and standing to the east of the original wattle church.

In this as in much else that he undertook throughout his reign, he was assisted by another member of the Wessex royal family, some say his brother, the learned Aldhelm, bishop 'to the west of the wood', as the chronicler described the land which lay on that side of the impenetrable forest of Selwood, stretching east from Frome and dividing the country as completely as an ocean. According to tradition, Aldhelm inspired Ina to build the first church by the well of St Andrew in a fold of the Mendip hills to the east of Glastonbury. It was on this site, the present city of Wells, that a bishopric was established during the reign of Edward the Elder (899–925), but Ine's name is still honoured on a brass plate let into the transept floor of the medieval cathedral.

Aldhelm was to die on 25 May 709 at the village of Doulting to the east of Shepton Mallet, while he was travelling from his palace at Sherborne in Dorset. When he was taken ill, his companions laid him in the little wooden church that stood on the crest of the Mendip plateau on the site where the medieval church was later built. There he died, and although his body was taken back to Malmesbury for burial because he had been a monk there, Doulting has always retained his memory. The church is dedicated to him, and below it, where the waters of the Sheppey spring out of the hillside, the village well, also dedicated to Ine's bishop, was long thought to have healing properties, being especially efficacious for diseases of the eye. Behind the basin of the public well, which for centuries provided the village of Doulting with its drinking water, you can still find traces of the little chapel and baptistry through which the water was channelled, with a flight of stone steps leading down to the spring. In recent years the Shepton Mallet Amenity Trust paid Wells Cathedral £1 purchase money for the well, which is now carefully tended.

On secular matters, there can be little doubt that Aldhelm helped Ine to formulate the laws which were to be the most significant aspect of his reign. They covered matters as diverse as incidents of homicide and the management of strayed beasts, as well as the administration of tenancy rights and the duties relating to military service and conscription. The laws also controlled the highways and restricted the trading routes used by merchants of various kinds; and several clauses were devoted to the management of woodlands. Fines were imposed for burning down trees and for cutting down any that were large enough for thirty swine to stand beneath them.

The last years of Ine's reign were troubled. The *Anglo-Saxon Chronicle* records that in 722 'Queen Aethelburh destroyed Taunton which Ine had built'. Aethelburh was Ine's wife, and writing in the sixteenth century Thomas Gerard explained that she was driven to that desperate action in order to expel the king of the South Saxons who 'having made himself lord of it [i.e. Taunton castle] used it for a bridle to keep in order the adjoyninge country which he had conquered'.

Four years later, Ine abdicated his throne in order to make a pilgrimage to Rome. He was to die there. He was succeeded by Aethelard, his brother-in-law, who gave his name to Aethelardstone near Ilminster, where he must have had a palace. It is still possible to follow the old Saxon road from that palace, known since the fifteenth century as Atherston, to Whitelackington.

After Ine's death the power of Wessex weakened, and the northern part of Somerset became vulnerable to the predatory greed of Mercia. In 733, a year in which the *Chronicle* notes an eclipse of the sun, Aethelbard of Mercia led a host into Wessex and occupied the royal town of Somerton. It was to remain in Mercian hands for the best part of a century and Pitminster, to the south of Taunton, is said to get its name from Pippa, a Mercian bishop.

In the decades that followed, the troubles with Mercia faded in the face of the Danish threat and their piratical raids along Somerset's coastline, and inland along the courses of the north-flowing rivers. Most of the major raids are listed in the *Chronicle*, but there is no doubt that there were many minor skirmishes which went unrecorded. One battle in which the Saxons proved victorious took place in 845, when the men of Dorset joined forces with the men of Somerset to fight against 'a Danish host at the mouth of the Parret and made great slaughter there and won the victory'. Tradition has it that the battle actually took place around Storgursey, but there is no doubt that the whole area around Bridgwater Bay was often to be the site of conflicts.

Some thirty years after that Saxon victory there was another triumph when Hubba, the most notable of the Danish pirates, was finally killed. Several places in both Devon and Somerset claim the site of his ultimate defeat and his burial place. Combwich, again at the mouth of the Parret, is one of the most likely contestants for his final battle, and a tumulus at nearby Cock Farm has been taken for Hubba's burial mound. In his *Book of Exmoor* (1903), however, F.J. Snell reported that 'others hold that a tumuli near the sea at Storgursey is Hubba's grave'. If anyone was thinking that Wick Barrow, now at the entrance to Hinckley Point Nuclear Power station, marks the place, they were clearly wrong, for there is no doubt that tumulus belongs to the Bronze Age.

The hypothesis that Combwich was the scene of Hubba's final defeat is strengthened by Asser, biographer of the great King Alfred (871–899), a man who devoted most of his reign to ridding his country of the menacing Danes. Asser believed that in the final onslaught on Hubba, the Saxons had mustered in the hill fort near Cannington. Then, forced by concern at the lack of any water supply, they decided to take the offensive, surprising the Danish army by night and killing Hubba and eight hundred of his men.

Early in May of 878, Alfred, who had built a fortification at Athelney, a low hill just standing out of the marshes to the east of Taunton, decided in his turn to take the offensive. With men from Somerset, Wiltshire and Hampshire he moved east towards Selwood and engaged the Danes at Edington, fifteen miles to the south of Chippenham, and scored a conclusive victory.

The defeated Danes, as we learn from the *Chronicle*, gave Alfred

> preliminary hostages and solemn oaths that they would leave his kingdom, and promised him in addition that their kin would receive baptism; and they fulfilled this promise in the following manner: three weeks later the king, Guthrum, came to him, one of thirty of the most honourable men in the host, at Aller, which is near Athelney, where the king stood sponsor to him at baptism; and the removal of the baptismal fillet took place at Wedmore, and he was twelve days with the king, who greatly honoured him and his companions with riches.

Aller church stands on a low island in the wet lands to the north-west of Langport. It is some way out of the village along a farm lane, and both the church and the farmhouse garden have a ha-ha separating their higher ground from the moors. The oldest part of the present church is a former south doorway, which belonged to the twelfth-century church and is generously embellished with Norman dog-toothing. It is now preserved inside the much restored church.

There is nothing at Aller to commemorate the baptism of

Guthrum, but it is generally agreed that the church stands on the site of a building erected around 878 to honour that event. It stands in open country now – all the woodlands are on surrounding hills – but the name of Aller (the Saxon for alder) suggests that it was then a place of alder carrs, which flourish on wet lands, and these scrubby trees probably provided the timber for the Saxon church. There is a local belief that some of these timbers still survive in the roof of the present church.

It has been suggested, with good cause, that Alfred chose the isle of Aller for the baptism because he was anxious that the Danes should not find the way across the marshes to his headquarters at Athelney. There was plenty of opportunity for spying. The whole baptismal ceremony took four days, followed by more than a week of feasting at Alfred's palace at Wedmore. At the end of that time, the ritual of removing the 'Chrisom' worn by the newly baptised took place. Secular business was also undertaken then, and during those days at Wedmore, Alfred drew up the treaty that assured Somerset a comparative peace from the Danes for many years.

It was to be broken in 918, when, we are told, 'a great pirate host came over hither from the south from Brittany under two jarls Ohtor and Hroald'. After several bloody skirmishes along the course of the Severn, penetrating into Herefordshire and Gloucestershire, they retreated back to the Severn Sea, and although King Edward had ordered the whole of the north Somerset coast to be fully guarded and alert, the Danes 'landed secretly by night on two separate occasions, once east of Watchet and again at Porlock, and on each occasion the English struck them so that only those few escaped who were able to swim out to the ships. They encamped on the island of Steep Holm until the time came that they were short of food, and many men perished of hunger, since they were unable to obtain provisions.' To escape that predicament, the survivors mustered their strength for further raids on the coast of South Wales.

Traditionally, Battlegore on the western outskirts of Williton is given as the site of the battle of 918, although it is almost certain that the iron-age hill fort to the west of Watchet was used as the Saxon stronghold. Yet it is most likely that the battle spread over wide stretches of the surrounding country. Writing in the sixteenth century, Camden noted that a field called Knap Dane in the parish of Nettlecombe, beneath the Brendon Hills, got its name from the number of Danes buried there after the fearful slaughter of 918. As for the Danish leaders, Ohtor at any rate is said to have lived on in Somerset place names. Othery on the road between Street and Taunton, and Oath near Aller, both claim to derive from Ohtor the Dane.

Three generations later, in 987, Watchet was attacked again, and this time the Danes were successful, slaying 'Goda the Devonshire thane ... and many with him'. Ten years passed and the Danes raided Watchet again and 'wrought great havoc by burning and killing people'. Nor did their attacks stop at the coast, for the *Chronicle* entry for 1016 tells us that 'Eadmund (then recently made king) fought against the host at Penselwood'.

However, despite the invaders attempts to conquer the Saxons on the edge of the forest of Selwood, the north coast remained the most vulnerable area. Miss Eardley-Wilmot, in the course of her work on Exmoor, has retraced the Herepaths (the routes along which the Saxon armies marched) in this area and, in particular, she has shown how the forces moved from the western edge of the Brendon Hills to Porlock Bay.

Although the Danish raids continued for well over a century after the death of Alfred on 26 October 899, in the twenty-eight years of his reign he did much to hold the Danes at bay as we have seen, and a greater part of that effort was centred in Somerset. We must also remember, however, that he was a great scholar, law-giver and man of letters. Somerset has a reminder of this aspect of the King in a small pendant, which some might call a book-marker, and which is generally known as the Alfred Jewel. It was found in the marshes around North Petherton.

The little medallion bearing the legend 'Alfred me fecit' and inscribed with a figure taken to be St Cuthbert is now in the Ashmolean Museum in Oxford. You can see replicas of it both in the Tribunal Museum in Glastonbury and on display in North Petherton church when it is not being worn by the mayor for civic functions. The conjecture that the figure it bears is the representation of the Northumbrian saint is derived from Asser, the priest from St David's, who became Alfred's friend, Latin teacher and biographer. He tells us that when Alfred was at Athelney before his decisive battle at Eddington, he had a vision of Cuthbert, which heartened him in his endeavours. This tradition partly explains the veneration for Cuthbert in the Glastonbury and Wells areas of the county. Wells city church is dedicated to the saint and a copy of the life of Cuthbert is believed to have been lodged in the vanished library of Glastonbury Abbey.

In connection with Cuthbert, we must remember that while Alfred was attacking the Danes in Somerset, the monks of Lindisfarne, then the target of repeated piratical raids, were carrying the uncorrupted body of their beloved 'Cuddy', who had died over two hundred years before, throughout the mainland before finally finding a resting place at Durham. Some say that they actually came as far south as Somerset, although it is more likely that the dedication of the Wells city church is due to the medieval connection with the See of Durham.

As a law-maker, Alfred took what was best and still appropriate from the laws of Ine; and his sense of democracy and justice was such that when he came to make his will, he summoned the West Saxon *witan* (the assembly of wise men) and asked that nobody should be constrained by either love or fear of their monarch from letting him know if there were any rules of common law that limited his freedom in making bequests.

During the first half of the tenth century, it was a Saxon churchman, Dunstan, a nephew of Athelm, the first Bishop of Wells, rather than a monarch who had the greatest influence in Somerset. He was born around 909 in the present village of Baltonsborough, near Glastonbury, where a paved path from the church leads to his supposed birthplace in what is now Main Street. His father Heorstan had an estate, and Dunstan was educated at the abbey. He was to become a member of the court of Alfred's grandson, Aethelstan, and thereafter to remain, whether in or out of favour, closely connected with the monarchy. In his early years, Aethelstan's niece, Dunstan's kinswoman, Aethelfleda, built herself a house to the west of the abbey church of Glastonbury and there entertained members of the royal court.

At the age of twenty-six, Dunstan had his first taste of royal disfavour. He was expelled from the court on the grounds of his reputed fondness for secular literature, whereupon he made secret monastic vows, was ordained priest and for four years lived a hermit's life at Glastonbury. In 939, Eadmund I, Aethelstan's brother, who had become king of Wessex in that year, had an almost miraculous escape from death while hunting in the Forest of Mendip. The story is told in the *Axbridge Chronicle*, and from that we learn that one day, presumably in the sort of low cloud that frequently covers the Mendip plateau, the king followed a stag to the very edge of Cheddar Gorge. On the exact spot from which the pursued stag plunged to its death, the king's horse checked his gallop. Certain that his life had been spared by divine grace, the king related the miracle of his escape to his nobles, assembled, presumably, in his palace of Cheddar, and declared it to be a sign that Dunstan should immediately be brought back into favour. Accordingly, the priest was installed as Abbot of Glastonbury, and the king made rich endowments to the monastery, which Dunstan governed according to the rule of St Benedict. During that time, Glastonbury Abbey was rebuilt from stone quarried at West Pennard, and Dunstan also turned his attention to reviving and enlarging the monasteries at Pennard and Athelney.

Dunstan's strict monastic reforms were to lead to his falling out of royal favour for a second time. In 956 he was exiled by Eadmund's older son Eadwig, only to be recalled when the younger Eadgar succeeded to the throne three years later, and gave Dunstan the bishoprics first of Worcester and London, and then the archbishopric of Canterbury. Despite his elevation, Dunstan never lost his concern for Glastonbury, and in

965 he was in a position to influence Eadgar to give lands at High Ham, near Langport, to the abbey. The local people, confusing Eadgar with Eadmund, explain that the miracle at Cheddar was responsible for this gift.

Born at Edgarley on the outskirts of Glastonbury, Eadgar was schooled by Dunstan. He became king when he was only sixteen, and partly because of his youth and partly on account of his scandalous relations with two young nuns, his corontion was deferred for fourteen years. When it took place in Bath in 973, Dunstan officiated, thus laying a precedent for the part played in subsequent coronations by the Bishops of Bath and Wells. Eadgar was only to live for two years as a crowned king. He died in 975 at his birthplace and was buried in Glastonbury. In 1052 his body was exhumed and declared to be incorrupt, the blood still uncongealed. This evidence of sanctity, together with the records of the work he had done at Dunstan's behest for the revival of the monasteries, brought about his canonisation. A shrine was dedicated to him in Glastonbury where his feast was honoured on 8 July ever year. He must surely also have been remembered at Combe St Nicholas where his second wife Aelfryth owned land. The Saxon font near the south porch in the church there is thought to date from his time.

For 988, the entry in the *Anglo-Saxon Chronicle* reads: 'the holy archbishop Dunstan departed this life and attained the heavenly'.

Despite some insensitive Victorian restorations, many Somerset churches retain evidence of their Saxon origin. I think especially of the fragment of a Saxon cross now facing you on the north wall as you enter the tiny church of Rowberrow beneath Dolebury hill fort; the less obvious Saxon fragments in the church at Holcombe; and the shaft in the church at West Camel, whose lands, together with those at Ilminster, were given to Muchelney Abbey by a charter of Aethelred (the Unready) in 995. Glastonbury remained the most important monastic centre in the county and during the tenth century four of the Bishops of Wells came from that abbey.

The most significant evidence of a secular Saxon building in the county is at Cheddar, where the remains of the royal palace occupied by Alfred and his descendants for at least two centuries is marked out in the grounds of the Kings of Wessex School. It was used as a hunting lodge for excursions into the Forest of Mendip, where, as the fourteenth-century *Axbridge Chronicle* relates, there were in the time of King Eadmund 'a good many deer and different sorts of other wild animals'.

Excavations indicate that this palace consisted of a series of wooden buildings arranged around a two-storey hall twenty-five metres in length. That hall had a central hearth beside which the king and his leading thanes sat to dine. It was built early in the ninth century, and it is most probable that Alfred entertained Guthrum here after the baptism at Aller, although we know that the king also had a palace at Wedmore. There were probably similar halls to the one at Cheddar in Somerton and Frome.

Other evidence of the Saxons in Somerset is clear in the landscape, where the hillsides still bear the signs of terrace cultivation and strip farming. To the east of Wookey Hole, in the field above the former village school that has now become a foolishly-sited old peoples' home atop a hill, there are signs of such lynchets in the same sheltered dip in the hills which the Roman villa occupied.

Apart from farming the land, the Saxons quarried the hills for building stone, and no doubt worked the Mendip lead mines, although we have no direct evidence for that. We do know, however, that there were Saxon iron-workings at Bickenhall, on the edge of the Blackdown Hills, and at Whitestaunton near Chard. Clearly, there were a number of small Saxon settlements as well as isolated farms and huts around the royal palaces. They are not easily discernible but there was certainly a settlement at Peasedown St John to the south of Bath, and a hearthstone from near Eckweek is now on display at the Radstock museum.

Most of our knowledge of Saxon land use and holdings comes from the survey carried out in 1086, twenty years after the Norman conquest, but still a reliable record, village by village, of the farming in the county in the early years of the eleventh century. Many farms and water-mills still marked on the large scale maps are listed in Domesday Book, together with the population and status of the manor, the numbers of cottars, villeins and serfs, the numbers of animals they owned, their farm implements and the extent of the land they worked. I have not listed them here, for the extent of the survey was so thorough and its details so minute that the figures are best arrived at in individual studies of particular villages and farms. I would, however, like to draw attention to the one water-mill listed in the Domesday survey which is still working, albeit restored in the nineteenth century after years of idleness. It is at Priston, also to the south of Bath, and it is now open to the public in the summer.

The first Saxon churches were mostly built of timber, but during the eleventh century there seems to have been a spate of church building in stone. At that time, Giso was Bishop of Wells and the House of Godwin was a powerful force in Wessex. It was then that Edith, wife of Edward the Confessor and a member of the Godwin family, built, at her own expense, a new stone church for the Saxon burgh of Milverton. The only traces of it left in the present church are a few stones in the north-east corner of the Lady chapel. More significant evidence of Anglo-Saxon ecclesiastical building has been found at Muchelney, proving that this foundation, which was to be so powerful throughout the Middle Ages, had a very early origin. The same holds true for Glastonbury which has a Saxon as well as a Celtic and medieval history, indeed Dunstan is reported to have been responsible for the rebuilding of a considerable part of the Celtic Abbey.

Above all there are substantial traces of a Saxon Cathedral at Wells, excavated in the early 1980s. It appears to have been built above a Roman/Christian mausoleum, and was to form the east end of the cathedral up to the eleventh century. Several parish churches throughout the county also bear evidence of being built on Saxon sites. The great-towered church at Chewton Mendip, for instance, has stones bearing marks of Saxon workmanship. They were used by the Normans in the building of the chancel and the south porch.

As well as the traces of their buildings, the Saxons left Somerset a legacy of their language in the place names, such as Shipham, from *sceap ham*, a sheep enclosure, which on the whole are common throughout the country. There are also isolated words surviving most strongly in certain areas and arising mostly out of the nature of the land. The misty rain which so often envelops the Somerset moors is often referred to as *liprey*, a word deriving from the Anglo-Saxon *liper*, which strictly means sea-spray. One can understand how the meaning came to be transferred as the sea-going Saxons straggled across the swampy moors. Domesday certainly makes reference to the marshlands, writing off the land around Wedmore with the phrase '*ibi morae quae nihil reddunt*', a bit of dog Latin which can be roughly translated as 'where nothing can restore the wasteland'. The draining of the Somerset marshes was to begin in earnest in the Middle Ages, but it would seem that in some areas, the Saxons, particularly in the area inland from Burnham, started some drainage schemes.

Unlike the Celts, whom they replaced and who made most of their settlements on hilltop enclosures, the Saxons came to build fortified towns on the plains, usually by rivers for ease of transport. Sir Frank Stenton's study of Anglo-Saxon England reveals that Axbridge and Langport were both originally part of a national defence system holding out against the Danes, and that in both places most of the inhabitants were tenants of the Crown. This in no way diminished the importance of the towns. Axbridge, which lay in the royal manor of Cheddar, was in effect governed by its thirty-two burgesses. Langport became a burgh around 890, and in the south of the county, Milborne Port which was again essentially a royal manor, had rights of minting the coinage during the reigns of both Aethelred the Unready and the Danish Cnut.

By that time, mints were established at several other burghs in the county; notably Crewkerne, South Cadbury, South Petherton and Watchet. It was during this period, too, that the mint was set up in Bath, a city that was originally a part of Mercia, but which seems to have become part of Wessex towards the end of Alfred's reign. By the tenth century, as we have seen, coronations were held here. In recording the consecration of Eadgar as king, the Parker version of the *Anglo-Saxon Chronicle* tells us that the event was conducted 'by a great assembly in the ancient city of *Acemannesceaster*, also called Bath by the inhabitants of that island'.

In the case of Bath, the Saxon city and the present one share the same site by the river, but in other cases the present town may well be on different ground. It seems most likely, for instance, that the Saxon burgh of Axbridge lay somewhat to the south of the present town, overlooking the narrowest part of the Axe valley and so only a little way down river from the royal palace at Cheddar.

By the eleventh century, the uneasy and powerful house of Godwin – a family whose place in eleventh-century Wessex is comparable to the twentieth-century Kennedys in Massachusetts – dominated Somerset, owning manors, among others, at Crewkerne, North Curry and Capton. Endlessly battling for power among themselves, their family feuds were eventually to lead to the success of the Norman invasion in 1066. Fourteen years before the Battle of Hastings, Harold Godwinson collected a band of soldiers in Ireland and landed at Porlock. Recording that event, the *Anglo-Saxon Chronicle* tells us that when Harold landed his nine ships on the stony beach of Porlock bay, 'many people were gathered to oppose him, but he did not hesitate to provide himself with food. He went inland and slew a great part of the inhabitants and seized whatever he pleased in cattle, captives and property'. The purpose of Harold's attack was to destroy Aelfgar, Lord of Porlock, a son of Leofric Earl of Mercia and the sworn enemy of the Godwins. Harold must also have been largely motivated by greed for extra power. Lord of Dulverton and, as Earl of Wessex, owning estates that amounted to about an eighth of Somerset, he was still hungry for more and coveted full command of the coastal stretch of Exmoor. His family were to lose by his action, for his sister Eadgyth (Edith the Fair), wife of Edward the Confessor, was to forfeit her manor of Selworthy after Harold's raid.

Porlock was to be scarred by that invasion for many years. In 1750, when Collinson came to write his *History of Somerset*, he reported that the local people could still point out vestiges of the buildings partly destroyed by Harold's mercenaries.

Although Harold was only to be king for a matter of months before the fatal battle at Senlac, near Hastings, his mother Gytha, who also owned many estates in the West Country was one of the most powerful women in the land. At the time of William's landing she was dwelling in the fortified town of Watchet (probably on the site of the coastal Iron Age fort), and when the news of the defeat of her son reached her, she is said to have retreated to the island fortress of Steep Holm.

However, the Godwins were not prepared to let Harold go unavenged or to acknowledge Norman supremacy without a struggle. Two years after William was crowned king, they led a Saxon rebellion against the Norman overlords, concentrating on the manor of Montacute near Yeovil. The choice of that place goes back to the reign of the first Cnut, for it was in about 1035 that Tovi, the then Lord of nearby lands, became convinced that he had found a fragment of the True Cross buried in the angular, wooded slopes of St Michael's Hill, from which Montacute gets its name. Tovi also owned land in Essex, and it was to the manor of Waltham that he carried the holy relic, and there he built a church to house it. When Tovi died both that church (Waltham Abbey) and the sacred relic were passed on to Harold Godwinson.

Convinced that the fragment possessed miraculous healing powers, which he had experienced himself, Harold honoured it by enlarging Tovi's church. It was there, after the defeat at Senlac, that he was to be buried, for on the eve of the battle he had gone to Waltham Abbey and prayed before the relic. Indeed, he is said to have gone into battle with the cry of 'The Holy Cross' on his lips. Some argue that this induced an over-confidence in the Saxons which caused the day to go to the Normans.

After the Norman victory, the lands of Montacute, then owned by the monks of Muchelney, were given to Robert of Mortmain, William's half-brother. He immediately built a castle on the summit of St Michael's Hill. The Saxons took this as desecration of the mound in which the fragment of the Cross had lain. Determined to revenge such a calculated blasphemy, they selected Robert's castle as the starting point for a general uprising. It was not successful. The castle remained in Norman hands, but by the end of the century it was given to the monks of Muchelney when some of their lands were returned to them.

Despite such pockets of rebellion, the Domesday survey shows a fairly settled agricultural pattern in the years following the Conquest. Apart from the significant matter of the draining of the moors, that pattern was to form the basis of life in the county during the Middle Ages.

V

From the Conquest to the Reformation

Sampford Arundel is a scattered village beneath the Black-down Hills on the Somerset/Devon border. Its name embodies the transition from the Saxon to the Norman era, when the manor of Sampford (the Saxon sandy ford) was given to Roger Arundel, who led the central section of William's army at the victorious battle of Senlac. Twenty years after that battle, Domesday Book was to record that the male population of the manor consisted of five slaves, eleven villeins, and six cottars.

The same 1086 survey for the Exeter area also lists animals. From it we learn that the Exmoor village of Luccombe boasted one horse, six swine, one hundred sheep and fifty goats. As for the land, there were fifty acres of woodland, five of meadows and two hides of ploughland. The Lord of the Manor, previously owned by the Confessor's queen, Edith, was Ralph de Limesi who was rewarded with several grants of Somerset land for his part in William's conquest.

Queen Edith had also owned Milverton on the south-eastern edge of the moor. This was then a market town, at a time when there were only seven in the county. Like any settlement of any size, it also boasted a mill. As I have noted, we have to go north-west to Priston on the outskirts of Bath to see the only mill recorded in Domesday that has been restored to working condition.

The Domesday survey was all-embracing, giving us a clear picture of eleventh-century land management and settlement patterns for the 612 manors in the county. Drawing the wider implication from it, we find that in 1086 a large proportion of Somerset was in the hands of the Church. Much of it was held by bishoprics and religious foundations in France, but the native Glastonbury Abbey controlled at least an eighth of the county. This sets the tone for the whole period from the Conquest to the Reformation, which is predominately the picture of a landscape dominated by the religious houses; although the royal hunting forests, extended by the Norman kings, also accounted for wide stretches of the county.

Although, as we know, the Saxon kings exercised a right to hunt the deer on Mendip from their palace at Cheddar; and the seventeenth-century Somerset chronicler, Thomas Gerard, informs us that the three bugles depicted in the church window at Dodington to the north of Nether Stowey formed the crest of a family listed as foresters in Domesday; it was the reigning Normans who really established the five hunting forests of Somerset. Although the county was then thickly wooded, the term forest (from the Latin *fore stare*, standing outside) did not imply trees as it does to us. The almost treeless uplands of Exmoor, whose beeches date from a much later period, is a case in point.

The other Somerset forests reserved for the Crown were Mendip, Selwood, Quantock and Neroche on the edge of the Blackdown ridge. None of these forest was mentioned in the Domesday survey, although there is a mention of a royal deer park at North Petherton (to which, three centuries later Geoffrey Chaucer was appointed under-forester); and of a certain Godric, who was a forester at Withypool in the heart of Exmoor, although the latter was not fully established as a royal forest until 1204. It was to remain Crown property until 1815 providing venison for generations of royal feasts.

There are records of at least three thirteenth-century perambulations of the Royal Forest of Exmoor; in 1279, for instance, twelve knights rode round the perimeter. Possibly William de Plessey was one of their number on an earlier occasion. He died in 1274, but during his lifetime he held the king's bailiwick on Exmoor. High up on the moor at Hawkridge, the church, which has a very fine Norman door, contains a coffin lid inscribed in Norman French, which has been ascribed to him. It tell us, frustratingly, that 'William . . . . lies here. God have mercy on his soul. Amen'.

From 1295, until her death in 1308, a woman, Sabina

Pecche, held the post of warden of the Royal Forest of Exmoor. She inherited that title from her father, Richard de Plectis, whose grandfather William, Thomas Gerard tells us, was an overseer of all the royal forests in the county. It does not seem likely that Sabina was active as a forester, her duties being carried out by her husband, Nicholas, who acted as her deputy.

Of the other Somerset forests, Selwood and Neroche were both wooded and contained fallow deer. These, together with red deer, roamed over the Mendip plateau, which was abolished as a royal forest in 1338. Long before that, John had sold the hill above Cheddar to the Bishop of Bath and Wells, although he retained for himself the southern escarpment near Axbridge, which is still known as King's Wood.

The woods themselves, both in Selwood and Neroche, as well as those outside the forests on the banks of the Avon, were subject to occasional clearances throughout the Middle Ages, the trees being cut down and their roots grubbed out or burnt. This process of turning wooded land into areas for cultivation was given the legal term 'assarting'. It is referred to in various documents of the period, confirming that when woods that had formed part of a royal forest were converted to tillage, the process had to be sanctioned by the King. It was in this manner, in 1252, that Henry III sanctioned the prior of Bruton to clear that part of Selwood Forest which was contained within the manor of Brewham, with the proviso that 'the doe with her fawn and others of the king's deer have free entry and exit'.

Outside the forests, as we have seen in the case of North Petherton, the King had hunting preserves. The lands around the important crown holding of Somerton were loosely described as a forest although the only game that was prevalent there was hares. Other deer parks belonged to the Church, such as those at Westbury-sub-Mendip, to the south of the Forest of Mendip, and Evercreech, on the edge of Selwood. They both belonged to the Bishop of Bath and Wells, while the deer park at Pilton was in the hands of Glastonbury Abbey. On the southern edge of the county, where Somerset meets Dorset, the Bishop of Salisbury owned a deer park near Chardstock. It is still traceable in the area known as The Parks, across the River Kit to the south-west of the church in that village. In 1298, trespassers broke into the park, and the Bishop had no hesitation in issuing a mandate to excommunicate them. During the reign of Henry VI, a certain Robert Hyndely was appointed as park-keeper there. He received twopence a day for his services, and at Christmas time he could choose between six shillings and eightpence, or a new robe.

Together with the setting up of the hunting preserves, whether forests or deer parks, went the establishment of the castles, fortified buildings on raised earthworks, far more impressive and sophisticated than anything the Saxons erected on the Celtic hill forts. One such Norman fortification set up on the site of an earlier one was established in 1067 by William I's half brother, Robert of Mortain, at the western edge of the Forest of Neroche. It is in Forestry Commission hands now, in an area of broad-leaf planting, and open to the public at any time. So you can clamber over the great outer earthworks, originally part of the Saxon encampment here; walk through the Norman bailey, now occupied by eighteenth-century farm buildings, and climb latter-day steps contrived for your convenience in order to arrive at the high, conical motte, later to be used as a site for beacon fires. From there you can look north across the trees to Taunton Deane and east over Sedgemoor to the sea. The castle mounds have long been grassed over, for Robert only remained here for twenty years, abandoning Neroche in favour of Montacute.

The banks of Richmont Castle by the public footpath that runs through the woods on the northern slopes of Mendip at East Harptree, are in danger of being completely eroded by motorcyclists. That fortification once stood high above the waters of the River Chew, which since the nineteenth century have been carried overground, in this place, to the reservoirs supplying Bristol. The Norman castle, built on this strategic position in 1138, was held by Sir William de Harptree, as a stronghold for Matilda. By means of one of the clever tricks, of which he was master, Stephen, who had successfully laid siege to Bristol, drew Matilda's supporters away from Richmont. The castle survived that onslaught and stood until the reign of

Henry VIII, when its owner, Sir John Newton (whose tomb you can see in the porch of East Harptree church) pulled it down and presumably used its stones to build himself a fine modern mansion.

As the Middle Ages advanced, other castles were to grow out of fortified manor houses. One such is at Farleigh Hungerford, a few miles south-east of Bath on the Wiltshire border. From the reign of William Rufus to that of Edward III, the Montfort family held the manor here. In 1369 it was sold to Sir Thomas de Hungerford, the first Speaker of the House of Commons. He immediately set about fortifying his manor house. In so doing he was acting against the law, a crime for which he received a royal pardon in 1383; meanwhile, in 1372, he built the church at Wellow, on lands which he is thought to have acquired at the same time as he established the manor that bears his name.

Dominant and impressive as these Norman castles and fortified manors undoubtedly were, it was the power of the religious houses established in the early Middle Ages which was the real force in the county. Apart from Glastonbury, most of these religious houses sprang from foundations outside Somerset. This was true of Cleeve Abbey, to the west of Watchet, a Cistercian foundation set on lands belonging to William de Roumare, Earl of Lincoln, who had established the Lincolnshire abbey of Revesby. From there, at mid-summer in 1198, twelve monks led by Abbot Ralph journeyed south-east to set up their new monastery in the valley of the Washford river, beneath the northern slopes of the Brendon Hills. They dedicated it to the Virgin Mary and, in the Cistercian tradition, named it Vallis Florida. It was to flourish, in time adding to itself lands in North Devon and Cornwall, as well as in parts of Somerset to the east around Huntspill and along the Parret valley.

The parish church at Cleeve (now known as Old Cleeve) still came under the jurisdiction of the Bishop of Bath and Wells, but the monks from Cleeve Abbey officiated there as they did at the pilgrimage chapel on the shores of Blue Anchor Bay and at Queen Camel church near Yeovil, well to the south-east. Naturally, Old Cleeve church had the closest connection with the abbey, and it is still possible to trace long sections of the cobbled path from the village of Washford, by the abbey ruins, under the bridge of the West Somerset railway, to the steep 'cobblers' steps', at the top of which you will find that the stones are discernible at the edge of a field and along the verge of the line that climbs up to the hill above the village of Old Cleeve. At the crest of that hill, the stump of a stone cross marks the place where the monks are thought to have considered establishing a church of their own.

Like those of Muchelney Abbey to the east, the monks at Cleeve were skilled and imaginative tile-makers, who have left intricate, delightful and sometimes fantastical examples of their work for us to enjoy. In addition to those which are displayed at Cleeve Abbey, you can also see some of their work in Old Cleeve church, which also boasts the only medieval font cover in Somerset.

At about the same time as the Cistercians came to Cleeve, the Carthusians were becoming established in Somerset. One of their foundations was at Hinton Charterhouse on the edge of Bath. The monks there had lead-mining concessions on the Mendips, and so gave their name to the settlement of Charterhouse around the area of the Roman lead mines. Here in Longwood, now one of the Somerset Trust's nature reserves, they had a fish pond, still known as the monks' pool.

To the south-west of Frome, Carthusians were established at Witham, and from there gave Somerset its best known and most loved saint. Although Hugh is chiefly associated with Lincoln, where he became bishop in 1186, he spent the previous eleven years at Witham. A monk of the Grande Chartreuse, he was called to be prior of Witham foundation by the invitation of Henry II in 1175, for this was one of the religious establishments that the King founded in reparation for the murder of Thomas Becket. Even after Hugh eventually took up his appointment at Lincoln, he would return to Somerset each autumn to refresh his spirits.

A champion of the poor and unfortunate (he is remembered in Lincoln for the protection that he gave to the harassed Jewish community); he was naturally disturbed at the hardships which the enforcements of the forest laws caused the poor people of Witham, whose lands lay within the Forest of Selwood. Commenting on the Latin derivation of the name 'foresters', he declared, 'Yes, that is the right name for them, for they will remain outside the kingdom of God.'

Another religious order in the county at this time was the Augustinian Canons who settled at Moorlynch, Taunton and at Barlynch, near Dulverton. This last monastery, founded by William de Say in the twelfth century, was to obtain lands around Morebath in Devon and to have control of the churches of Winsford on Exmoor and Hillfarence and Bradford-on-Tone to the north-west of Wellington.

The church of the manor of Sampford Arundel, where I started this exploration of medieval Somerset, was given by the Arundel family to the Augustinian Canons of Canonsleigh, just across the border into Devon, at the end of the twelfth century. Apart from its thirteenth-century tower, this church is now almost completely Victorian; although it does contain an extraordinary medieval carving of two hands holding what appears to be a heart, and which could indicate a rare heart burial. There is nothing left, however, not even a sanctuary ring on the door, to serve as a memorial of the dreadful event in 1225, when Nicholas Arundel, a tyrannical Lord of the Manor, fled to the church pursued by the villagers he had wronged. When the priest refused to grant him sanctuary, the villagers set on him and killed him, despite the retribution which they must have been aware such an action would call down on them. In fact twenty-four villagers were sentenced to death for that murder, and of those only five escaped, fleeing into the dense woods of the Tone valley.

In the same year further violence took place on the edge of Somerset's Exmoor in the church at Oare, primarily associated with R.D. Blackmore's *Lorna Doone*, for, according to that ever-popular novel it was here that Lorna was shot on her wedding day by Carver Doone. The historical killing was in some ways a reverse of what happened at Sampford Arundel, for in this case, Robert, Lord of Oare, murdered Walter, the chaplain.

In Somerset as elsewhere, the Middle Ages were the

centuries of church building as well as of the establishment of monastic foundations. Most of the parish churches, not completely destroyed by the Victorian restorers, contain traces of Norman and Early English architecture. One trace of each church's past that usually remains is the carefully recorded lists of the priests who have served there since its foundation. Very occasionally it is possible to know something of the men behind the names. One who is known to us is Wulfric (obviously a Saxon) who became a priest in his birthplace of Compton Martin on the northern slopes of Mendip, and served there for five years from 1120. He then went to the south-west and became an anchorite at Haselbury Plucknett to the north of Crewkerne, where he lived in a cell adjoining the parish church. Supported by the Cluniac monks of Montacute, he adopted a penitential regime, consisting of rigorous fasting, the wearing of chain mail and frequent immersion in cold water. Through these extreme measures he acquired a reputation for paranormal powers and was visited by royalty anxious for the benefits of his healing powers and prophetic insights. Henry I and his queen, Adele, were among the people who sought him out in 1130. Three years later, Wulfric was to prophesy the death of the King, and to greet Stephen as monarch even before he had claimed the throne. This did not save him from many admonishments from the holy man during his disastrous and disputed reign. After Wulfric's death, the monks of Montacute claimed his body, but his disciple, Osbern, saw to it that the anchorite's cell should become his tomb. So, for many years Haselbury was a place of pilgrimage where Wulfric was honoured as a saint. His cell was still in existence when Thomas Gerard visited the church in 1633.

It is the minor features of the village churches that tell us most about the people who worshipped there in the Middle Ages. So at Priddy on the heights of Mendip the church, set on a knoll above the village and built in 1352, still retains an echo of its medieval past in the form of a stone ledge by the wall where the old and frail might sit, the floor being covered with rushes and unencumbered by pews.

Storgursey, on the desolate flat lands to the west of

Bridgwater Bay, has one of the most remarkable churches in the county. The name of the village is a corruption of Stoke Courcy, which evolved because the original territory known as Stoche fell into the hands of William de Courcy, who married the granddaughter of William de Falaise who had it as a reward for his loyal support to William the Conqueror. The original Norman church, probably built by Falaise in the final years of the eleventh century, makes up the transept and crossing of the present building. To the east, the floor rises quite steeply to the chancel, which formed the choir of the priory set up here by monks from Lonlay, a French Benedictine Foundation. The nave to the west is a Tudor addition.

My greatest delight in the medieval churches of Somerset lies in the evidence of the vitality of the local craftsmen. You will find it mirrored in the plentiful, exuberant heads of the Green Man, a fertility symbol that crops up on roof bosses and bench-ends, and which is even the focus of the double squint at Stogumber. Even more forceful examples of such imaginative frenzy are to be seen in the gargoyles (which are functional water-spouts); and in the creatures, known in Somerset as 'hunky-punks' which have no functional purpose other than to ward off the devil. These lively grotesques are seen climbing the towers and adorning the north, or devil's side, of the church roof. You can see them at their most majestic and fearsome in the form of the great beasts of Kilmersdon and at Pilton near Glastonbury.

The carvings on the medieval fonts are particularly splendid. It is worth finding your way to the remote church of Lullington, on the edge of Orchardleigh Park, to the north of Frome, both for the sake of the magnificent Norman door and for the twelfth-century font. The latter is adorned with all the monsters and demons of hell waiting for the unbaptised soul to fall into their clutches. Another, later font, well worth seeking out, is in the church at Nettlecombe, which stands in the grounds of the Field Studies Council's residential centre below the Brendon Hills. This font was carved in about 1470 and has its place in a chapter on medieval Somerset because of its connection with Chaucer. The representations of the seven

Two of the massive rose-coloured stones, forming the Stanton Drew circles beside the River Chew. *Mick Sharp*

Notice the ammonite to the left of the entrance of the Stoney Littleton long barrow. *Mick Sharp*

Arthur's Camelot? Aerial view of the hill-fort in the village of South Cadbury. *West Air Photography*

The cliffs of Cheddar Gorge: a landscape happily preserved by the National Trust. *Aerofilms*

Frequently reconstructed, Tarr Steps, Exmoor's famous clapper bridge, thought to date from the early Middle Ages. *Mick Sharp*

The stone ramparts of Dolebury, rising to 20 feet, overlook the route from Mendip to the Bristol Channel. *Mick Sharp*

Where Exmoor meets the sea, sheep graze above the wooded cliffs of Porlock Bay. *Peter Burton/Harland Walshaw*

Wells Cathedral from the gardens round the springs that give the city its name.

A mitred fox on a Brent Knoll bench-end records a quarrel with the Abbot of Glastonbury. *Peter Burton/Harland Walshaw*

Glastonbury Tor, crowned by the 13th-century tower of the lost church of St. Michael. *Somerset County Council Library Service*

Massive yew hedges set off the golden Ham stone of Montacute House. *Peter Burton/Harland Walshaw*

Under construction in 1864, the Clifton Suspension bridge was attacked for desecrating the Avon Gorge. *Reece Winstone Archive*

Throughout the nineteenth century, Bristol's busy waterways extended into the heart of the city. *Reece Winstone Archive*

Bath as Pepys knew it: 'It cannot be clean . . . so many bodies in the same water.' *Copyright British Museum*

The eighteenth-century Royal Crescent, work of John Wood the Younger, overlooks the city of Bath. *Martyn James*

sacraments of the church on this font are more usually found in East Anglia. Their presence here is said to have come about through Geoffrey Chaucer's daughter-in-law, Alice, whose grandmother was Lady of the Manor of Nettlecombe. After the death of Geoffrey's son, Alice married again and became Duchess of Suffolk, but she still retained an interest in the Nettlecombe church.

More relevant to the true medieval era are the two effigies of crusaders in this church. Simon Raleigh's crossed legs resting on a lion indicate that he died in battle. He was in fact killed in 1260. Nearby is John Raleigh, a seven-foot giant, lying beside his wife, Maud. It is from such church effigies, mostly of crusaders and their ladies, that we have the most vivid impressions of Somerset's nobility in the Middle Ages. They are not all fighting men. In the east of the old county, at Norton St Philip, there is the effigy of a man who, in the place of armour, wears a robe and a high fur hat. There is an ink-horn at his waist. He is thought to be Sir John Fortescue, a fifteenth-century barrister, who became Lord Chief Justice of England.

A less well-authenticated, and much more extraordinary, effigy is to be seen in the church at Chew Magna to the north of the Mendip Hills. This is a cross-legged, wooden figure, once painted in brilliant colours. It is supposed to be a representation of Sir John Hautville, the tyrannical, thirteenth-century lord of Norton Malreward, a village to the north-east, whose lands were said to have been his reward for hurling the great stone across the country from the hill fort of Maes Knoll, a little to the north, to the road beyond the stone circles of Stanton Drew (see page 11).

Whatever the true origin of the effigy in Chew Magna church, it is treated with more respect than that of another and later Sir John, scion of the Merriot family, Lord of the Manor, and patron of the church at Bradford-on-Tone for forty-one years from 1350. His elbow, together with the holy water stoop, was simply cut away and discarded by Victorian restorers in order to make space for pews.

The first vicar of that church, established in 1216, was a Fleming, Theodoricus Teutanicus. Later, when the parish was served by Augustinian Canons, Bradford bridge was built for the convenience of the monks whose journey from Exmoor culminated in a crossing of the Tone.

Those monks, and the men from the other religious houses travelling to their associated churches, were not the only people to be journeying to spiritual goals. As we have seen, several shrines in Somerset, as well as the growing collection of relics in the great abbey at Glastonbury, were the objects of pilgrimage for people throughout the country. One such 'Pilgrim Church' which specifically met their needs was at Otterford, on the eastern edge of the Blackdown Hills, halfway between Exeter and Glastonbury. Wealthier and more adventurous pilgrims even sought holy places much further afield, joining in the journey to Compostela in north-west Spain and travelling through Somerset to Weymouth in order to embark on that journey. The gathering point for the start of such an expedition was in the south of the county; and the naming of Palmer Street in South Petherton is said to bear witness to one of the main collecting places.

I have concentrated mostly on the churches of village parishes for the insight that they give us into the history of medieval Somerset. I do not feel it is really appropriate here to add to the great mass of literature that has been written about the great city churches of Bristol, south of the Avon; Bath Abbey; and, above all, the magnificent thirteenth-century cathedral at Wells. However, the actual building of that cathedral is a vital part of the history of medieval Somerset.

The first Gothic cathedral in England, Wells took one hundred and sixty years to complete, and must have been a continual source of employment from 1180 when the work was started. By 1229, the building was completed from the apse to the west front; but the well-loved stone steps leading to the chapter house, and the chapter house itself, were not finished until 1340. It was about that time that the famous figure-of-eight arches were constructed in the transept, in the hope that the central tower would thus be rendered strong enough to hold a spire to rival the one at Salisbury, an attempt reluctantly abandoned. At least, in 1390, Wells had the honour of installing its intricate and elaborate clock, now the oldest timepiece of its sort still functioning.

Even in the grandeur of the cathedral, the individual craftsmen had scope for a lively and sympathetic humour. The stone capitals of the pillars are all worth studying. Among the beasts and monsters which lurk among the stiff-leaved foliage, you will find an unfortunate man with the tooth-ache; another with a thorn in his foot; and a series forming a sort of medieval strip cartoon telling the tale of a theft from a local vineyard. Most interesting of all is a head in the north aisle, which is said to represent Adam Locke, one of the master masons concerned in the building of the cathedral.

The adjacent Bishop's palace has a history going back before the completion of the present cathedral, for it was in 1207 that Bishop Jocelyn, a native of Wells, chose that city rather than Bath for his residence. With permission from King John, who held the land for the Crown, he made a park in the meadows around St Andrew's Well, whose springs give the city its name. In a few years, he built his living quarters there. They still form a part of the modern palace.

In 1290, Bishop Robert Burnell, Chancellor of England under Edward II, built the great hall, which was to be rendered roofless at the time of the Reformation, and further destroyed by the removal of the south wall in the nineteenth century. In its heyday, this gaunt ruin was the scene of magnificent feasts, at which royalty were frequently entertained.

There was inevitably friction between Wells and Glastonbury, and within Wells itself, between the cathedral and the city. It was the Bishop, Ralph of Shrewsbury, deservedly unpopular for his conduct during the Black Death, who originally had the moat constructed in order to save himself from attacks by the people. He even found it necessary to provide the gatehouse on the inner side of the drawbridge with a portcullis and a chute from which boiling oil or scalding hot water could be poured on his attackers.

At least one of the Wells priests died during the Black Death. His memorial can be found engraved on one of the lower pillars of the west front. There are several theories as to how this louse-born typhus fever came to Britain, but most historians agree that it entered through the West Country ports in the late summer of 1338, the chief suspects being Bristol and Malcombe Regis – now Weymouth – in Dorset. Bristol, with over ten thousand inhabitants, was certainly the largest port in the West Country; and the city records encapsulated in *The Little Red Book of Bristol* relate that during the months of pestilence fifteen of the fifty-two councillors died. They were, of course, among the wealthiest of the citizens, the death rate among the poor would have been much higher and could well have risen to somewhere between thirty-five and forty per cent. Whatever the toll, it was sufficient to cause the city to be neglected and it was recorded that grass grew high in Bristol streets.

Most of our knowledge about the ravages of that epidemic come from church records. Five years after the plague had subsided, King Edward III wrote to the prior at Witham granting him permission to hire secular labour and to rent out his monastic farms because the priory had lost all its servants and retainers 'in the last pestilence'. Their deaths had resulted in a great part of the Carthusians' land remaining 'waste and untilled' while such corn as had been sown 'had miserably rotted as it could not be gathered for lack of reapers'.

On the whole, however, the plague was not altogether a complete disaster for the monastic houses because those lay people who survived did not just have the melancholy task of burying their dead; they also, if they were of any standing, had to pay fines to their landlords out of their inheritance. This meant that very often the church stood to profit, and indeed during the plague months, one cell of Bruton priory received fifty head of oxen and cattle, one for each tenant who had died.

No estimates are possible for the numbers of deaths among the peasants and serfs, such as those who would have worked on the Witham lands during the years of the sickness. In fact, the only class of people of whom we do have records is the clergy themselves. From the records of new appointments at that time it has been calculated that 47.6 per cent of the beneficed clergy in the diocese of Bath and Wells must have died between November 1348 and June 1349, when the pestilence seems to have run its course.

And what was their Bishop, Ralph of Shrewsbury, doing during that time? Well, in January 1349, he wrote a letter to all the priests in the diocese. It was mostly concerned with the administration of the last sacrament in those parishes which had been left without a priest. In such circumstances, the worthy Bishop decreed, it was permissible for the dying person to make confession to a layman 'or if no man is present, then even to a woman'. Despite that liberal sentiment the Bishop also took the opportunity to criticise those priests who would not come forward to take the place of their colleagues who had perished of the Black Death. Meanwhile, he himself was writing not from Wells but from his summer residence at Wiveliscombe in the plague-free, western part of his diocese, where he had taken refuge in November 1348.

In December 1349, when the plague had fully subsided, Bishop Ralph came in triumph to Yeovil for a special service of thanksgiving. He was not a welcome visitor. The rectory where he lodged was put under siege and his entourage attacked by 'sons of perdition' bearing 'bows, arrows, iron bars and other kinds of arms'. After the adherents of the church had come to the Bishop's rescue, no less than sixty people had to do penance for the affray, which had been simply a gesture against Ralph himself and the wealthy classes who had been able to flee the infection.

In the following decades, when the countryside was still feeling the effects of a more than decimated population, the market towns were beginning to grow. Several Somerset towns, now often no more than villages, were important trading centres during the Middle Ages, most of them holding charters granted during the thirteenth century. At Chardstock, for instance, a weekly market was held under a charter granted by the Bishop of Salisbury in 1218, about the same time as Bishop Jocelyn of Wells founded the new town of Chard.

It is Ilchester, however, which we last looked at as a Roman settlement, which was to take the lead among the Somerset towns, although it was always in competition with nearby

Yeovil and Montacute. Its ascendancy lay partly in the fact that during the thirteenth century several local monasteries had invested in property within the towns walls, and a Dominican priory was established on the town lands. Until the end of that century, the town was able to support at least four goldsmiths and two dyers and was enjoying the wealth created by a small Jewish community who came to trade there.

It is interesting to speculate as to how much these growing towns were affected by the French wars. Were members of the growing middle class drawn into them, or were they simply the concern of the nobility aided by the desperate mercenary soldiers who could find no other source of livelihood and adventure? The latter must remain anonymous. For the former, we turn again to the church effigies, such as that of Lord John Harrington, in Porlock, who could trace his family back to the Danish Osulf of Northumbria. Lord John went to France with Henry V, but was taken ill during the Siege of Falaise and came back to England, where he died in 1417. His wife, Elizabeth, a member of the Devon family of Courtenay, lived on as Lady of the Manor for another fifty years.

As the Middle Ages drew to a close, with the coming of the Tudor dynasty, the divisions between town and country became more marked; but both were to bear the imprints of medieval settlements to the present day. Of course, the land bears the marks of medieval agriculture throughout the country, but because the northern part of the county was so often under water, Somerset presents a rather special case. So I would like to start off by looking at what we know of the draining of the moors at that time. As with so many other aspects of land management, the drainage of the swampy ground to the south of the Mendip hills was in the hands of the church or ecclesiastical foundations, Glastonbury Abbey, Athelney and Muchelney owning at least two-thirds of the area, which was quite a different landscape from 'the levels' that we see today.

The monks built walls, or embanked causeways, to strengthen the banks of the rivers as well as digging drainage ditches. Evidence of their work to the west in Sedgemoor can be seen along the Parret on the moors near Westonzoyland, between that village and the nineteenth-century pumping station. Later canalisation of the rivers flowing through the Somerset moors to the east has changed the landscape substantially from its appearance in the Middle Ages. This can be demonstrated by the existence of the substantial fish barn owned by the Abbot of Glastonbury, close beside the manor house at Meare where he had his summer residence. The Brue flows neatly beside it now between high artificial banks, but when the abbot's fish were drying out in his stone barn, the river flowed through a wide lake, which is how Meare got its name.

The monks knew how to make use of their waterways. By 1316, a sea route to Glastonbury had been formed by the construction of the Pilrow Cut, from the Brue near Tealham Moor to the Axe at Buddlesham, and the tidal river that once flowed north with the Hartlake and the Sheppy through the Panborough/Bleadney gap was diverted into Meare Pool.

As for the Axe, until the eighth century it had been navigable as far as Bleadney, three miles out of Wells, and in 1200, Richard I approved the construction of a wharf at Rackley near Axbridge, which is still discernible by the river bank there. In the fourteenth century there was a wharf by the Axe at Wedmore, and another at Bleadney.

To the west, when the River Tone was controlled, the wet lands around it were reclaimed to the benefit of the Dean of Wells and the Abbot of Athelney. We have already noted what measures were taken to control the Parret. In addition to the river bank walls, sea walls were being put up around the coast, and *clyses* (the local name for a sluice) constructed. The eventual result was that the moors were no longer salty marshes, but had become freshwater bogs interspersed with pasture. The inland areas were gradually being reclaimed and the drained areas enclosed. This process was furthered in 1235 by the Statute of Merton, which allowed the Lords of the Manors to enclose waste or common ground, provided that the tenants had sufficient pasture for their small numbers of cattle. This made it possible for drainage ditches (*rhynes*, as they are called in Somerset) to be constructed.

In 1304, Edward I convened a Commission of the Sewers for Somerset with responsibility for the drainage watercourses between the main rivers and the farm ditches. This meant, in fact, that the Lords of the Manors delegated the work of drainage to their tenants as an addition to their regular customary and statutory services.

All this activity was confined to the clay belt, for the peat area was considered useless. The peat moors around Westhay, which have now been so ruthlessly exploited, were left alone. There is little evidence that much was taken from them in the Middle Ages. At that time, apart from being used as fuel, the peat which had been accumulating for centuries was allowed to go on building up and some of the vegetation found in the peat now dates from as late as 1300.

Horticulture at that time did not depend on having plants grow in unnatural soils, as it does today with such devasting effects for the peat moors. However, some strange ideas about landscaping were manifest. In 1243, for instance, a group of small elm trees was planted in front of the ornate west front of Wells cathedral.

Domestic gardens were rare. Only one, at Langport, is recorded in the Domesday survey; and we have no way of knowing what cultivated land surrounded the lost medieval farms. Two such on Mendip can still be quite easily traced. Dursden, which gave its name to Dursden Drove running from Rookham above Wells, was flattened in the 1970s, while Andrews Green Bottom, nearby, above Ebbor Gorge, was destroyed in the eighteenth century. The banks of both are still easily discernible. Recently, extensive archaeological work has been done on two other medieval farmsteads at Ramspits in the parish of Westbury-sub-Mendip. They both seem to have been deserted from the middle of the fifteenth century and stand on the eastern side of Lynchcombe beneath Deer Leap lane as it runs past Ebbor Gorge. It has been suggested that all these Mendip farms once served as 'sheilings' or summer residences for the herdsmen when the cattle grazed the upper pastures.

On Exmoor, the deserted farm of Mousehanger near Winsford was probably at the centre of a hamlet in the fourteenth century. It has long since disappeared, as completely as have the villages at Witcombe, to the east of Ham Hill and Holcombe in east Mendip, where the isolated Norman church stands by the grassy earthworks of the original settlement. The church is now visited in spring time for the wild daffodils in the adjacent woods.

One aspect of medieval agriculture, which Somerset shared with much of England and Wales, was the concentrated breeding of rabbits. For centuries conies were a highly prized source of food, a delicacy considered far superior to chicken. Special hillocks known as pillow mounds were constructed in which the creatures could make their burrows, and these were guarded by wardens who protected them as fiercely as the foresters who were responsible for the King's deer. You can still see these pillow mounds on Exmoor in front of the aptly named Warren Farm near Simonsbath; and high up on the headland of Brean Down to the north-east. The rabbits of that spectacular headland were important enough to be mentioned in a document of 1361 in which Robert Brene, the Lord of the Manor, assigned them to one, Thomas Hege.

As in the rest of medieval England, the crops in Somerset were grown in a three-year rotation in an open field system. Some of these remained in evidence until the nineteenth century. As well as these great open fields, hillsides were terraced in the twelfth and thirteenth centuries to produce arable crops for the growth in population that occurred with more settled conditions and agricultural improvements, and which was to be wiped out by the Black Death. Yet, signs of these terraces are still visible at Westbury-sub-Mendip, on the southern escarpment of Mendip, an area which is still used extensively for market gardening, and which for many years in modern times was the main source of English strawberries.

In other areas, and particularly in the west of the country, sheep and cattle rearing increasingly took over from arable farming, and a pattern of enclosed land gradually took over from the open fields. By the end of the fourteenth century much of the land on the south-eastern part of Exmoor around Brompton Ralph and Clatworthy was almost fully enclosed.

VI
Tudor Somerset

The name of Henry Whyttoksmeth appears in a will drawn up in the Mendip village of Binegar in 1508. He is described as a clothman, and is one of many people pursuing that trade and craft by harnessing the power of the waters springing from the underground rivers of the limestone hills. Cloth-making at this time was being carried out extensively throughout Mendip. Croscombe and Chewton Mendip were two other important centres of the industry.

The story of the full flowering of the textile trade in Somerset, and its decline as similar sources of water power in the south Pennines energised more profitable mills, belongs to a later chapter. Here, I simply want to note that the county's emergence from the feudal, land-based hierarchies of the Middle Ages was encouraged by the growth of a powerful middle class enriched by the sources of wealth and employment supplied by the wool trade.

Mendip has wide pasturage for sheep to offer in addition to its source of water power. Although the lead in the soil can prove fatal to cattle, sheep are not affected by it because they graze solely on the blades of grass and do not touch the infected soil around the roots as cattle do. So the monks of Hinton Charterhouse could safely keep flocks of sheep around the lead mines which still bear their name; and forty years after the Dissolution of the monasteries the monks' sheep of nearby Green Ore were mentioned by a witness before an Elizabethan Court of Exchequer.

Although enclosures on a large scale did not take place in the county until the late sixteenth and seventeenth centuries, some land was reserved for pasturing sheep and cattle on quite a large scale long before that. Brompton Ralph, below the

Brendon Hills which was enclosed by 1343 is one such example.

When enclosures became more frequent, they were enforced for a variety of purposes. In many areas the three-field system of communal crop management was giving way to a four-field arrangement. When that happened, encroachments were frequently made on the common land. These new enclosures were not exclusively designed as sheep pasture. At East Quantoxhead, for instance, land was taken away from the people in order that rye could be cultivated; and further west, at Outmoor and Doniford near Williton, water meadows created in the fourteenth century were providing models for further land improvements in order to supply food for a growing population.

We have to remember that these re-allocations of land were taking place at a time when Henry VII was increasing his demands on both church and people in order to fill his coffers and establish the Tudor monarchy. In the rebellious western parts of the county this encouraged active support for Perkin Warbeck's uprising in 1497. The active participation of both clergy and land-owners in that revolt was to result in a vicious circle of discord as more money, in the form of fines, was collected by the Crown. Hugh Luttrell of Dunster had to find a sum of £200, while the Sydenhams of Brympton (near Cannington) got away with a mere £33. They were both more fortunate than Lord Audley of Nether Stowey, a notorious trouble spot, and Alexander Hody of Gothelney, who were both executed for their part in the rebellion. On behalf of the church, the Abbot of Athelney had to pay £66 and a similar sum was extracted from the borough of Bridgwater. North Petherton was fined the exorbitant sum of £505 and Taunton was close behind with a demand for £441.

The dissatisfaction that these demands engendered was not in any way ameliorated by the King's subsequent tour through the county. He stayed at the Deanery in Wells and made a visit to Glastonbury before venturing further afield to Bridgwater and Taunton, where he lost £93 in a game of cards with the abbot. Could that have been a face-saving way of reimbursing the church in Somerset for the money he had taken?

All this while the increased wealth of the county, brought in by the wool trade, was put into the building and aggrandisement of the parish churches. In the mid-fifteenth century, St John's at Glastonbury was enhanced with no less than six altars; and from 1486 to 1514, St Mary's at Taunton was the recipient of several generous bequests. Puxton, in the neighbourhood of Woodspring Priory, which was consecrated in 1539, was the last of the pre-Reformation churches to be built, and still retains the base of its stone screen.

The church at High Ham was completely rebuilt during 1476; the Elizabethan rector, Adrian Schael recording in the church register for 1598 that it was made possible by money from John Selwood, Abbot of Glastonbury and some personages and parishioners who 'did bountifully and readily contribute charges to the same'. The benefactors included a former rector, John Dier as well as Sir Amyas Paulet, who also assisted the church at Langport to carry out a similar rebuilding project. That same Sir Amyas had the misfortune to be acting as magistrate in 1500 and to order the Vicar of Limington, near Ilchester, to be put in the stocks for 'insobriety or otherwise promoting a riot'. As the young priest was none other than Thomas Wolsey, he took his revenge, on becoming Chancellor, by imprisoning the aged Sir Amyas for six years.

Most of the Somerset towers, tall and splendidly decorated, are the chief glory of the Tudor church building. John Leland, when he travelled through the county in 1535 made particular note of 'the goodly new high tourred steeple' at Chewton Mendip. The last of the great towers of east Somerset was completed at Batcombe in 1540. It is 87 feet high, and was the final glory of a church whose nave had been rebuilt some years earlier when the two aisles and the clerestory were added. As a sign of loyalty to the dynasty which created the prosperity to make this possible, the font is marked with the Tudor Rose.

Inside the churches, the local craftsmen seem to have been given a free hand, and took advantage of it to execute exuberant carvings particularly on bench-ends and roof bosses right through the Tudor period. In St Michael's church at Milverton, you can see representations of Biblical scenes and characters together with likenesses of Henry VIII and his children, Edward VI and Mary Tudor. Among the commoners represented is a man taking a swig from a tankard and thought to represent a Church Ale Feast, a fund-raising event which took place in the nave of the church before the introduction of pews, and which was later confined to the Church House. At Brent Knoll the figures on the bench-ends actually form a sort of strip cartoon representing the contempt that the parish felt for their landlord the Abbot of Glastonbury, portrayed as a fox in ecclesiastical vestments.

It is, however, at Crowcombe in the Quantocks that you will find the most complete and lively set of Tudor bench-ends in a county rich in such carvings. These were carved in 1534 and include marvellously wild representations of the Green Man, nature fertility symbols prissily referred to as foliate heads.

Roof bosses on the whole are more restrained and often used for heraldic purposes. In Evercreech, the ceiling, which is thought to have been first painted in 1548, bears the crest of the Duke of Somerset, Lord Protector during the reign of the young Edward VI, among the hovering angels. At least one other example of Tudor craftsmanship is worth seeking out. It is at Bishops Lydiard, where there is a fine fan-vaulted screen, engraved along its length with an inscription of the apostles' creed. It is thought to have been made in Taunton in the sixteenth century.

Tudor effigies inside the churches tell us more of the landed families, who financed most of these expansive building schemes. At Rodney Stoke near Cheddar, beneath the southern escarpment of Mendip, a chapel built on to the north side of the chancel houses the tomb chests of the Rodney family, whose fortified manor house stood by the church. Here is Sir Thomas, who died in 1478, dressed in armour, with his eight children around him. Nearly half a century later, the tomb chest of Sir John was set under a typically Tudor cusped arch. Up to the time of the Reformation it was thought to have been used as an Easter Sepulchre.

The monastic houses vied with the churches in extravagant building plans. Between 1496 and 1503, when the masons Robert and William Vertue were employed by Bishop Oliver King to rebuild Bath Abbey, more construction and restoration was going on at Cleeve, Montacute and Woodspring. At Muchelney the extravagance and mismanagement over the building works and the general running of the monastery were so great that the abbey collapsed through debt, a few months before the order for the dissolution of Somerset's twenty-three monastic houses came into force.

The Dissolution itself was not carried out without bloodshed. In Taunton and Bridgwater there were executions of those who had protested against the Royal decree, but only Hinton Charterhouse and Glastonbury took a firm and organised stand against it. Their refusal to comply was quickly quashed. Abbot Whiting of Glastonbury, a wise and much loved old man, was dragged through the main archway of his abbey and taken to the top of the Tor to be executed with two of his monks. Parts of his mangled body were displayed at Bridgwater, Bath, Ilchester and Wells. His chair, built to a pattern that was to remain traditional in Glastonbury to the end of the twentieth century, is displayed in the Bishop's Palace in Wells.

The Dissolution bred generations of vagrant unemployed, as the landless monks and lay brothers were joined by those who had lost both tenure and common rights through enclosures. Some fifty years after the monasteries were closed, Stryne was reporting on an 'infinite number of wicked, wandering people', who generally disturbed the peace of poor countrymen, obliging them 'to keep a perpetual watch on their sheep folds, pastures, woods and cornfields'.

On the other side of the coin, the Dissolution and the subsequent re-allocation of monastic lands provided a source of private wealth that lasted through several generations. Humphrey Coles was one such entrepreneur to take advantage of the situation. He took over the farmland around Pitminster and Corfe, which had previously belonged to Taunton Priory. There, on rising ground, he built a great house for himself.

Together with his son and grandson, he lies in effigy in Pitminster church. All three men served a term as High Sheriff of Somerset.

Their neighbours, the Seymours of Hatch Beauchamp on the edge of the Forest of Neroche, were to rise to national prominence when Lady Jane became the third wife of Henry VIII. Her brother, Edward, was promptly made Viscount Beauchamp of Hache. By 1531, he had become Sheriff of the County, and as the Duke of Somerset he acted as Protector during the reign of his nephew, Edward VI.

Further west, Edward Rogers was well rewarded for his services to the Tudor Court by grants of land from the despoiled Cannington Priory, which he came to inhabit. The fine doorway that he gave to his splendid mansion still stands although the rest of the house has been rebuilt during the centuries. Rogers had to leave home during Mary's Catholic reign, but he returned at the accession of Elizabeth and, until his death ten years later, was able to enjoy lands extending as far as the Manor of Porlock.

Despite such disturbances of land ownership and common rights, and the confusion in the parishes caused by the removal of married priests during Mary Tudor's attempts to bring the nation back to Roman Catholicism, agriculture and industry continued to expand. In south Somerset, particularly around Crewkerne and South Petherton where work on the land was combined with the weaving of sail cloth, market towns and villages grew ever more prosperous. To the north, a great Cloth Fair was held at the cross roads of Norton St Philip where the George Inn now stands; and by the time of Elizabeth the weaving of linen was established alongside the woollen industry.

At the same time, the livestock fairs generally increased in importance. At Binegar, the fair, which was primarily concerned with horses, lasted a full week. Elsewhere, the summer lanes were filled with drovers and their beasts as sheep, pigs and cattle were driven to market.

This prosperity contributed to a spate of building, as the wealthier families built themselves fine new manor houses and spacious farms. They were built as the Crown released its hold on the forests and as the land was cleared of woodland. Much of the timber for the building work came from oaks formerly growing in the monarch's preserve. Thus the 'disparking' of the royal game enclosure at Poundisford, to the south of Taunton, during the reign of Henry VIII, enabled the merchant adventurer, William Hill, to set about building a great house to rival that established by his stay-at-home brother. In his case, the building materials came from the ruins of the abandoned Taunton Priory, and with these materials he set up a substantial house surrounded by 127 acres of the former deer park, and designed in the form of an H, which could be taken as a tribute to the King.

Combe Sydenham, in the Brendon Hills near Stogumber, is one of the greatest of all Somerset houses. Built by the Sydenhams in 1580, and home of Sir Francis Drake's wife, Elizabeth, its E-shaped frontage is popularly believed to be designed to mark the Queen's initial, although as we see below, this was not necessarily always the case. It stands on land once owned by Cleeve Abbey, and is now open to the public during the summer months, as is the great mansion at Montacute to the south-east. Owned by the National Trust, the latter is built of the honey-coloured Ham stone and set in a formal garden. Edward Phelips, who was to become Speaker of the House of Commons and Master of the Rolls, established his dynasty here. No one who visits Montacute can forget the entrance to the Great Hall, divided from the passage leading from the main door by a stone screen, or the wall at the further end of the Hall covered by a plaster frieze showing an early version of the practice of a Skimmity Ride, immortalised by Thomas Hardy in *The Mayor of Casterbridge*. In this instance, the hen-pecked husband, who tried to sneak a little beer, is being paraded round the village by his dominant wife.

Barrington Court, to the north of Ilminster, is also owned by the National Trust. Built of Ham stone in 1514, during the reign of Henry VIII, its E-shaped frontage gives the lie to the popular belief that this scheme of architecture was always a tribute to the Virgin Queen. The twisted finials and chimneys lend a particular charm to this two-storey building.

Apart from these magnificent houses, the county is rich in smaller Tudor and Elizabethan manor houses and farms, such as Dodington Manor on the northern slopes of the Quantock Hills, Colinshays Manor and Horseley Farm in the south-east of the county, which stand beside the River Brue between Bruton and South Brewham.

In the seventeenth century, Thomas Gerard was to praise the formal garden that Edward Phelips laid out at Montacute. It was only one of the many Tudor gardens of Somerset, most of them no doubt inspired by William Turner, a Dean of Wells Cathedral and better known as the father of English botany. A Northumbrian, born in Morpeth, Turner was educated at Cambridge where he became friends with Nicholas Ridley and Hugh Latimer. These two encouraged his devoutly held Protestant beliefs and were indirectly to establish his botanical interests, for the practice of his Faith led, both before and after the reign of Mary Tudor, to enforced absences from England. He first studied botany seriously in Italy and thereafter collected plants throughout the continent, actually establishing a garden in Cologne during his second exile.

A plaque for him has been placed on the wall of the old Deanery on the north side of Wells Cathedral green, where he created his best recorded garden. It was not made without trouble. In 1551, he wrote: 'I am dene here in *Wellis*, but I can get neither house nor one foot of land' and complained of being 'pened up in a chamber of my lorde of bathes wt all my household servants and children as shepe in a pyndfolde'. He was forced to leave Wells during Mary's reign. He returned on the accession of Elizabeth, only to be suspended for noncomformity in 1564. By that time, his garden was completed.

Nothing is to be seen of it now, for it was shamefully cleared out one Sunday morning in the 1960s to make a building plot for new houses for the Wells' canons. However, a similar garden at Lytes Cary, north-east of Ilchester is in the care of the National Trust and open to the public. It has been planted with the species that would have been familiar to Henry Lyte who created it, and is much as it was in the seventeenth century. Henry Lyte was another early herbalist and published a translation of a Flemish herbal in 1578, which he dedicated to Queen Elizabeth 'from my poore house at Lytescarie'. A copy is on display in the Great Hall.

These gardens were being planted and tended at a time of national concern about the power of Spain. From 1584 until the destruction of the Armada there was a constant fear of invasion. The coastal defences were kept under continuous surveillance and three thousand Somerset men were provided with arms and trained at weekly musters to meet the expected attack.

It is said that the Spanish Armada was first sighted by a Bridgwater skipper, who immediately gave the news to Sir John Popham, the Lord Chief Justice, who lived in Wellington. He informed the Queen, urging 'haste, haste, haste, post haste, and again I say, haste, haste'.

From Combwich, the seventy-ton *William* sailed out of the mouth of the Parret to join Drake's fleet; and throughout the county the prepared beacons on the hilltops blazed out the message of the Spanish threat. They were to flare again in 1588 as part of the national rejoicing at the Armada's defeat. There were some families, however, for whom Drake's victory was not wholly welcome. They were those who had not subscribed to the Act of Uniformity of 1559 and preferred to pay the £20 a month fine for non-attendance at the parish church, their spiritual needs being met by Catholic priests hidden in their houses. Many such arrangements were connived at, so the threat of Jesuit infiltration was taken very seriously and with good cause.

In Spain, a Somerset blessing on the mission of the Armada was given by Robert Parsons, then Rector of the English College in Rome, a position he was to hold until his death in 1610. The son of a Nether Stowey blacksmith and educated in Taunton, he was to become a Jesuit and a friend of Edmund Campion. Another Nether Stowey man to become a Jesuit was actually executed with Campion at Tyburn in 1581.

In the following century the religious differences were to erupt into the bloodshed of the Civil War. In Somerset that national disaster was to be compounded by the local tragedy of Monmouth's doomed uprising and the subsequent reprisals executed by the notorious Judge Jeffreys.

VII
Wars and Rebellions

The landscape in which the wars and rebellions of the seventeenth century took place in Somerset has been described for us by Thomas Gerard, born in Trent, now just across the border into Dorset, who toured the county in 1633 describing the parishes according to the various river basins. He wrote of the solitary wilderness of Exmoor, 'the more commodious for staggs who keep possession of it'; of the market at Minehead; the harbour at Watchet; and he waxed particularly eloquent about the prosperity of Taunton and the delights of the orchards surrounding the town and the cherry gardens flourishing in the 'rich red earth'.

Although Gerard made no mention of them, he must have been aware in his travels of the many new crops that were beginning to be grown in the county at this time. We know about them from the farm and market account books, where clover and other vetches are mentioned for the first time in any significant amounts. They could not have been quite so noticeable to a traveller as hops, which were now being grown for sale to small brewers in Yeovil; or the tall, yellow flowers of woad, once imported from France, and now breaking the green of summer meadows in much the same way as the rape fields do today. Woad, which dyes blue, was needed for the expanding cloth industry, which also created a market for hemp and flax and for teazles which were used to card the nap on the cloth. In the 1990s, the last two crops are appearing again: flax, which is now used in the manufacture of linoleum, makes welcome patches of delicate blue in the landscape; and teazles are found to be much more gentle than mechanical, metal carders.

The new agricultural improvements, which were to come to

fruition in the next century, generally involved the planting of increased crops of root vegetables such as carrots and turnips. The sheep, initially kept solely for their wool, had their part to play in these new methods of arable farming. Gerard must have come across flocks being driven in the mornings off the upper pastures, where they had spent the night grazing, in order that they could manure the fields for planting.

We have to remember, however, that these changes were taking place at a time when fifteen- to twenty-ton barges could still float up the Parret to Langport and when most of the Somerset moors still lay under water for a greater part of the year. James I drew up a plan for draining and enclosing much of Sedgemoor, but it was never put into action; and although the Dutch engineer, Vermuyden, who was to be responsible for draining the fens of Lincolnshire, also had schemes for Somerset, nothing came of them until the following century.

The King was no doubt motivated to consider the plight of north Somerset by the great flood of 1607, when the sea swept inland the whole way along the coast to the east of Combwich. At Berrow, a milkmaid was forced to take refuge on a small island which she shared with mice, shrews and other wild creatures.

At about this time, dramatic changes were also going on inside the parish churches. Beside the despoiled remains of Muchelney Abbey, the ceiling of the village church was being extensively decorated by a local artist, who favoured flamboyant and buxom angels, dressed in the costumes of the time. They are still there to delight or shock us.

A more general change in all churches was to be introduced in the reign of Charles I, when Archbishop Laud decreed that the altar, which had been moved into the nave at the Reformation, should be returned to the chancel at the east end of the church. Moreover, it was to be surrounded by a rail, which would prevent it being profaned by the dogs accompanying their masters from outlying farms to the compulsory church services. Some churchwardens also had to act as dog whippers when these animals got out of hand.

This new dispensation is particularly apparent in the church at Rodney Stoke, near Cheddar, where the finely carved altar, dating from 1634, draws attention to itself with an exaggerated version of the particular bulbous legs of Jacobean design. In this church the rood screen and loft were built as late as 1625, and the balustrade still exists, as does the octagonal, wooden font cover put in place two years later to preserve the consecrated water.

Nearby at Croscombe, between Wells and Shepton Mallet, the little hillside church has an almost complete set of Jacobean furnishing including high box pews, an ornate pulpit and a marvellous screen surmounted by the Royal Arms of James I. A more modest church at Catcott, to the north of the Polden ridge, also retains its Jacobean pulpit, altar rails and pews. The latter, which are made of elm wood are unusual in having folding extensions, which could be pulled out to form bench seats for servants and children.

The beginning of the seventeenth century was the start of the long era in which the importance of lengthy sermons was encouraged if not enforced, and many Somerset pulpits, well worth looking out for, date from this time. At St Bridget's church near the coast at Breane, close to Weston-super-Mare, the finely carved pulpit dates from 1620 and the one at Langford Budville, between Wellington and Milverton, must have been installed at least six years earlier. For it was in 1614 that the churchwardens bought the vicar an hour glass so that his sermon time could be monitored, although it is uncertain as to whether the running sands rationed the time the parson spoke or prescribed the amount of time he should spend on his feet. Perhaps it was the latter, for in 1623, the curate, Thomas Wygood, was doubly reprimanded for neglecting to give his monthly sermon and for refusing to take the village children through their catechism.

Once again, it is the effigies of members of the great families that show us something of the people who worshipped in the churches under the new dispensation. At Curry Rivel, to the north of Langport, in the thirteenth-century church that dominates this crossroad village, you can see the effigies of Marmaduke and Robert Jennings, who died in 1625 and 1630 respectively. They have been immortalised in what Pevsner calls 'very rustic work', obviously by the hand of some local craftsman. Their ladies do not lie with them, but their joint children, three girls and three boys, kneel by their tomb.

A more notable citizen of this time was Robert Gray, whose monument of 1635 in St Mary's church in Taunton bears an inscription, opening with the couplet:

> Taunton bore him, London bred him,
> Piety trained him, Virtue led him

and concludes

> Taunton blessed him, London blessed him.
> This thankful town, that mindful city.

So much for the respectable; but even before Cromwell's rule, Puritanism was making itself felt in church government, and those who fell foul of its dictates could be humiliated and even treated with great cruelty. In 1633, for instance, the curate of Cannington, one Tobyas Calloe, was arrested for riotous behaviour at a Church Ale Feast and locked up in a small, stone hut from which he was rescued by an equally riotous gang of his cronies from East Quantoxhead. At that juncture, the church council ordered that anyone who could lay his hands on a horse should ride off in pursuit of Calloe. I'm afraid I have not been able to follow that story further, but I can tell you that it was about this time that Sir Thomas Richards, Chief Justice of the King's Bench, made an order in Taunton denouncing 'Revells and Church Ales as well as bear and bull baiting'.

Sexual immorality was most severely punished. Young Joane Walters of Bridgwater was only one of the victims of the high moral tone of the time. In 1617, she was whipped behind a cart through the streets of the town on account of unchaste conduct. The seventeenth-century witch hunts were even more sinister. Instigated by James I himself, they were to continue long after his death in 1625. In 1632, a seventy-year-old Wincanton woman was hanged for her part in the organisation of a black mass in which the participants seem to have done nothing more reprehensible than walking backwards around the church, three times. Twenty-five years later, there was another witch hunt in Wincanton, when Elizabeth Style of Stoke Trister was condemned for her participation in a coven.

In the following year at Chard, Jane Brook was hanged on 26 March for allegedly causing the serious illness of Richard Jones, a Shepton Mallet lad, by putting a curse on the boy.

The pious firmly believed that witches had the power to take on animal forms. In 1633, Julian Cox, a Quantock woman from Triscombe, was tried before Judge Archer in Taunton because a huntsman was convinced that she had changed herself into a hare that he was hunting.

It was against such a backdrop of superstitious fears that the Civil War began in 1642. Like many another county, Somerset was divided in its loyalties; although in the years leading up to the hostilities there had been a general stand against the levies of Ship Money by the Crown. It was the Somerset-born, John Pym, who led the Parliamentary opposition to Charles I, and who was among those who drew up the Petition of Right in 1628. With most of the Somerset gentry he was firmly behind the Parliamentary order that the county should raise a militia. When it came to declaring allegiance in war, however, things looked differently and many Somerset land-owners supported the King. Although on the whole, the north of the county was for Parliament and the south for the Royalists, there were many exceptions. Wells, for example was strongly Royalist, while only eight miles away, Shepton Mallet was equally strongly, and more effectively, behind the Parliamentary cause.

In the first year of the war, there was a skirmish at Marshall's Elm, and another the following year at Chewton Mendip. In July 1644, Sir John Horner of Mells, to the west of Frome, reluctantly entertained Charles I, who was making what proved to be an unsuccessful recruiting drive in the county. In that same year, John, half-brother to Sir Edward Hungerford, was put in charge of the Royalist garrison, stationed in the castle of Farleigh Hungerford, beside the road that leads out of Somerset towards Trowbridge in Wiltshire.

At the same time, Sir Edward, the rightful lord of that castle, commanded the Wiltshire Parliamentary forces.

John Hungerford depended on Bristol to sustain the garrison, so when Prince Rupert surrendered that city to the Parliamentary forces on 11 September, 1645, he was left without any means of support. Four days later, apparently without any bloodshed, Sir Edward resumed control of his castle and installed a Parliamentary garrison. The castle, part of which dates from the fourteenth century, is open to the public and in the chapel, which contains the Hungerford tombs, you can see the effigy of that Sir Edward, dressed in full armour.

Somerset's best known Parliamentarian is, of course, Admiral Robert Blake, son of a Bridgwater ship-owner and born in the house in the town centre which now houses the Blake Museum. He was to rise to such prominence in his naval career and as a friend of Oliver Cromwell, that when he died at sea after his last victory against the Spanish at Santa Cruz in April 1657, he was buried in Westminster Abbey. He was so hated by the Royalists, however, that after the Restoration his body was thrown into the streets.

During the Civil War, Blake also served on land. In 1644, he held Taunton against the Royalists, and, during that siege, it was probably he who ordered that the one pig left in the town should be whipped around the walls in order to delude the besieging army into thinking that there was a herd of swine at the citizens' disposal. In the April of the following year, the Royalists withdrew to Langport, where they were defeated by Parliament's new Model Army.

After the Battle of Worcester, which concluded the Civil War, the King's son, who was to return to England as Charles II in 1660, was sheltered in Somerset by Edward Kirton of Castle Cary and led to safety by Edward and Robert Phelips of Montacute. But it was the Revd Dr Henry Byam, rector of the Exmoor parish of Luccombe, who had been arrested by Blake early on in the hostilities, who escorted the exiled Prince to the Scilly Islands and later to Jersey. There, Byam acted as chaplain to Prince Charles until the garrison was forced to surrender to the Parliamentary forces.

At the Restoration, Henry Byam returned to his parish, and eventually became a Canon of Exeter and a Prebendary of Wells. He did not enjoy these honours for long, for he died on 16 June 1669. His memorial in Luccombe church was composed by his contemporary, Dr Hamnet Ward, who also published a collection of Byam's sermons, most of which were preached in the presence of the exiled Charles.

Despite the skirmishes and battles of the Civil War, Somerset industries flourished during the seventeenth century. Before the hostilities started, the county was so wealthy, that in 1630, when it was assessed for Ship Money, only Devon, Yorkshire and London had to pay more; and by 1637, at which time he was giving employment to over one thousand people, John Aske of Fairfield House, between the Quantocks and the coast, was said to be the wealthiest clothier in England.

At the same time, the county was growing rich in mineral wealth. In 1665 the Mineral Court, which had jurisdiction over the lead mines in the Forest of Mendip, met in Wells on 1 April. The main purpose of that meeting was to swear in the jurors who were called upon to enforce the complicated laws which governed the working of the mines, whose activities do not appear to have been in any way disrupted by the hostilities. Other mines, in the west of the county, also seem to have been operating during the Civil War. In 1633, Gerard reported that 'a Dutchman hath found out Mynes of excellent Alabaster which they use much for Tombes and Chimney pieces. It's somewhat harder than ye Darbeshire Alabaster, but for variety of mixtures and colours it passeth any, I dare say of this Kingdome.'

All this wealth, together with the trade going in and out of the port of Bristol, naturally brought pirates sailing up the channel along Somerset's coastline. The Parret ports were affected by their activities, and one of Admiral Blake's greatest services to his country was to clear the seas; an operation that was also enforced by the gun emplacements on the rock of Steep Holm. While the pirates were being suppressed, the press gangs engaged in building up Charles I's navy were also busy in the towns along this coast from Bristol to Watchett.

It was also during the seventeenth century that paper-making, stimulated by the rapid increase in the demand for printed material, became established in Somerset. The mills were powered by the same swift-flowing limestone waters that were later to turn the machinery for the cloth mills. Paper was also being made in the west of the county, and still is, at Watchet, on the headland near St Decuman's church.

In Somerset, the bloodshed of the Civil War is less keenly remembered than the fearful slaughters that took place in connection with the uprising of Charles II's illegitimate son, James, Duke of Monmouth. This was to lead to the so-called Pitchfork Rebellion of July 1685 and the subsequent reprisals taken by the cruel and dyspeptic Judge Jeffreys.

The Revd Andrew Paschall, vicar of Chedzoy, was convinced that some fearful disaster was heralded, when an earthquake shook his house; an event followed by the portents of the night sky above Westonzoyland when, at the 1684 winter solstice, several false suns were seen above the moors. Furthermore, in 1679 a number of Siamese twins had been born around Sedgemoor, and this was taken to portend grave trouble.

Sedgemoor is, of course, the focal point of the tragedy. If you go to Westonzoyland now, you can walk along the droves, beside the drainage rhynes, until you come to the site of the Battle of Sedgemoor, the last full-scale armed confrontation on English soil. The space is now fittingly and movingly supplied with memorials to all the men of Somerset who have fallen in wars throughout the centuries.

It is a sad place even in summer: the flat expanse of the drained moor reminds the visitor of the one channel which, as students of the battle know, was said to be responsible for the downfall of Monmouth's strategies. To the north, the ridge of the Polden Hills marks the skyline, and it was to those modest heights that some of the more fortunate of his followers managed to escape from the massacre of his troops. One in particular, a certain John Swayne, a native of Shapwick, is said

to have literally leapt to freedom. The extent of his phenomenal long jumps is indicated with little marker stones, which
you can detect among the undergrowth if you follow the
public footpath sign into the woods above Moorlynch, from
the south-eastern edge of the road running along the Polden
ridge. Many of the other survivors were held prisoner in
Westonzoyland church, where several of the wounded were to
die. The names of all these prisoners – there were some five
hundred of them, bolted in behind the heavy wooden door – are
recorded here; and no amount of flower festivals can totally
obliterate the impact on this church of that terrible, crowded
incarceration of young men, who had set out with such high
hopes on behalf of the popular Protestant Duke, who was
going to save their livelihoods from rapacious landlords.

At a rough estimate, of the three thousand Somerset men
who followed the Duke into battle, three hundred were killed
at Sedgemoor, and another thousand died either in trying to
escape or as the result of the summary executions ordered by
Jeffreys. Many of those who survived that rough justice were
sent as cheap labour to the West Indies.

In 1685, in the great hall of Taunton Castle, where the
County Museum is now housed, Jeffreys tried over five
hundred Monmouth supporters. Among his victims was one,
William Haynes, from the wealthy wool town of Beckington,
three miles to the north of Frome. He was ordered to be
transported, and on 24 October of that year, he was put
aboard the *John* at Bristol and taken to Barbados, an island on
which you may still hear Somerset accents. There he was sold
to a planter, whose name is recorded as Henry Quintyne.
Among the other prisoners in the hold with Haynes was one of
the eight rebels from Whitelackington, brought to justice at
the same time. This man, John Rogers, also destined for
Barbados, was sold to a Major Johnson. The clothier, William
Selfe, another Beckington man, whose trial came up at Wells,
was transported to Jamaica as was George Miller of Whitelackington.

Miller was perhaps more fortunate than Charles Speke of
Whitelackington Manor, who was sentenced to execution for

refusing to swear against his fellow land-owner, Edmund Prideaux of Forde Abbey, for his part in 'aiding and assisting the rebels against the king'. Speke was reprieved, but the order came too late. Before it reached Somerset, he had been hanged at Ilchester.

It was on 23 September 1685 that Judge Jeffreys held his last court. It took place in Wells, on the site of the food market to which farmers from the outlying villages brought cheese, corn and bacon for sale. For the purpose of the trial, a screen was erected at one end of the market, behind which the judge sat, while business, presumably, continued on the other side more or less as normal.

The county is full of places where Jeffreys held his summary courts. Nowadays, the most obviously accessible are the George Inn at Norton St Philip and the Mermaid Hotel in Yeovil High Street. At both these places you may still eat and drink where that much loathed servant of the King and scourge of Somerset took his refreshment. At the George, they will tell you the fearful story of a local man, who held the door open for Jeffreys, after the trial was completed, and who was somehow swept along with the prisoners. Being unable to convince anyone of his innocence, he was executed beside them.

It seems to me almost blasphemous that the route of Monmouth's progress through the county is now marked with the brown tourist notices pointing people to the route of the 'Pitchfork Rebellion'; for the appalling slaughter of innocent young farm workers, fearful of the powers of the landed gentry, is still bitterly remembered here; indeed, for many years no member of the Royal Family dared to visit Taunton.

After Monmouth landed at Lyme Regis on the Dorset coast on 11 June 1685, he immediately started to journey north into Somerset, where he had previously been acclaimed and entertained by the Sydenhams of Brympton d'Evercy near Yeovil, William Strode of Barrington Court, and the Spekes of Whitelackington. It is also possible that the philosopher, John Locke, who in 1661 had succeeded his father as squire of Bellerton near Chew Magna was also involved in the discussions which led to Monmouth's bid for the throne; although he fled to Holland, two years before the fatal encounter at Westonzoyland.

By four o'clock in the morning of 17 June 1685, the streets of Taunton were packed to welcome Monmouth, who had spent the previous night camped outside the town. When the Duke entered, the happy people threw flowers at the feet of his horse as he rode in triumph to take up his lodging at Captain Tucker's house by the Three Cups Inn. The following day, twenty-seven young Taunton girls, each carrying a Bible, came to present themselves, and the following day the Protestant Duke of Monmouth was declared King of England. On 21 June he marched out of Taunton with his triumphant followers to Bridgwater, where the Mayor, standing by the market cross read out a further proclamation, confirming that Monmouth was king. His tour of the county as a ruling monarch came to an end when James II's army pursued him through Frome, Shepton Mallet and Wells, and so back to Bridgwater, where plans for the final encounter were laid.

Despite all this turmoil, following so swiftly on the tumult and bloodshed of the Civil War, the seventeenth century was the era in which many of the great houses of Somerset were established and embellished. At Simonsbath, in the middle of the Forest of Exmoor, James Bovey, a London merchant, took advantage of the land laws of Cromwell's Commonwealth to build himself a great house, which is now a hotel. At the Reformation, Bovey obviously lost his freehold, when the Forest was reclaimed by the crown. Nevertheless, he remained at Simonsbath until his death in 1696.

Other Somerset households were more directly affected by the Civil War. In the autumn of 1642, the lawyer, John Turberville (of the family whose name Hardy borrowed for Tess) acquired Golden or Gaulden farm at Tolland, between the Quantocks and the Brendon Hills. It is open to the public now and you are able to appreciate the grandeur of the plasterwork that he installed, which happily escaped undamaged during the time that the house was used as a garrison. His initials are inscribed over the door between the hall and the room generally referred to as the chapel.

In the early 1650s, Lord Poulet added a fine banqueting hall to his house at Hinton St George to the north of Crewkerne. That house replaced the earlier two-tiered 'Manor Place' described by John Leland during his tour through South Somerset in the sixteenth century. The new manor house was begun around 1630, and was embellished six years later with one of the extravagantly decorative plaster ceilings that were so fashionable at that time. This magnificent family house is built of the golden stone from Ham Hill, near Yeovil, and Lord Poulet's hall has a roof glazed with lead ore from Mendip. During the latter part of the seventeenth century, some more modest buildings gradually appeared throughout the county.

It was the opinion of the Quaker, John Whiting, that if there had been religious freedom in England after the Restoration, the fearful massacre of Monmouth's rebellion and its terrible aftermath would never have taken place. The tragedy was made almost inevitable by the Act of 1664 which declared all forms of worship outside the Church of England to be illegal. Defiance of that law was widespread. In Somerset, the gaol at Ilchester, which stood on the north bank of the river, could not contain the numbers of Quakers and other Nonconformists, who were not prepared to make concessions to the demands of Caesar.

There had been a substantial number of Quakers in the county for some years. When George Fox came to address a meeting in Taunton in 1663, he was able to report in his journal that it was 'very large'. The year before that visit, a Crewkerne Quaker had made a valiant stand against tithing, and in the same year Taunton produced its own brand of Nonconformist fervour, for George Newton, the vicar of St Mary Magdalene's, together with his assistant Joseph Alleine, refused to give their allegience to the Book of Common Prayer. In this he had the support of many other Puritan clergymen, such as Laurence Musgrave of nearby Angersleigh, on the edge of the Blackdown Hills. Having been deprived of his living without any form of compensation, Newton immediately started a dissenting group in the town. Seven years later he was joined by twelve ministers serving a congregation of three hundred and fifty dissenting souls.

That experience seems to have been typical throughout the county, for despite the severity of the prosecutions, secret groups of Nonconformists continued to grow. So that by the time there was a temporary abatement of the severity of the laws in 1669, over a hundred such groups were counted in the county as a whole. By 1672, when the Declaration of Indulgence gave freedom of worship to those meeting in specially licensed premises, there were at least 144 such designated places.

One of the first buildings to be registered in this way was Taunton's Baptist chapel in Mary Street. In the eighteenth century, it was replaced by the Unitarian church, where the young Coleridge came to preach. In the same year, George Newton's dissenting congregation built their own meeting house in Paules Lane on the same site where they had previously gathered for worship in defiance of the law.

By 1680, reactionary opinion had strengthened in the town and there were serious attempts to stamp out Nonconformity. Newton was the main target. Led by the Mayor, the self-righteous upholders of the Church descended on Paules Lane and gutted the new building, carrying away all its wooden fittings – pulpits, tables, seats and pews – and ritually setting them alight in the market place.

Nine years later, the Act of Toleration put an end to such desecrations. At Trudoxhill, to the south-west of Frome, a small cottage was publicly converted to a place of public worship. The Congregationalists still meet there.

In the next century, religious tolerance abounded, partly perhaps because of the intense intellectual scorn for enthusiasm, rife among the intellectuals of the time. That stance was not shared by the Somerset agricultural labourers, cloth workers and miners, as is evident from the response given both to the Quaker, William Penn, when he preached in Wells market place, and to John Wesley during his tours of the county.

VIII

An Age of Reason and Romance, Squalor and Elegance

By the eighteenth century, the conscious divisions between rich and poor were firmly established, as agriculture gave way to industry in many places and as the labourers became more fully aware of their rights. This trend was as marked in Somerset as elsewhere, and here as in other places throughout the country it was accompanied by the rise of Nonconformity, and in particular by the itinerant preaching of John Wesley.

In this county, his most enthusiastic support was drawn from the Bristol brickyards and the coalfields of northern Mendip. It was in 1739 that he first visited the coal mining area in Pensford, walking into the village with twenty-three companions. As he was unable to hold a meeting in the church, as he had hoped, he held his meeting in the main street near the medieval bridge, now by-passed by the main road. He was to return to this village on at least twenty-four further occasions and must have regarded it as a challenge, for his appeal to the working men drew the wrath of the mine owners and landed gentry, who were often the same people. One meeting, which he was holding in a field, was disrupted when a bull was driven in among the worshippers.

In 1745, Wesley visited the miners of Coleford, near Frome; after he had been there one miner reported that 'a society began to be formed, a mighty outpouring of the spirit fell on the people'. Both Charles and John Wesley were to visit the village several times in the following years. On 6 August 1746, Wesley preached at Oakhill near Shepton Mallet and was most moved by the response of the villagers. On 28 March 1749 he returned and again found to his delight 'a great peace and a people loving one another at Oakhill'. It was not to last. Four years later, when he returned to the 'little Societies' in

Somerset, he found there had been a back-sliding and that 'many once alive have been drawn back to perdition'. Nevertheless, Wesley's tradition did remain alive in the area, and in nearby Ashwick, in a hamlet charmingly known as T'Other side of the Hill, you will find a cottage that bears his name and where he is said to have preached. One of its rooms was used as a chapel and services were held there on Sunday afternoons until 1973.

Although George II was adamant that 'no man be persecuted for conscience's sake', Wesley had strenuous detractors in Somerset as elsewhere. Among his most active persecutors in the county were John Free, Vicar of East Coker near Yeovil and Augustus Toplady, curate at Blagdon on Mendip and best known as the author of the hymn 'Rock of Ages, Cleft for me', which he is said to have composed while sheltering from a thunderstorm in Burrington Combe, where annual services are still held to commemorate the event.

Despite such opposition, John and Charles Wesley were able to count many Church of England clerics among their supporters. One of John's most valued friends was Dr Coke, curate of North Petherton, in the heart of agricultural Somerset. John Wesley was 86 when he made his last visit to Somerset in 1789. On that final tour, he preached to the coal miners once again as he journeyed from Midsomer Norton and Coleford on his way to Frome through Vobster, Mells and Buckland Dinham.

In contrast to the poverty and squalor in which the mostly illiterate coal miners of north Somerset eked out their precarious lives, the lot of the wealthy landed gentry was one of unbelievable elegance and sophistication. The high living of the latter groups was shared by the visitors who were coming in increasing numbers to take the waters in the newly designed city of Bath. While the Wesleys devoted themselves to the souls of the labouring poor, their aristocratic convert, Lady Huntingdon, determined to spread adherence to Methodism among the rich. In 1765, she opened a chapel in Bath, which was attended in the following year by Horace Walpole and also by the Revd John Penrose, a Cornish clergyman whose gout brought him to take the waters in Bath. The chapel, in whose services only the invited might participate, stands in the north-eastern part of the city by the building which now houses Bath's Museum of Naive Art.

Somerset's most notable native dissenting minister in the first part of the eighteenth century was undoubtedly Henry Grove. He was born in Taunton in 1683, where he eventually ran the dissenting academy in which he had once been a pupil. In the autumn of 1714, he contributed four essays to the eighth and final volume of *The Spectator*. One of these, on the subject of Novelty, was mentioned at Mrs Thrale's dinner table in April 1776, when Dr Johnson observed that it was one of 'the finest pieces in the English language . . . yet we do not hear it talked of. It was written by Grove a dissenting teacher.' To which Boswell, in recording the discourse, commented, 'He would not, I perceived, call him a *clergyman* though he was candid enough to allow very great merit to his composition.'

Among the Somerset 'clergymen' was one who certainly would not acknowledge a dissenting minister as a colleague. I am thinking of Richard Graves, rector of Claverton, who in 1799 wrote an open letter to his son at university. In it he commended the lad for declaring his allegiance to the Thirty Nine Articles and advised him to steer clear 'of speculative and controversial points, which would only puzzle and perplex you'.

Despite the activities of the Dissenters and the general refurbishing of the churches during the Jacobean period, a certain amount of church building went on in the county during the eighteenth century. We learn of some of it from John Collinson, vicar of Long Ashton, who published his parish by parish account of Somerset in 1791. Some of the buildings that he wrote of, such as the 'church of modern erection of one pace, plain and simple to a degree' at Walton-in-Gordano have disappeared. In that case the eighteenth-century church was replaced in 1839, and the church that Collinson wrote of had in its turn replaced the medieval parish church which stood at a short distance from the beach. Collinson was pleased with the modest building that served the parish in his time. He tells us that it had 'a turret and one small bell' and that it was 'the perfect place of worship for the inhabitants'.

That church was obviously catering for a congregation more modest in its expectations than the one that attended the great church at Martock, which was enhanced at this time by a great stucco altar piece. This was provided by John Butler, a privy councillor in Nova Scotia, who wished to make a suitable presentation to the town of his birth.

Collinson tells us little of the great sixteenth-century angel roof of Martock church, which Pevsner reckoned to be the finest in the county, but he waxed eloquent on the 104 pews with which it had recently been furnished, and the 'very handsome new organ, erected at the expense of the inhabitants', which he declared added 'greatly to the dignity of the church'.

Among other churches to be embellished in the eighteenth century was the medieval building at Kilmersdon whose west door is studded with the date of 1766. However, by far the most elegant and complete building of this period is to be found at nearby Babington, standing beside a somewhat earlier great house, built when the original village was cleared and the land emparked. The church, which was in the gift of the Knatchbull family, was built around 1750. Its roof is crowned with an octagonal tower topped by a stone cupola.

Although we know little of the congregation of that isolated church, we do have records from several parishes of the games of Fives that were regularly played in the churchyards. This West Country version of the original *jeu de paume*, the precursor of Real Tennis, became popular in the seventeenth century, and by the eighteenth it seems to have become a craze that caused great concern and displeasure among some clerics. As early as 1633, a complaint was made at the Taunton sessions about the practice of playing this 'idle game' in Williton and so defacing the church 'to the great dislike of the inhabitants'. At Martock in 1745, the churchwardens were instructed 'to prevent Fives playing in ye south side of ye church'. The players, naturally, promptly moved to the north side and according to the vestry records, caused, such 'wickedness, swearing, quarrelling and fighting in the churchyard' that the only remedy was to dig a ditch across 'Ye Fives Place' and for the sum of three shillings have the sexton fill it with rooting docks and nettles. That seems to have put an end to the game in Martock, but the same method at Wrington was not so successful. Fives continued to be played there until 1824, when the churchwarden, a Mr James, requested that he be buried in the middle of the pitch with a large headstone marking the grave.

In other places somewhat less extreme measures were adopted to prevent Fives players desecrating the churchyards. When Parson Woodforde, whose Norfolk diaries are better known than those he kept during his youth in Somerset, was curate to his father in Castle Cary, he noted that the churchwardens were granted leave to dig up the Fives place. However, a few years earlier in 1764, when at the age of twenty-four, he served as curate in neighbouring Babcary, he was happy to entertain his supper guests on one July evening with games of Fives in the churchyard.

The sensible solution, which was soon arrived at, was to build special Fives towers. Most of these, such as the one at South Petherton, date from the early nineteenth century, but at least two, that at Stoke sub Hamdon (behind the Fleur de Lys public house) and the one at Bishops Lydiard probably date from the late eighteenth century.

As well as being a bit touchy about games in the churchyard, most Church of England clerics in the eighteenth century were as sensitive as ever to threats of Papism, and were harsh on any glimmer of sexual immorality. In 1767, Parson Woodforde 'received a letter from Edward, Bishop of Bath and Wells to desire me to transmit to him a correct list of Papists or reputed Papists with an account of their age, sex, occupation and time of residence in the parish of Castle Cary, with all convenient expedition at Wells, in order to its being laid before the House of Lords next session'.

In the February of the following year, the young man had to officiate at a public penance undergone by one Sarah Gore, who had a child out of wedlock.

The secular buildings of the eighteenth century, including the follies erected in the newly enclosed parklands, are faithfully recorded by Collinson. The one that literally dominates the landscape of east Somerset beyond all others is Alfred's Tower. It was built early in the 1700s by Henry Hoare on a spur of a hill to the west of his mansion at Stourhead. A three-sided brick building, it is 155 feet high and there are 121 steps leading to the top. It was erected in honour of Alfred the Great's victory at nearby Penselwood, and as Collinson observed it stands 'on an eminence commanding the most beautiful inland prospect in the kingdom, and to which description would fall very short in doing proper justice'.

In other parts of Somerset, many of the great houses belonging to the old county families were falling into ruins. Writing of Combe Sydenham in the Brendon Hills, Collinson tells us that 'A considerable part of this old pile is in ruins, with ivy creeping through the fine old arches and stair cases. In the centre is a tower, and there are the remains of a noble kitchen. Part is modernized and inhabited by a farmer.' The same fate befell the Horners' Elizabethan manor at Mells to the west of Frome. Pevsner, in his description of the buildings in that village, quoted a report from the *Gentleman's Magazine* of 1794 which recorded that 'Half the old house is mouldering in ruins, the rest is occupied by a farmer.' Lytes Cary, near Somerton, now in the hands of the National Trust, was described by Collinson as a great house of the past. The Lyte family had sold their fine fifteenth-century hall in 1748, and for the best part of two hundred years, it too was used as a farmhouse. It was bought and restored by Sir Walter Jenner in 1907.

On the other hand, some medieval and Tudor buildings were being brought up to date in an altogether grander fashion. Marston Bigot, to the south of Frome, which had long been in the possession of the Earls of Cork and Orrery, was transformed into a Palladian mansion in 1713. That great house was allowed to fall into a ruinous state, but it was fortunately restored in the 1980s.

As trade increased many unlanded business families were able to build themselves substantial houses, such as the pleasing two-storey Somerton Randle on the outskirts of Somerton, in whose grounds a Shakespearean production is now staged annually at midsummer.

Towards the end of the eighteenth century, Thomas Joliffe employed Capability Brown to landscape the parkland surrounding his new mansion of Ammerdown. The classic gateway to his old house at Charlton still stands by the roadside above the feudal village of Kilmersdon. The building of Ammerdown, on the ridge to the east of the village, was begun by Joliffe in 1787 and completed four years later; the following year its proud owner, became High Sheriff of Somerset.

By that time it had become generally fashionable to replace old manor houses by grand mansions. Sometimes, as in the case of Ammerdown, these were built at a distance from the original family home. On the Mendip plateau, the Hippsleys deserted their thirteenth-century manor, which still stands by the disued church at Emborough, and in about 1750 they built themselves an imposing stone house, with four Tuscan columns adorning its entrance, a few miles away at Ston Easton. This mansion has now become a hotel where visitors can enjoy the splendid plasterwork and magnificent columns of the interior. Mansions such as Ston Easton and the manor house (now demolished) at Chewton Mendip built for the Waldegrave family in the 1780s were largely financed out of the flourishing industries of the time, and in these specific cases directly from the wealthy lead mines and the coal measures of north Somerset. More and more men were being employed in the coal fields and the lead mines were all intensely active, although the dire effects of lead and allied substances were already being noted. At Rowberrow, near Shipham, where calamine was mined, the surrounding foliage was destroyed by the poisonous fumes sent out during the refining of the mineral. Collinson observed that 'Very little wood thrives near the village'. Iron works were also flourishing on Mendip from the middle of the eighteenth century. At Pitts Farm, above Ebbor Gorge, the entrance to one such iron ore mine is still visible with a pit prop at the entrance supporting the roof.

Although coal had been dug at Kilmersdon intermittently

from the fifteenth century, it was not until the seventeenth that it was extensively mined around Farringdon Gurney and Midsomer Norton. By 1681 something like a hundred thousand tons a year were drawn from the north Somerset mines and this amount was substantially increased in 1736 when coal was found at Radstock. Here in the mines, then generally known as the coal works, men influenced by Wesley's preaching would pause for prayer before starting the day's shift. A Timsbury collier, whose house was used regularly for Methodist meetings, was killed in a pit accident in 1786. The men who discovered his body reported that they found him in an attitude of prayer.

Quarries were another major source of wealth at this time, as they have been ever since, to the great detriment of the landscape. Ralph Allen of Prior Park, who had initially made his fortune by re-organising the Post Office was in a position to invest in the Combe Down quarries. From 1725 they had supplied the now famous golden stone for the new buildings of Bath. Now that quarry work is almost completely mechanised it is difficult to imagine how hundreds of men were once employed on this back-breaking, dangerous work. The eighteenth-century artist George Morland's painting of a contemporary quarry works, which shows a scene somewhat on a par with the slaves employed on building the pyramids, is displayed in the gallery on the upper floors of the Bristol Museum.

Apart from minerals and stone, the other great resource of north Somerset was its water power. It was this that enabled numerous water-mills to flourish, many of which were used to meet the ever increasing demand for paper. The strip of woodland at Stoke Bottom, near Oakhill, contains the sparse ruins of forty houses, a flourishing village in Collinson's day when both a log-wood and a paper-mill provided work for the inhabitants, and a fortune for John Billingsley, the owner of the land and a substantial force in the county.

To the west, paper-making was on a much smaller scale, and was even carried out by farmers as a winter occupation. William Wood of Snailholt near Watchet was recorded in 1750 as being both a cider- and a paper-maker, with seven men working for him. During the nineteenth century, that family business grew and eventually moved to the site further down the valley which it occupies today.

Towards the end of the century gunpowder was needed to deal with the 'American troubles' and the Napoleonic wars, as well as Britain's growing imperial ambitions. The north Somerset powder-mills, whose furnaces were fed on charcoal made from the wood of such limestone loving trees and shrubs as black alder, spindle, poplar, willow and dog-wood, met that demand.

The manufacture of cloth was, however, still the staple industry of the county as a whole. Although Collinson recorded three paper-mills and four grist-mills in Cheddar, he noted that in that village, 'Many of the poor are employed in spinning and knitting hose'. Gradually, such work was becoming mechanised. On 8 July 1773, Parson Woodforde went 'up into South Cary to the Royal Oak to see Mr Nevil's grand machinery, being the whole of the woolen manufactory, from one end of it to the other, and all in motion at once. It is very curious indeed – three thousand movements at one going – composed by Mr Nevil himself, and which took him ny thirty years in completing it.'

Flax and hemp were now added to wool as extra resources in the county's textile trade. There was a rope walk at Yeovil, and sail cloth and webbing were being manufactured at Crewkerne. More delicate operations were undertaken in Martock and Yeovil, where gloves were manufactured; and around 1780, Vansomner and Paul, silk merchants of Pall Mall, established a silk weaving factory in Taunton. The serge trade came to Wellington in the middle of the century when a disastrous fire had disrupted the industry in Tiverton across the Devon border. In 1754, the Tone fulling-mills were established, and the great ponds which supplied the mills are now part of the town's parkland.

In general, the lot of the working people was worsened by the drift from farms to industrial towns. The agricultural labourer was certainly very poorly paid but so long as he was connected with a farm, he did have some measure of security and a settled home as well as land on which he could grow some of his own food. This was not always the case for the people working in the mines and mills. As always, poverty and poor housing led to an increase in crime, and more and more people fell foul of the law and were sentenced to prison terms. There was some thought of building a prison for such defaulters in Wells, but it was abandoned for a site to the east of Shepton Mallet.

That prison – which still exists today, and which was to become notorious in World War II, when it was the focus of *The Dirty Dozen*, a novel more widely known as a film – had a bad reputation from the start. When John Howard visited it in 1773, he reported that it was 'a shocking place; built on a marsh'; he found the sanitation to be very primitive, even for that time, and complained that the cells were like pig sties. A keeper told him that the place was so unhealthy that he buried three or four prisoners every week.

Despite the increase in industry, Somerset remained predominantly an agricultural county, and the eighteenth century was to bring many changes to both the farms and the landscape. The great storm of 26 November 1703, which killed Bishop Kidder and his wife in their palace in Wells when they were crushed by a falling chimney, brought chaos to the north Somerset moors as waves crashed through the sea walls. A Commission of the Sewers for Somerset was convened to consider plans for draining the moors. On 14 November 1709, they met in Axbridge, and on 27 June 1726 they held a session in Wells, in which the controversial matter of defining and allocating the responsibility for keeping the rhynes and drainage channels clear was inconclusively and heatedly discussed. On 3 August, the meeting was re-convened at the George in Glastonbury, when a little progress was made, the discussion being restricted to a consideration of dealing with the watercourse from the Brue, which flowed under the settlement of Beckery to the south of the town. In general, the committee's procedures seem much like the discussions that go on today in the planning of the much-needed ring roads round the county's medieval towns and villages, including the city of

Wells, for it was not until 1770 that the systematic drainage of Sedgemoor and the Brue valley went into operation.

Even then nothing happened smoothly. The land-owners were expected to meet the cost and it was very high; so it is no surprise that there was some concerted opposition before the Act for the draining of King's Sedgemoor was finally passed in 1791. It was then that the great engineering works, which diverted the rivers Parret and Cary into King's Sedgemoor Drain were begun. It is an enormous stretch of water, fifteen feet deep, fifty-five feet wide at the surface and ten feet wide at the bottom. Throughout the centuries it has been carefully maintained and still serves its initial function, although members of angling clubs now join the solitary herons on its banks. To appreciate the full grandeur of this utilitarian waterway and to see the extent of the land it drains, stand in the middle of the footbridge, which crosses it to the north-east of Westonzoyland, and which can only be reached by walking a mile or two along the old droves between the feeding rhynes.

These ditches were dug in the eighteenth century, and like the main drain they still play a vital part in preserving the moors and acting as 'wet fences' for the cattle grazing the reclaimed pasture. From a height, such as the top of Glastonbury Tor, you can see the pattern of rhynes and droves along which the herds were taken, making a chequer-board of the landscape.

Most of our knowledge of the farming practices of late eighteenth-century Somerset comes from John Billingsley's report in 1795 for the newly formed Board of Agriculture. This north Somerset land-owner had a keen interest and an important part to play in all the new developments that were taking place around him. His home was Ashwick Court, near Oakhill, a mansion that was sadly, partially demolished in the 1960s, leaving a few bare walls and gaping windows. At least you can see his memorial in Ashwick church.

In his report, Billingsley commended his fellow land-owner, Thomas Joliffe of Ammerdown, for his 'melioration' of barren land 'by summer fallowing and turnips'. Many such agricultural improvements were linked to enclosures, and much of the loss of Somerset's common land began in the eighteenth century. Early in 1722, legal notices were given out in St John's church in Glastonbury regarding the enclosure of Glastonbury Common Moor and Baltonsbury. They were in fact enclosed on 2 May, and shortly after that date some of the old commoners defiantly drove their cattle on to the land, which had by then been specifically 'hayned', that is reserved for the growth of hay.

There is no doubt that many people suffered hardship as a result of enclosures. On 22 December of that same year, the public-spirited Wells doctor, Claver Morris, distributed £20 at the Rose and Crown Inn at Glastonbury to those people whom he felt had been unfairly treated.

Enclosures must have benefited some of the smaller farmers as well as the great land-owners. However, until the latter part of the century, the average farm size was something under forty acres, and only a very few farmers were responsible for as much as one hundred acres. Such an acreage would be considered a really sizeable holding. Many of the smaller farmsteads have gone the way of Ashwick Court, but there are a few traces of lost farms. High up on Mendip, above Ebbor Gorge, you can just make out the outline of the house and the immediate garden of the dwelling place where a William Green lived when he was farming in 1766. The site is still known by the family name.

The new improved farming methods led to greater business taking place at the fairs and markets throughout the county. New livestock fairs were inaugurated, one of the busiest being held at Woolavington, four miles north-east of Bridgwater below the Polden ridge. This fair was established in 1777, and was held annually on 18 October. It specialised in cattle, sheep and young colts. In that same year the Bath and West Agricultural Improvement Society was founded. Its first public exhibition in 1790 was devoted exclusively to fat sheep. Naturally, John Billingsley was one of the most distinguished of the founder members of that Society. He was also a great champion of enclosures, mainly because he thought it was in this way that flocks of sheep could be increased on upland farms such as that belonging to William Green, who no doubt kept the now extinct, hardy, fine-woolled Mendip breed.

Although sheep dominated the 1790 show, Somerset's long reputation as a source of dairy products was at its height. In 1785, the September fair at Frome, which operated under a charter of 1270, was specifically designated as a cheese fair. It still takes place as a general agricultural show with one large marquee reserved for cheeses that can come from as far afield as Scotland, although the cheeses are still made to Somerset recipes. Collinson confirmed that the fertile moors around Cheddar had provided the area with an opportunity to become 'justly celebrated for making cheeses . . . superior in quality to most in England'.

The increase in both industrial and agricultural productivity drew attention to the difficulties of conveying goods and animals along the appalling roads of the time. Dr Claver Morris always made a special note in his diary whenever he managed to get his horse to go at more than six miles an hour, and he frequently commented on the near-impassable state of the Timsbury road, on which he was forced to travel when he made his regular visits to the coalfields.

It was initially because of the increased output from these coalfields, that the gentlemen of Somerset contracted 'canal mania'. John Billingsley was naturally there at the very beginning and was one of the most persuasive advocates. He took the chair at the first meeting of a canal committee, held at the Old Down Inn near Emborough in 1792. In 1794, the plan that was then discussed was authorised, the proposed course surveyed by the brilliant, young Scottish engineer, John Rennie, and in the following year, construction began.

The implementation of the enclosures and the struggles with the authorities that had to take place before road improvement plans and schemes for canal construction could be put into practice, forced Somerset land-owners to become politically active. In 1766, already suffering from the ill-health which was to force his resignation two years later, the elder Pitt visited Bath. 'The sum of things is that I am fitted more for a lonely hill in Somersetshire than for the affairs of state,' he confessed. His son, who succeeded him some twenty years later and who was to become renowned for his tax reforms, is honoured by a monument on the hill to the west of Curry Rivel for his part in reducing the tax on cider.

As for the doings of lesser politicians, we have James Woodforde's account of the Somerset version of Eatanswill. On 12 October 1767, the curate noted in his diary that he went to Bridgwater in order to attend a meeting to elect 'two proper persons to represent this county in parliament'. Sir Charles Tynte and Lieutenant-Colonel Cox, an officer in the Somerset Militia were selected. They were opposed by a Mr Trevelyan, who in the following December gave a dinner at the Ashford Inn 'to his friends which are the lower sort of people'. In the following March, Lord Ilchester and Lord Berkeley of Bruton gave a more resplendent dinner for the two official nominees. Two weeks later, Mr Trevelyan stood down.

The elder Pitt was not the only notable national figure to visit the county during the eighteenth century. The outstanding natural features of the limestone hills of Mendip were becoming famous, and people in the south and east of England wanted to see the wonder of Cheddar Gorge for themselves. It was described by Collinson as 'certainly the most striking scene of its kind in Great Britain'. These same visitors would naturally also go to nearby Wookey Hole, as tourists do today, and find, as Collinson wrote, that the 'entrance is narrow but soon opens into a very spacious vault, eighty feet in height – the whole roof and sides of which are incrusted with sparry concretions of whimsical form, and present a grand appearance to the spectator, who is lit by tapers through the dark subterraneous passage. From the crevices of the roof perpetually distil drops of crystal water, which by its petrifying quality form in some parts large projections of strange rude figures.'

Long before Collinson broadcast the charms of Wookey Hole to the world the place was a popular attraction to visitors. When Alexander Pope came there earlier in the century, he was so taken with the 'sparry concretions' that he had a man shoot some of them down in order that he might carry them off to adorn his grotto in Twickenham.

Although the people of Somerset were no doubt impressed by

such notable visitors from the world of literary London, they were not without cultural stimulus of their own. For as well as commenting on boxing matches, cock fighting at the Ansford Inn and performances by the mummers, James Woodforde writes of his opportunities to enjoy the theatre. At Castle Cary in the July of 1766 'an insolent saucy mob' admittedly spoilt his pleasure at a performance of *The Provok'd Husband or a Journey to London* which was given at the Court House; but three years later, between 14 May and 6 June, at the same place, he was able to relish uninterrupted performances of *The Beggar's Opera, Hamlet* and *Richard III*. There were no doubt other delights in the space of years between.

Decades before Parson Woodforde tells us of theatre in Castle Cary, the Wells doctor, Claver Morris, was regularly attending and participating in musical evenings held at the time of the full moon, so that members of his circle might have an easy journey between Wells and Shepton Mallet. The road they took passes beneath Sharpham Park, standing above the village of Dinder. This was where Henry Fielding was born in 1707. Although the family moved to Dorset, when the future novelist and playwright was still a very young child, and although he was to spend most of his adult life in London, he set much of *Tom Jones* (completed in 1748) 'in that part of the western division of this kingdom which is commonly called Somersetshire'. Squire Allworthy is a Somerset man, living in a house built in the Gothic style, which his creator assures us 'was as commodious within as venerable without', a prime example, in fact, of the manor houses that were being built throughout the county at this time.

It was at the end of the century that the landscape of Somerset had a most significant part to play in the transformation of English literary sensibilities. For it was during the brief years that Coleridge and Wordsworth spent in the Quantocks that the concept of *The Lyrical Ballads* was conceived and most of the best poems in that volume were written. It was at the Bell Inn at Watchet that *The Ancient Mariner* was dreamed up, and St Decuman's church on the nearby headland is always taken to be the one for which the wedding guest was bound.

The young Coleridge and his wife had been living in Clevedon until he was taken under the protection of Tom Poole, the radical tanner of Nether Stowey, who settled the little family in a cottage of his own on 31 December 1796. In the following July, Wordsworth and his sister, Dorothy, took a year's lease on Alfoxton, a large country house, now a hotel, near the Quantock village of Holford.

Much has been written about the years that these two literary giants spent in the West Country, and I should particularly like to recommend Tom Mayberry's book, *Coleridge and Wordsworth in the West Country*. It is he who disproves the commonly held notion that Ash Farm, across the Devon border from the tiny hamlet of Culbone, was the place where Coleridge was staying when he was disturbed by the 'person from Porlock'. It seems to have been far more likely that the poet was taking a few days respite from the crowded Nether Stowey cottage in the farmhouse at Withycombe, nearby Ash Farm, and now totally demolished. In company with other writers on this literary period, Tom Mayberry draws our attention to Dorothy Wordsworth's journals and to her descriptions of long country walks taken with the two poets. Other books give directions for following in Coleridge's footsteps through Somerset in the August of 1794 while he was still at Clevedon; but few people on today's roads would wish to tramp out from Nether Stowey, as Coleridge did, to preach from the black oak pulpit in the Unitarian chapel in Mary Street, Taunton; or follow him east to perform the same duty at the Dampier Street chapel in Bridgwater.

Coleridge's cottage in Nether Stowey, now owned by the National Trust and open to visitors during the afternoon is true to its literary tradition. Until the mid 1990s it was occasionally manned by Edmund Blunden's brother, Lance, and inhabited for part of the week by Derrick Woolf, the editor of the poetry journal *Odyssey*. There, and at the Coleridge bookshop in the centre of the village, you can browse among books and papers relating to the poets of that period and to Wordsworth and Coleridge in particular. Regular literary events are held in both places.

A contemporary account of Coleridge's time at Nether Stowey can be found in the diaries of William Holland, who was rector of the nearby parish of Over Stowey. He thoroughly disapproved of both Tom Poole and his protégés. 'Satan himself cannot be more false and hypocritical' than Poole, he wrote; and he described Sarah as looking 'so like a friskey girl or something worse that I was not surprised that a Democratic Libertine should choose her for a wife.'

As Bath grew in elegance during the eighteenth century, it naturally attracted many painters. Thomas Gainsborough lived there from 1759 to 1785, and was most probably known to the wealthy widow to whom the nineteen-year-old Mary Wollstonecraft acted as companion in 1778. Social life does not seem to have been greatly affected by the Napoleonic Wars, although the threat of invasion was strong enough for gun emplacements to be set up on Steep Holm and at the end of Brean Down. Because of their practice of taking long nocturnal walks, Coleridge and Wordsworth were considered by some of their Quantock neighbours to be French spies; and Bath society must have been kept well aware of the threat from across the Channel when the aged Fanny Burney chose to settle there after the death of her husband, the French refugee officer, General Alexandre Gabriel Jean-Baptiste d'Arblay.

No doubt William Holland had some pleasure in using the threat of a Napoleonic invasion to encourage local suspicion of Wordsworth and Coleridge, whose nocturnal walks in the Quantocks led some people to regard them as French spies, for in common with much of the rest of the country, Somerset was nervously preparing for a French landing. The gun emplacements, which still stand on the island of Steep Holm, remind us of the real fear that 'Boney' would sail up the Bristol Channel. When that threat was removed, and Napoleon's army surrendered, one of the most notable trophies of the war was the Rosetta stone, unearthed by French troops in the Nile delta in 1799. It was to be deciphered by a Somerset man, the talented polymath, Thomas Young, born at Milverton on the eastern edge of Exmoor on 13 June 1773.

IX

Industry, Agriculture and Victorian Values

Queen Victoria first came to Somerset as a tiny baby in 1819. Her visit is proudly recorded on the outer wall of the George Hotel in Ilminster. It boasts that it was here that the great queen spent her first night in a hotel. She was, in fact, being taken to Seaton in Devon at that time, and considering the state of the roads in the West Country, her journey must have been hazardous as well as uncomfortable.

The century of growth and change was dependent on improved means of communication, so before looking closely at the growth of the Somerset industries and the first stirrings of mechanised farming in the nineteenth century, I should like to make a brief survey of the transformation of the county's roads, chart the short history of its canals and describe the establishment of the railways.

Throughout the first half of this century, the various Turnpike Trusts, empowered by the related Acts of Parliament, gradually resulted in the formation of a network of new roads throughout the county. By 1851, the Chard Trust, to instance one of many, was responsible for forty-five miles of local roads starting out from the town in all directions. Even short distances, such as the five-mile stretch of the London road, and the seven-mile Axminster road were served by gates and bars at which the tolls were collected. These have disappeared, but many of the toll houses, such as the one at Snowdon Hill on the Honiton road, are still standing. Chard local history group have recorded that in the middle years of the century, those tolls were collected by a widow, Mary Mitchem, who lived in the house with her daughters, one of whom, Lois, helped her mother to collect the dues.

To the north-west of Wells, the local trust, established in

1854, maintained twenty-one miles of road from Wells to Highbridge near Bridgwater, as well as the five-mile road to Cheddar. The two highways met at Portway Elm, a junction that still exists, although the tree has gone. Some planners argued that it should be incorporated into the proposed Wells ring road, a project which has been mooted and discussed for nearly as long as it took the original Wells and Highbridge Trust to get clear of debt, a matter that was only concluded in 1870.

The most spectacular transport development in the early years of the nineteenth century was the growth of the canals. The only one of these, apart from the much restored Kennet and Avon to the south of Bath, to have retained its course and its water for any length is the Bridgwater and Taunton canal, running through fairly flat country and now used for pleasure boating. It was in 1966 that the Somerset Inland Waterway was founded with the express aim of opening this particular waterway up to navigation.

In 1827, when the barges first moved along that canal from Firepool, in Taunton, to Huntworth, a mile to the south of Bridgwater, it was intended that their voyage should be the first part of a great scheme that would link the Avon at Bristol with Taunton. That project never materialised and nor did the full extent of the Grand Western canal, which was designed to link Taunton to Exeter *via* Tiverton. The stretch of water along level ground from Holcombe Rogus through Devon to Tiverton was completed in 1830 and now has been classified as a Country Park. The Somerset stretch, running for part of its course beside the River Tone as it flows west from Wellington, had to traverse much more hilly country and was also obstructed by important land-owners. In particular, the owners of Ninehead had no wish to have the canal, on which part of their fortune was based, running too close to their mansion. This meant that an aqueduct had to be constructed, over the driveway, and a series of lifts and overland mechanical incline contrivances had to be devised in order that the tub boats, many of them filled with bricks from the new Taunton yards, could be lifted from one level to another. Most of this tortuous route can still be followed, although only strips of marshy ground indicate the bed of the old waterway. Nevertheless, the course provides some fascinating detective work for amateur industrial archaeologists.

In its early years, the Bridgwater Taunton Canal Company ran into serious trouble with the Tone Navigation Commissioners, who were acting under an agreement drawn up in 1698 which sponsored navigation on the river as an 'Incouragement to Trade and an Exceeding benefit to the Poor'. In 1828, when the canal company took possession of the river, they ejected William Goodland, an inspector of the Tone navigation from his home in Bathpool, bringing an Act of Trespass against him. His case was first heard by the circuit judge at the Wells Assizes and was then taken on to be heard before the judges of the King's Bench at Westminster.

For part of the route, the course of the Somerset section of the Grand Western runs parallel to the railway. This is also true for almost the whole stretch of the Bridgwater to Taunton canal, whose course was followed closely by the railway engineers, except for the stretch of country where the canal looped westward to North Newton.

In the east of the county, the canal building was specifically linked to the carriage of coal. The first such waterway was opened early in 1805 and ran from Paulton to Limpley Stoke near Bath, where it joined the Kennet and Avon canal. Ten years later, a tramway was laid along the towpath to ease the task of the horses drawing strings of eight or nine tub boats loaded with coal to Midford Wharf.

In the south of the county, a canal from Chard was opened in 1842. It ran north to join the Bridgwater Taunton canal at Creech St Michael. This waterway was one of the last to be constructed, for by the middle of the century, the waterways were being superseded by the railways.

By 1841, the Bristol and Exeter railway had reached Highbridge near Burnham-on-Sea; and twenty years later the Somerset and Dorset railway was formed to provide a through route from Burnham to Poole in Dorset, so linking the Bristol and English Channels.

The work, first on the canals and then on the railways, brought itinerant 'navvies' into Somerset. Brunel, who at one time had tried out agricultural labourers for his work on the cutting at Bleadon between Weston-super-Mare and High-bridge, found that the job was far better done by the travelling workmen, although he was to form a very high opinion of native Somerset navvies.

Naturally, there was considerable friction between the local inhabitants and the despised, apparently over-paid incomers. The outcast plight of the 'navvies' was to become the concern of Victorian philanthropists and evangelists, who have left us a record, *The Fisherman and His Net*, which describes their missionary work on the North Somerset coast. One of their number made a diary entry for 13 July 1865 in which she happily noted: 'I went down to Brean Down. On my way thither I met with two navvies who made themselves known to me and said, "We spent many a comfortable hour when you used to read and speak to us at the Thorne cocoa-shed." ' You can still get cocoa at the foot of Brean Down, and very welcome it is too after a walk along that high promontory to the nineteenth-century gun emplacements at its western edge.

As for the collieries, those around Radstock were served by a broad gauge branch line, projected by the Wilts, Somerset and Weymouth railway. Part of this line, between Radstock and Frome is currently being revived by railway enthusiasts, who are reconstructing the route along which coal was taken east. The coal going south was still taken along the Parret and Yeo rivers.

Coal mining, which had started as a major operation in the county in the seventeenth century, increased rapidly during the nineteenth and was centred almost exclusively in the Rad-stock, Midsomer Norton, Coleford area. The mines were all to be closed in the 1970s, and twenty years later an excellent private museum, devoted to the Somerset mines, was opened in Radstock. It is from that museum's publication, *Five Arches*, that much of my background information about the history of the east Somerset coal mines in this and the next chapter has been gleaned.

Although most of these mines continued to operate until the 1960s and 70s, one had a much shorter life. In April 1860, a shaft was sunk at Vobster Breach in the Nettlebridge valley near Coleford. Seven years later, two coke ovens were constructed there. The purpose of that venture was to produce coking coal for the Westbury Iron Works. These ovens were the only ones to be built in the Somerset coal fields; however, they were only in use for seven years, for in 1874 the colliery had to be closed. The almost vertical seams of coal constituted a serious hazard for fire damp and the risk of continuing operations was unacceptable. In addition to the ovens, the ruins of several buildings connected with the colliery still remain, although in the summer months they are hidden by almost impenetrable vegetation.

In the west of the county, on the Brendon Hills, extensive iron ore mines were being worked, the ore being exported to the steel works of South Wales. One of the first of these mines to be opened was in 1852 at Raleigh's Cross on the eastern edge of the Brendon ridge. It was to be in operation for some thirty years, during which time five cottages for the miners were built nearby. Some communal leisure activities were provided: there was a reading room and a separate institute, where meetings could be held in a hall above the boiler house. Near to the little settlement was the large locomotive shed and repair shop. A twelve-foot high bridge, supported on cast iron columns, stood above the northern escarpment of the hills, and it was from this construction that the ore was tipped on to waiting railway waggons which conveyed it down the steep incline to Watchet harbour, three quarters of a mile away, at a gradient of 1:4. The remains of this incline railway are still standing by the isolated chapel which once served the mining community. The railway was completed in March 1861. In November 1883, the Raleigh's Cross mines were closed, but it was not until 1907 that the mining villages were finally demolished.

In the east of the county, the iron works at Mells, established by the Fussell family in the early years of the century, were producing edge tools which were renowned throughout the country. On 15 July 1828, John Skinner, rector of Camerton on the northern outskirts of Radstock, walked from Whatley, where he was then staying, on a visit to Nunney in order to buy a scythe for his garden. In his diary he recorded that he did so because the best of such tools 'in the county, perhaps in the kingdom, are made by the Fussels who have mills at Mells, Nunney, and Little Elm'. The remains of the iron works have been carefully preserved. They stand to the east of Mells village, at the side of Mells River which runs through to Vallis Vale by Great Elm pond. It is a pleasing, romantic, riverside walk now, a Somerset version of Derbyshire's Dovedale, with the hart's tongue fern covering the limestone cliffs above the little waterway. For the iron workers tramping to the grindstones and the blistering forges the valley must have presented a less pleasing prospect.

You can see evidence of Fussell's work at Chantry. James Fussell, who died in 1845, built the house, which is now the home of the novelist, Anthony Powell. On the church which James Fussell established on his land for the convenience of his workers, one of the angels adorning the spire carries a stone replica of a Fussell tool.

Some slate was quarried in the county. At Treborough, on the northern slopes of the Brendon Hills, the quarries which had been in operation since the Middle Ages (in 1426 they supplied two thousand slates to Dunster Castle) were extended to meet the increased demand for the stone. By 1850, some two acres of the hill were being quarried and this was bought by a William Pritchard, who came south from the slate quarries of North Wales. Eight years later, with two fellow countrymen to assist him and with the aid of local labour, he was producing six hundred tons of slate annually. William Pritchard died in 1882 and is buried in Treborough churchyard near to one of his workmen, Isaac Chedzoy, killed in a quarry accident in 1875 at the age of forty-five.

In the middle of the nineteenth century, the Mendip lead mines received a new lease of life when it was discovered that the slag left over from mine workings going back at least to Tudor times could be re-smelted. In 1854, Nicholas Ennor, a

Cornish engineer, came to Mendip from his work on the Brendon Hills and within three years had acquired the Priddy mineral rights. There you can still see the remains of a surface flue which Ennor devised. It runs along the hillside, an uncovered ditch now with some remnants of stone-work left. Once, smoke heavily charged with lead vapour poured through the cavity, leaving deposits on the side walls before being expelled from the tall chimney whose base still stands.

When the Mendip Mining Company was working at Charterhouse in the 1860s, it was found that at least a quarter of slag, from workings that went back to the Romans, could be smelted in this way. Here you can actually walk along the flues in which, at one time, wretched children from the Cheddar workhouse scraped lead, heavily charged with arsenic, from the walls. In 1865, the Charterhouse workings yielded over three hundred and twenty tons of lead, but there were only twenty years of life left to the mine. By 1880, the lead mine at Priddy was the only one left working on Mendip and it was to close early in the next century.

The 1870s saw the end of the calamine mining at Shipham and Rowberrow, which in the last years of the eighteenth century had produced zinc for use in the Bristol brass foundries. By the middle of the nineteenth century, the activity was reduced to a few isolated miners working their own grooves in the area. When these were worked out, the two villages, whose whole livelihood had depended for so long on the mines, fell upon desperately hard times.

These mining activities and various aspects of the cloth trade were for centuries the main Somerset industries. During the nineteenth century, the textile mills became more diversified in their operations. By the 1830s, sheep were no longer the only source of raw material, for silk worms were now being reared in boxes arranged in tiers in sheds or 'magnaveries', one of which was built at Over Stowey to supply the textile mill at nearby Holford Glen, on the northern edge of the Quantocks, which was one of the first to turn from wool to silk.

When the woollen trade of Exmoor collapsed in 1834, largely due to the loss of the monopoly contract which

Dulverton had enjoyed with the East India Company for supplying serge to China, the three-storey mill in Chapel Street was turned over to the manufacture of crêpe. This was a fashionable way of treating silk, which was crumpled and usually dyed black to be sold for mourning garments and funeral trappings. At the start of the operations in Dulverton, the crêpe manufacture employed seventy people, but the industry was to be short-lived. By 1851, only thirty-four people worked in the mill, and ten years later the number had dropped to eleven. By 1879, the industry folded and the mill was taken over by the still surviving Dulverton laundry.

In the south of the county the production of lace rapidly became one of the main industries. There were four lace mills operating in Chard in 1851. The largest of these, a six-storey building, still stands. It belonged to the Holyrood Mill Company and employed over three hundred workers. Chard lace was always entirely machine made, and it bore slight resemblance to the more sought-after and expensive hand-made pillow lace, produced across the Devon border in Honiton. Nevertheless, it was greatly in demand for net curtains and dress trimmings, while a special silk lace was produced for bridal veils and more expensive clothes.

There have always been extensive tanneries in the county, the leather – especially in the southern part of Somerset – being used for the manufacture of gloves in particular. The glove industry in these parts flourished from the late thirteenth century, when we have a record of a William Glover of Montacute. It carried on until the outbreak of World War II. In the nineteenth century, the glove workers had to endure appalling conditions. The Beam men, as they were called, had to spend hours stooping over a beam in order to scrape the skins so as to make them clean and pliable for the cutters and stitchers, and in the 1860s the glove workers were expected to put in a fourteen-hour day.

Much of the glove making was carried out in Yeovil, which was described in 1852 as being 'a very dirty and a very stinking place'. The more prominent citizens were fully aware of the town's appalling reputation and some twenty years previously had formed a Yeovil Town Improvement Commission. One prominent glove manufacturer, Thomas Dampier, was among the Commissioners. He was, however, a rather infrequent attender at the Commissioners' meetings and was one of the chief objectors to their proposal, in 1831, to the raising of rates so that essential improvements could be carried out. Nevertheless, his son, who combined glove making with brewing, was mayor of the town four times between 1856 and 1862. The dreadful condition under which the Yeovil glove-makers laboured were not much improved, however, and became a matter of national concern. As late as 1902, when Rider Haggard published his survey of rural England, he found it fitting to include comments on their working conditions, based on a conversation he had had with Mr J.D. Adams, the town's Medical Officer of Health.

While these industries continued to grow in the towns, the north Somerset landscape was undergoing further alterations as the drainage of the wet lands became more effective and widespread. Between 1770 and 1830, the moors were all enclosed, and rhynes were cut to serve the double purpose of field boundaries and drainage, and access droves were formed between them. None of this was straightforward, and much of it depended for its success on the canalising of the rivers.

The greatest problem was to keep the water levels even. By 1818, some steam pumping was operating in the Lincolnshire Fens, and some twelve years later such a pump was in operation on the moors near Westonzoyland. Its purpose was to control the flooding of the Parret, an operation that had to be sanctioned by an Act of Parliament. It was not until 1834 that the *Taunton Courier* was able to comment favourably on the steam engine and the benefits it had brought to farmers. The Westonzoyland pump of 1867 has now been restored to working condition by enthusiastic industrial archaeologists, who show it off to the public from time to time.

In the north-east of the county, sea flooding has always been a hazard. After the severe flood of 1876 which affected Sedgemoor as well as the Brue valley and the levels between Glastonbury and Highbridge, the Somerset Drainage Act was passed. It established eleven new Internal Drainage Boards, so bringing the total number for the county to nineteen. Each Board, which had powers to levy its own rates, was individually responsible for the maintenance of all the rhynes and sea walls in its area.

Unlike the fens, where the land saved from the sea is used almost exclusively for the growing of vegetables, the Somerset farmers have generally used the reclaimed land for pasture. The county has always been noted for its dairy products and especially for its famous Cheddar cheese. The nineteenth century saw a great growth in cheese manufacture. Although it was still farm-based, cheese schools, run and supervised by the farmers' wives, were sending cheese makers out nationwide. One of the most notable of these cheese schools was tutored from 1890–1900 by Edith Cannon, daughter of a dairy farmer. Her classes were held at model farms throughout the county, such as the one at Haslebury Plunkett, which extends on rising ground above the church. Edith, who was born in 1868, won the champion prize at the Frome Cheese Show, when she was nineteen. Her two younger sisters also became tutors in the cheese-making schools; and one of her students went on to become the founder of the dairy-processing firm of Cow and Gate, which still has an extensive plant in Wells. Techniques for making the traditional Cheddar cheese spread to Scotland, then to Canada; and although it is now produced almost everywhere in the Western world, its traditional origins are honoured and remembered each September at the Frome Cheese Fair.

Undoubtedly the greatest agricultural change to take place in Somerset during the nineteenth century was the Crown's sale of the Forest of Exmoor to Frederic Knight, a Worcestershire business man. Knight built the farms on the high moor, most of which are still in operation. It was he who organised the planting of the beech hedges and windbreaks that are now such a marked signature of the moor. One of these farms, Pinkworthy, beneath the swamps of The Chains, where the Exe rises, is now owned by the County Council and run as an educational centre; but most of the others are still working farms. To stock his farms, Knight imported hardy beasts, favouring Highland cattle and Cheviot sheep. The latter were driven south to their new grazing grounds. The northern shepherds came with them. That is why at two of Knight's more remote farms, Tom's Hill and Larkbarrow, it is possible to see the circular stone walls of a sheep stell, built in the northern fashion.

The whole episode was re-enacted for television in the 1980s, when the TV journalist, presenter, traveller and dog-handler, Aza Pinney, walked fifty-two Cheviot sheep, flocked by Gertrude the leading ewe hogg, from Hawick, in Roxburghshire, to Simonsbath, in the middle of the moor, a distance of some four hundred miles. One of the most attentive viewers of that programme was Mrs Little, daughter of the shepherd who originally brought a flock of hardy northern sheep to the moor. When I met her, she was still living in Simonsbath and was still loyally convinced that no one could handle sheep like her father.

Despite fluctuations in farming fortunes, the rural population of the county was relatively untouched by the terrible poverty that hit the townspeople in the middle years of the century. Although rural housing conditions were frequently appalling – there is an account of a family of thirteen sharing an attic apartment in Montacute village in the 1870s – people in the Somerset countryside were better off than their counterparts in many other areas of the United Kingdom. Even in the middle years of the century there was nothing to compare with the disaster of the Irish famine years, yet the want of potatoes (for the blight spread through all Europe) was felt sorely. Arthur Hull, one of the leading citizens of Chard, noted in his diary for 14 January 1847: 'Distressing times, people half-starved, want of potatoes, corn so dear'. Three months later he was reporting the Bristol riots.

Although the nearest Chartist branch was in Bristol, still in tumult from the riots of 1830, there was considerable support for the movement in the south of the county, particularly from the over-pressed workers in the textile mills. On 19 August 1842, the Chartist newspaper reported a meeting in Chard attended by over a thousand people. It was followed by a picketing of the mills and the advent of a troop of yeomanry from Ilchester, called in by the mayor.

In these middle years of the century, unemployment was rife in the towns, forcing many men to turn itinerant. A good number of them found casual work on the new railways, and Brunel, who was then constructing the cuttings for the Great Western, found these Somerset men to be 'the most powerful, fearless and most enduring workmen to be found in any country in the world'.

Other workers, deprived of both agricultural and industrial employment emigrated to Australia, taking advantage of the almost free passage to the antipodes. In those desperate middle years of the century, whole families left Somerset to start again in unknown lands. Among them, according to a record of the village of Street, near Glastonbury, for the years 1844 to 1909, was one John Baker, an agricultural worker who took his twenty children with him when he sailed from England.

As always, unemployment led to crime. Many of those who lacked both work and the basic necessities that would enable them to leave the country landed up in Shepton Mallet prison, Bath gaol or the House of Correction in Taunton. In 1823, treadmills were supplied to those institutions, and prisoners sentenced to hard labour were forced to operate them. At least they were spared the more painful tasks of stone breaking or untwisting lengths of rope.

At the other end of the spectrum, the large land-owners had considerable wealth and leisure at their disposal. Much of it was spent in the frequently misguided but usually essential restoration of the medieval churches. Writing of Old Cleeve church, in his history of Exmoor, John Lloyd Warden Page declared that he could 'well remember the day when the nave, falling with the fall of the ground, sloped boldly from the west door to the chancel. But the "restoration" has changed all that, though there still appears a slight, a very slight rise.'

Among the greatest Somerset land-owners of the nineteenth century was the Portman family, whose great house at Orchard Portman, on the eastern edge of the Blackdown Hills, had to be vacated after a fatal typhoid epidemic. The dwelling was subsequently destroyed and the family moved to Staple Fitzpaine, where successive Portmans took on the traditional nineteenth-century role of squirson, controlling both village and church. They enclosed most of the former Forest of Neroche in order to breed racehorses, claiming that the pasture was too rich for deer. In addition, they had become such extensive land-owners that the villagers claimed that a traveller could journey from Staple Fitzpaine to Portman Square in London without ever leaving Portman land.

Naturally, this family had an important part to play in the restoration of Staple Fitzpaine church. While doing so they demolished the nearby church at Bickenhall, transferring the monument to the Elizabethan, Rachel Portman, who is buried in the old churchyard there, into the chancel of Staple Fitzpaine church.

Church building in this era was not only a matter of restoration. Hornblotton, between Glastonbury and Castle Cary is a purely Victorian church. Built in the early 1870s, it has a tiled belfry and interior walls of red and white plaster. Some twenty-five years after that church was built, Sir Thomas Acland, owner of the Holincote estate in the north of Exmoor, supported the restoration of one of the moor's three totally remote churches. Stoke Pero stands over a thousand feet above sea level and there seems to have been a church on the site since the sixth or seventh century, although the building that the Victorians restored dates from the thirteenth. On the wall of the church you will see a picture of a donkey. It immortalises Zulu, who earned his fame during the time of the Boer War by plodding twice daily from Porlock to Stoke Pero in order to bring timber for the new church roof.

Throughout the county you will find among the stained glass with which the windows of these restored churches were embellished, several examples of work by Burne-Jones and his students. The great Pre-Raphaelite artist himself designed a window in Kilmersdon church in 1878. Even after the painter's death, the firm of Morris & Co. continued to provide Somerset churches with windows in the Pre-Raphaelite style.

You can see examples of their work in the church of Over Stowey on the eastern edge of the Quantock Hills; while in Mells church, near Frome, a large piece of embroidery depicting a colourfully, sinuous Pre-Raphaelite angel was stitched by a Mrs Horner, lady of the manor and friend of the painter.

The most significant act of nineteenth-century church building in Somerset is surely that of Downside Abbey, which serves the Benedictine community and the school, both of which are linked with the mother house at Douay in France. It was when that community (largely made up of English Catholic exiles) began to suffer during the most bitterly astringent years of the Age of Reason, that the return to England was made possible by the offer of a refuge in Shropshire. In 1814, the monks came south into Somerset, journeying from Worcester to Bath, where the schoolboys were temporarily housed. Then the monks journeyed on, making use of the newly dug coal canal and travelling by barge to Paulton. From there they walked, through Chilcompton to their new home at Downside House near Stratton on the Fosse. Crowds of onlookers watched them on their way. Their abbey church was not built until 1872, complementing the chapel built in 1823 in an extension to the original late seventeenth-century mansion.

By the nineteenth century, most of the great houses had been established, yet considerable building and renovation was going on, some of it fairly ridiculous, such as the folly of Banwell Castle, inland from Weston-super-Mare. This Victorian fantasy comes complete with a crenellated wall and gatehouse. Other buildings were more solemnly pretentious. The old house at Orchardleigh to the north of Frome, for example, was pulled down in 1856 and replaced by a mock Elizabethan mansion. Its lovely extensive parklands were to fall prey to twentieth-century vandalism, when a hotel took over the property and started to lay out three golf courses. On the whole, the Victorian gardens fared better, such as the one that Charlotte Welman planned around Poundisford Park near Taunton.

In such spacious and leisured surroundings, the arts and sciences might well be expected to flourish. As early as 1816, Andrew Crosse of Fyne Court, at Broomfield on the southern edge of the Quantocks, was daring to forecast the possibility of radio-telegraph communication. His old house is now the headquarters of the Somerset Naturalist Trust and so its surrounding gardens and parkland are open to visitors. In Squire Crosse's day, visitors to the laboratory, now a lecture and exhibition hall, included Michael Faraday and other leading scientists of the time. The local people were more alarmed than respectful of the work going on at their door steps, and referred to their scientific landlord as The Thunder and Lightning Man.

There were several literary figures among the Somerset gentry of this time. It was to Combe Florey, between the Quantocks and the Brendon Hills that the Revd Sydney Smith retired from his post as Canon of St Paul's in London, and it was there that the jokester fixed antlers to a couple of donkeys in response to the remark by a local lady that his vicarage grounds would be improved by being transformed into a deer park. The house, which eventually came into the hands of Evelyn Waugh is now the home of his son Auberon.

R.D. Blackmore, who took Exmoor for his canvas, and in *Lorna Doone* created a story so universally popular that the niceties of its geographical and historical aspects are still being hotly debated, came from a far more modest clerical family. His father had been rector of Clayhidon in Devon, just across the Somerset border in a valley of the Blackdown Hills. Now people are still asking if the wild Doones sprang from a Sedgemoor fugitive or a wandering Scottish clan, and pondering if they really settled in the Malmsmead valley, where a monument to their creator has been placed. Some people will even take it for fact that Carver Doone shot Lorna in the remote and most beautifully sited church at Oare, where the novelist's grandfather was vicar from 1809 to 1842, and where another memorial to the writer was put up in 1928.

A lesser known Victorian writer, but one esteemed and encouraged by Charles Dickens, was the blind Alice King, a

poet and prolific novelist who was born at Cutcombe on the
western edge of the Brendon Hills. Her novels, which first
appeared in the 1860s, followed each other in rapid succes-
sion, three volumes at a time. They are mostly set in far-flung,
exotic places although her West Country origins are recalled in
the imaginary place-names of *The Lady of Winburne*. How
sad that when I went to look at her work in the Bodleian
Library, I should find most of the pages uncut.

Richard Jefferies, one of the greatest and most evocative
writers on the English countryside also had a Somerset
connection, although Wiltshire and Berkshire claim him for
their own. The painter, John William North, who lived at
Beggearnhuish House at Nettlecombe was a devoted friend of
Jefferies, and it was while the writer was staying with him
beneath the Brendon Hills that he gathered material for his
Red Deer, to be published in 1883. After Jefferies' death in
1887, his widow and son stayed in North's house and, I hope,
recalled happy memories from Jefferies' *Summer in Somerset*,
which was published posthumously in the *English Illustrated
Magazine*.

Strangely, it was not until the early twentieth century that
popular interest in Glastonbury's connection with King
Arthur was fully aroused. Tennyson set his *Idylls of the King* in
Cornwall, but Somerset gave him his inspiration for *In
Memoriam*, a far greater sequence of poems. It is in the
churchyard at Clevedon above the Bristol Channel that his
friend, Arthur Hugh Hallam, is buried; and it was looking out
over the Channel from that coastal village that the poet was
inspired to write the much-quoted and most moving quatrains
beginning 'Break, break, break,/On thy cold, gray stones, O
Sea'.

There are rocks on the coast at Clevedon and at Portishead,
but further west on the North Somerset shore, the receding
tide ebbs to reveal long stretches of sand. These unromantic
but spacious beaches were a natural goal for the new vogue of
the seaside holiday, pioneered by the Prince Regent at
Brighton and made possible by the ease of rail transport and a
rapidly growing middle class.

The two most popular Somerset resorts are still Weston-super-Mare (which gets its name from being above the moors, not the sea) and Minehead on the eastern edge of Exmoor. The former was the more accessible and indeed much of Weston was 'purpose built' with houses that could be offered for summer lets. However, Minehead, especially since a Butlin's Camp was set up there in the 1960s, has certainly had the longer life. At the end of the nineteenth century, both resorts were flourishing, and Somerset experienced the first inroads of 'grockles' and 'emmets' who were to flood the South-West after the two world wars of the following century.

X

In Peace and War: 1900–1960

Until plastic replaced natural materials for the making of containers of all types, Somerset basket makers had a vital role to play in the agricultural economy of the whole nation. The wet lands around Athelney to the east of Taunton are a particularly good environment for growing the willows, or withies, as they are called locally. Indeed, it was here, in 1827, that willows were first grown as a major British crop. They do still grow here, and in the autumn, when everything else is turning brown, you can drive past fields of willow, planted the previous spring and still in green leaf. They are not cut until January and are one of the few remaining harvests that cannot be undertaken by machine. For this reason, and because the ancient craft of basket-making is still kept alive if only as a tourist attraction, withies still provide a modest source of employment in the Athelney, Stoke St Gregory area. If you want to have a feeling for the industry in its heyday, read Berta Lawrence's *A Band of Green Withy*, a novel which takes the story of withy-growing up to the end of World War II, and visit the Black Smock Inn a couple of miles along the road beside the Parret from Burrow Mump. Black Smock is the name of a particularly fine species of willow and the inn stands in the middle of withy fields. For generations, it has catered for those whose lives were linked to that crop. As late as 1957, 1,500 acres of land around Athelney were devoted to withy growing. That area steadily declined to some 400 acres by the 1990s.

Willows grow best in wet lands, and so the industry did not suffer unduly from the fact that until 1940 West Sedgemoor was liable to be completely waterlogged for six months of each year. In the severe flood of 1929 all the moors around Athelney were under water for nearly three months and the disruption to people's homes and livelihoods was such that a national disaster fund was set up. The catastrophe led to the Land Drainage Act of 1930, when the Somerset Rivers Catchment Board was formed to take responsibility for all the main rivers in the county.

Peat-taking is another industry which has always flourished in the Somerset wet lands. It has now reached environmentally threatening proportions, which I shall discuss further in the next chapter. The most extensive build up of peat is on the eastern moors or levels, where it has provided a livelihood for several families throughout many generations, since commercial peat drying started in 1870. For decades the peat was mainly cut for fuel and for livestock litter during the winter months. It is only latterly that it has been commercially exploited for hobby gardening. The whole story of the peat industry is told at the Peat Moors visitors' centre at Westhay. That excellent little museum is attached to the Willows Garden Centre, formerly owned by Roger Rogers, who comes from a family which has long been linked with peat-taking.

Lime-burning, which had started with the improvements in agricultural techniques in the eighteenth century, was still practised regularly during the first half of the twentieth. The limestone for this purpose, which had long been quarried out of the Mendip hills for use as building material, started to be exploited for road works as the dusty country lanes gave way to macadamised surfaces. At the beginning of the twentieth century, three new quarries were opened in the village of Binegar alone, and stone was soon being conveyed from Binegar station to most of the southern counties of England. The first workings, which were owned by Reed and Son, were begun in 1900; the Dalley's quarry started operation in 1908; and, finally, in 1923, H. Matthews and Son opened up a quarry near Binegar bottom, which continued in operation until the 1970s. That site was long used for producing asphalt. At Gurney Slade, the quarry that Francis Flower's company worked throughout the 1920s was dedicated solely to producing stone for the limekilns. That quarry was to change hands several times, and was even closed down for a while, but it was re-opened in 1951 and continued work until the 1970s. Limekilns were operated at Evercreech, near Shepton Mallet until the 1960s. At Emborough, the first stone crusher to be built in the county was in operation by 1910; the new machine replaced the old men, who used to earn a few shillings breaking stones at the side of the road.

Mining, too, had a vital part to play in the economy of north Somerset. On the Mendip plateau, the St Cuthbert's lead mine stayed in operation until the 1920s, and around Radstock, the people's lives were dominated by the coal mines. These Somerset mines were notorious on two counts: the difficult nature of the twisted veins of coal in seams that were frequently no more than eighteen inches wide; and the brutal 'guss and crook' method of hauling the coal from the face to the waiting trucks. This barbarous practice was to remain in operation until World War II and is one of the greatest blemishes on Somerset's history.

A.J. Parfitt, whose book, *My Life as a Somerset Miner*, was published by the Miners' Office in Radstock in 1930, describes the guss as a kind of harness consisting of 'a piece of one inch rope, four feet in length. The rope had to be spliced . . . to form a girdle, with a piece of chain attached called a tugger'. The carter boys, some of whom, like Parfitt himself, were about twelve-years-old when they followed their fathers down the pit, had to make this harness for themselves. Then, with the rope girdle around their naked waists, they were expected to straddle the tugger and attach themselves to the putt – a shallow box mounted on iron runners.

Mark Starr was born in 1894, thirteen years after the future Labour leader, Ernest Bevin's birth at Winsford on Exmoor. Although the older man was to have the more glittering political career, Mark Starr's life was of just as much benefit to the working man. He started his mining career at the age of thirteen as a carter boy in Lower Writhlington colliery, harnessed to the infamous guss and crook. Like many another Somerset lad, he went across the Bristol Channel to work in the comparatively easier and less hazardous pits of South

Wales. He managed to escape from the mines in 1917, when the South Wales Miners' Federation gave him a scholarship to the Central Labour College in London. From then on he gave his energies to political education and to campaigning for the betterment of working conditions. In 1928 he emigrated to the United States, and in 1942 the Mayor of New York nominated him for the post of the city's first director of Adult Education. Unfortunately he did not get the job – the City's Board of Education jibed at his record as a 'labour protagonist'. He died in 1985.

It was small wonder that so many Somerset coal miners took the sons who carted for them and set off for the Welsh valleys. Working conditions underground were marginally better there, and at least the coal veins presented a more workable surface. Those who remained behind gradually organised themselves into a sufficiently strong body to protest to the management. In July 1907, three men – a Writhlington hewer; Fred Swift, a boot-maker from Midsomer Norton; and the Revd Geoffrey Ramsay, rector of Writhlington founded the Somerset coalfield branch of the Independent Labour Party. Keir Hardie, himself, came to Radstock in 1910 to address the miners, and the whole area was naturally affected by the Coal Miners' Strike of 1911. The Dunkerton colliery was always strongly militant, and in September 1927 the owners' lack of concern for their miners' safety led to riots. Dunkerton's history of political action goes back to April 1907, when some two hundred carting boys, aged between sixteen and twenty-two, applied for a pay increase on the grounds that the putts were heavier and the routes rougher than any other colliery in the district. The rate of pay was one penny for the first fifty yards of any stretch of the route underground and a subsequent halfpenny for each fifty yards thereafter. The boys demanded that this be increased to a penny rate overall. After eighteen months they came out on strike bringing the men out with them, for no coal could be brought to the surface without the carting boys. That strike continued for many months and remained peaceful until January 1909, when the manager's son, Edgar Heal, encouraged a group of blacklegs to return to work. This so annoyed the Dunkerton boys that they marched on the manager's house and fighting broke out. When Edgar Heal drew a revolver the boys hurled stones. The affray ended in their capitulation. Ten of the miners were sent to jail; Edgar Heal was acquitted from firing at the mob, and eventually work was resumed at the initial rates.

Things were so bad in the county during the General Strike of 1926, that refugees from the Radstock mines sought food and shelter in the Home Counties. By then the Somerset miners had a champion in Arthur J. Cook, who was born at Wookey, near Wells, on 22 November 1884. He started work as a young lad on the local farms and, once he started to read and think, he soon found himself the only radical in a Tory village. The book that set him on the path of social concern was Samuel Smiles's *Self-Help*. At the age of seventeen, he became so concerned about the fate of coal miners generally that he walked from Somerset to the Rhondda, thus following in the footsteps of all those Radstock miners who had crossed the Bristol Channel in search of better conditions. Twenty-one years later, Cook became General Secretary of the Federaton of Mineworkers.

It was not only the appalling conditions in the mines that stirred the people of Somerset to take political action in the early years of the twentieth century. The Nonconformists came out strongly against the Conservative Education Act of 1902 which, by introducing the payment of rates for voluntary aided schools, caused Free Church members to subsidise the Anglican and Roman Catholic schools in which their own members were forbidden to teach. 'Legalised plunder' they called it at the Indignation Meeting, which was held on Wrington green on 30 September that year. The indignation was mostly reserved for the way in which Nonconformists who had refused to pay the rate had their goods seized and sold by auction at the Golden Lion inn in the village. That same evening a pubilc meeting was held in the John Locke Hall with speakers from Bristol, Weston-super-Mare, Clevedon and Cheddar.

The unrest and dissatisfaction was general throughout the country and was to lead to the downfall of the Conservative government in 1906. In the election, the Conservative, Charles Foxcroft, had a rough reception throughout the Frome division for which he had hoped to be elected. At Twerton, he was pelted with turnips and managed to lose his bowler hat as he rushed for the comparative safety of his car. In Radstock, ninety per cent of the people turned out to vote for the Liberal, John Barlow, but although he and his party were successful the new Liberal government neglected to repeal the infamous act. Right up to the outbreak of World War I, Somerset citizens were being brought before the magistrates for refusing to pay the rates. Two miners were prominent among the defaulters: Joe Watts of Paulton and A.E. Chivers, secretary of the Writhlington collieries and treasurer of the Free Church Council.

In 1908, after the branch of the Independent Labour Party had been formed in Radstock, the Somerset Mines Association became affiliated to the growing Labour Party. Two years later, Fred Gould, who in 1923 was to be elected as the first Labour Member of Parliament in the South-West of England, became the first Labour Councillor in Midsomer Norton. By the end of World War I the councils of Norton and Radstock were both Labour controlled.

These changes naturally led to conflicts with the landed gentry who owned the mines. In 1907, Lady Waldegrave, whose family was the largest mine owner in the district, had got away with telling the old people attending an annual dinner in Radstock that they would get their reward hereafter for the pain and suffering they were bound to endure in the coming year. Such attitudes were no longer acceptable and in 1913 when Lord Waldegrave complained about the frivolous pursuits of the young men of Radstock who 'did nothing but laze about and smoke cheap cigarettes', he was soon brought to task by the Revd Geoffrey Ramsay. The socialist rector retorted that the men of whom the noble lord and pit owner complained could 'only afford the cheap and shoddy stuff', while as for taking part in manly sports, the only facility in the district was an obsolete pit yard only large enough for a game of marbles.

Lord Hylton of Kilmersdon, who owned over ten thousand acres of Somerset land, including the Writhlington mines, was accused of refusing to build houses for his workers or release ground for leisure activities.

In the south of the county, the lot of the workers in the textile trade was as hard, if less dangerous, than that of the miners in the north. Margaret Bondfield, who was to become the first woman chairperson of the T.U.C. was born in Chard. Her active socialism was no doubt inspired by the fact that her father, who had started work as a bobbin boy in the lace mills at the age of nine and who had worked for the same mill for sixty years, was sacked with one week's notice.

For the more fortunate, the Edwardian era and even the troubled 1920s wore a more pleasing aspect. It was in that decade that Barrington Court garden near Ilminster was laid out as part of a model estate, its design much influenced by the work of Gertrude Jekyll. Those gardens, now in the ownership of the National Trust, are open to the public, and so are the even more splendid gardens at Hestercombe, laid out by Gertrude Jekyll herself in collaboration with Edward Lutyens, who was commissioned by its owner, the Hon. E.W.B. Portman, to design a garden to set off the great house. Hestercombe is now the property of the Somerset Fire Brigade, who have made it their headquarters since 1953. During World War II American troops were billeted in the house and the gardens were naturally neglected, many of the original plants dying out. The garden restoration started in 1973, and subsequently the County Council welcomes the public to these formal terraces to the north of Taunton.

There are a few remarkable church interiors that date from this period. The most astonishing, to my mind, is situated at Charterhouse by the entrance to the mineries. It is a very small church, built in 1908 for the lead miners, and was designed to serve as a meeting place and school as well as a place of worship. Externally, it is little more than an uncompromising rough cast hut, but, inside, W.D. Caroë created a riot of intricate, interlaced Gothic woodwork. This can be seen on most summer, weekend afternoons, when the church is kept open.

The late Victorian and Edwardian eras, when Burnham-on-Sea became a fashionable watering-place, saw the development of many towns and villages. Wellington is a notable example. In honour of the Duke, who took the town's name for his title, the most expensive houses at the southern end of the town were built in the newly-styled Wellesley Park. The cheaper properties naturally grew up around the station road. The railway might be a thing of convenience and pride, but nobody wanted to live beside it. Most of the buildings in the town were based on the work of two architects, Edward Thomas Howard, and his son, Ernest Tom Howard. The latter lived until 1957 and continued to make his mark on the town until after World War II.

Before 1910, the Howards favoured the local red brick, faced with stone for those buildings which were designed to impress. They both paid great attention to detail and delighted in the introduction of such decorative features as stone or terracotta panels. Their builders often used a black lime mortar made with the admixture of ash from the boiler furnaces of a local factory. Their own house, 8, High Path, to the north of the town centre, still carries their shared monogram in its gable. The small detached building beside that house once served as their drawing office.

Like those in every other county in England, Somerset villages carry the marks of World War I in the tragic lists of the fallen inscribed on centrally placed war memorials, frequently built in the shape of tall Celtic crosses. The one memorial that must be peculiar to the county is the equestrian statue in the north chancel of Mells church. It was sculpted by Sir Alfred Munnings and it commemorates Lieutenant Edward Horner of Mells Manor, killed at the age of twenty-two. At least one village had cause for gratitude when that war ended. A thanksgiving window in Rodney Stoke church celebrates the safe return of all the men and women from that place, who served their country from 1914 to 1918.

As in World War II, when Italian prisoners of war worked on the farms, Somerset, during that earlier conflict, became in the broadest sense, host to foreign nationals. During

World War I, it was the Portuguese who came to Minehead to train the mules which were to be used as beasts of burden in Flanders.

The years between the wars bring us to living memories. The records of such recollections which began to be made on a large scale in the 1960s are now part of every museum's archive and give us a clear picture of the county in the 1920s and 30s. There are also many local historians who have taken on the task of preserving memories of the areas in which they have spent most of their lives. Such a one was Robin Athill, who spent most of his life on Mendip and who for many years taught English at Downside School. He was six years old when he first came to the county, living on the northern slopes of Mendip at Hazel Manor, a house that was burnt down in 1929. By the time of his death in 1994 he had become the acknowledged historian of the hills. As a child Robin Athill would have known people from the villages of Chantry and Whatley, who successfully petitioned the council in 1923 against the proposal to tar the local roads. Until 1913, the surfaces of the Somerset roads consisted simply of bare stone which covered the hedgerows with white dust in dry weather. Now, new roads and motorways have swallowed up much of the county, just as the reservoirs drowned whole farms and villages earlier in the twentieth century. The valley beneath the village of Blagdon was first flooded in 1916; and the large Chew Valley Lake drowned the village of Moreton and the buildings of Walley Court and Denny Farm just after World War II.

The traffic on the M5 now roars over land which once formed the hamlet of Edithmead, a little inland from Berrow and Burnham. Fortunately, that lost community found a chronicler in Phyllis Wyatt, who spent her childhood there between the wars. A tiny cluster of cottages, served by a church put together with sheets of corrugated iron, Edithmead kept its own character, although in one sense it died as a community long before the motorway traffic flowed over it. The last Harvest Home was held in the village in 1930. It was a splendid event, culminating in the Charleston being danced in the marquee, put up for the occasion. The last communal event of any description to be held in Edithmead was a celebration commemorating the Silver Jubilee of George V and Queen Mary. It took place in a large wooden building which usually served as a cow byre and general farm shed.

It is no surprise that Edithmead is not mentioned in Maxwell Fraser's *Companion into Somerset*, published in 1947; although the book does give a clear picture of the county just after World War II. When Miss Fraser visited Wookey Hole, for example, she found 'a pleasant footpath up a green, tree-shaded valley' heading to the great caves. They have now become such a tourist attraction that practically the whole centre of that village has been turned into one vast coach and car park.

Electric light was installed in the caves as long ago as 1927, and it was then that the underground caverns, through which the River Axe flows beneath the limestone hills, were first opened up to the public. Twenty years later when Miss Fraser went there, she would have seen signs of the ferns, encouraged by the artificial light, which now flourish on the wet rock.

When Miss Fraser came to Wookey Hole, H.E. Balch, the former Wells postmaster, was curator of the museum which he had founded in Wells. An amateur archaeologist, he became fascinated by the Mendip caves when he first went underground at the age of fourteen. The rest of his life was devoted to their exploration.

Before the formation of the Welfare State, the lot of many people, especially the old and poor, was as hard in Somerset as elsewhere. Retired farm labourers who had lived all their working lives in tied cottages faced a particularly bleak future. What lay ahead of them was the ultimate misery of ending their days in the local workhouse. A sad contrast to the rural idyll that we like to think existed in the countryside before the machines took over. Nevertheless, there is some reality in our pastoral dreams and much of it can be found in the books of Freda Derrick. She was the granddaughter of a farmer from Lympsham, near Weston-super-Mare, and although she lived most of her life in London, her pleasure was to write about the work of the Somerset craftsmen and to illustrate her books with the drawings she made as she cycled around the county on her holidays. One of these drawings is a detailed study of a thatcher re-roofing part of Muchelney Abbey, using withies to tie the wheat straws to the rafters. Every summer, Freda Derrick came to East Brent, returning to the place where she and her brother (who was killed in World War I) had spent their childhood holidays. She made that her base for her excursions round Somerset searching out craftsmen at work. It was her opinion that 'if the tools of the country mason, wheelwright, carpenter and smith pass into our folk museums and out of life, England will suffer a double loss'.

It was World War II, and the fear of invasion, that marked the Somserset landscape. Its monuments are in such functional buildings as the line of brick pill boxes along the southern slopes of the hills between Wells and Doulting; the concrete platforms at the end of Brean Down, where the fort established in 1867, when Napoleon III was the threatened invader, was reinforced for use against Hitler; and even the statue of Romulus and Remus suckling the wolf, which an Italian prisoner-of-war set up beneath Pen Hill above Wells.

People's memories of those war years are still vivid. It was a time when at least two women worked as railway signal-box operators in the Radstock area; and many others from all over the county were employed as land-girls on the Somerset farms. The farm workers up on Mendip knew the true secret of the grassy earthworks on the top of Blackdown, near Charterhouse. Looking now like Iron Age fortifications, they represent the site of the mock city of Bristol, designed to fool the German bombers and stop them flying north to their real target. One mine was in fact dropped there. It gouged out a very useful cattle pond.

The Italian prisoners-of-war were not the only 'visitors' to Somerset during World War II, for despite being on the flight path to Bristol, the county was an evacuation centre. Teachers came with the children from London schools, and among them was Kathleen Young, whose pupils were attached to a school in Cheddar. Writing two years before her death in 1991, Kathleen claimed that Mendip had become her favourite spot on earth. During the war years she had married a Charterhouse farmer, and walked daily through Long Wood and into Cheddar Gorge to get to school.

Mrs Jean Bryant of Norton St Philip recalled her memories of the war years for a village scrap-book. She remembered that when the air raid siren sounded, she and her family sheltered under the scullery table in her aunt's house listening to the shrapnel falling all along the road as the German bombers were cleared out of Bath and Bristol. This same aunt took in an old lady who had been bombed out of her home in Bath and who was found lying in the hedgerow by Hinton Charterhouse.

It was not only people who were given refuge in Somerset during those years. The Domesday records were kept in Shepton Mallet prison, which was then in the hands of the American army and gained the reputation of being 'the world's grimmest glasshouse'.

The American T.S. Eliot had a more pleasing connection with Somerset. It was in the inter-war years that he traced his ancestry to the Eliots of East Coker, a small village to the south-east of Yeovil, on the Dorset border. The American branch of the family stemmed from an Andrew Eliot who settled in Salem in 1660 and was to become a member of the jury at the infamous witch trials. T.S. Eliot, who had decided to become a resident in Britain during his years at Oxford in World War I, declared about a decade before his death in 1965 that he wanted to have his ashes buried in his ancestral village. So now there is a permanent memorial to him in the west end of the church. It is fitting then that he should have started the last stanza of *East Coker* (written in 1940 and forming the second of the *Four Quartets*) with the words 'Home is where one starts from' and concluded it with the much-quoted 'In my end is my beginning'. Despite some new building, East Coker is little altered from the days when Eliot came there and found the light falling:

Across the open fields, leaving the deep lane
Shuttered with branches, dark in the afternoon,
Where you lean against a bank while a van passes.

When T.S. Eliot was living and writing in London during the inter-war years an older, lesser, but more easily accessible poet had become a frequent visitor to the Quantocks. Henry Newbolt used to stay in the old school house at Aisholt, a little village which draws its name from the ash trees which surround it, and which Coleridge described as 'a green, romantic chasm', when he thought of renting that same house in order to be near his friends, the family of the Revd John Brice.

Newbolt was also a frequent visitor to the great house of Orchardleigh to the north of Frome. He is buried by the little church that stands on an island in the lake of the extensive parkland. Other writers who took refuge in Somerset during their latter years were the writer and biblical scholar Monsignor Ronald Knox and the poet Siegfried Sasson. They are both buried in the churchyard at Mells, a village they knew well as guests of their co-religionists, the Asquiths of Mells Manor.

For a while, H.G. Wells taught in Wookey Hole School, a hilltop building which has now, rather inappropriately become an old people's home. Compton Mackenzie lived for a while in a house in West Horrington overlooking one of the most beautiful wooded combes of Mendip. It was Edward Thomas, however, a man from Hampshire, who was to write most directly about Somerset. He did so in his *In Pursuit of Spring*, a book based on a bicycle ride into the county in the Easter of 1912. He wrote of the stones along the Polden ridge which mark the prodigious leap made by Swayne (see page 107) after the Battle of Sedgemoor. He laughed at himself for being so meticulous as to have to check up on Wordsworth and prove that there really is no weathercock on Kilve church, before going on to write the most perfect description of the shore at Kilve, where the sea seems 'hardly distinguishable, save by its motion, from the broad beach of gray pools, blackened pebbles and low rock edges'. In the park of the vanished Cothelstone House, he discovered the figure of Jupiter, which still stands on the hillside, the sole survivor of a group of statues sold off in the early years of the nineteenth century. He would have liked, he wrote, to have thought of the figure as 'a Somerset Pan or Apollo' but found it mainly pathetic and partly ridiculous. Surrounded by the indifferent cattle, I must confess that I find it enchantingly absurd and am glad that it was spared the fate of its fellows.

Painters as well as writers have celebrated Somerset. William Henderson is among them. He was born in Frome in 1903 and died in Wiltshire, four days before his ninetieth birthday. An idiosyncratic and unfashionable artist, he was a great colourist. Among his early tutors was Judith Lear, widow of the vicar of Mells and niece of Sir John Millais, whom he met at St Tropez.

In later life, Henderson recalled that as a child he had been invited to a Christmas party given for her son Peter by the widow of Captain Falcon Scott of the Antarctic. Scott's Somerset memorial is inscribed on the family tomb in the churchyard of the now 'redundant' church at Holcombe on the edge of the Somerset coalfields.

The inter-war years saw an increased active interest in the details of local history in contrast to the eighteenth- and nineteenth-century enthusiasm for the wide scope of antiquity. From Downside Abbey, Dom Ethelbert Hone, parish priest of Stratton on the Fosse from 1891 to 1940, was not only active in his own brand of Christian Socialism but also served for many years as chairman of the Somerset Archaeological Society. Dom Ethelbert worked with Arthur Bulleid on the archaeology of Glastonbury and with Dean Armitage Robinson in recording the medieval glass of Wells Cathedral. He is particularly valued for the work that he did on scratch dials, the primitive sundials marked out on the walls of churches.

Much local history is also contained in the memories and songs of living men and women. Cecil J. Sharp, that great collector of folk songs and dances, who discovered material from all over England until his death in 1924, started his work when he heard a song in Somerset. It was sung by John England in the garden at the Hambridge vicarage where he was staying, with his collaborator the Revd C.L. Marson.

Many more such songs were later to be discovered by Ruth Tongue and published in her *Chime Child or Somerset Singers* (Routledge and Kegan Paul 1968). Ruth Tongue was born in 1898 and spent her early childhood in Taunton Castle, where her father was the Nonconformist chaplain to the garrison. At a very young age she cultivated the habit of chatting to the local people, who would invite her to their homes. It was thus that she learned that she was a 'chime child', born between Friday midnight and dawn on Saturday. Such a one has special divine protection and, as well as being exceptionally musical, has the gift of controlling animals.

We owe may romantic folk-tales to Ruth Tongue as well as many charming Somerset songs and carols. One of these stories was told to her in Kilmersdon in 1962 by a lady who explained that the Lady Chapel in the church there was built after the Lord of the Manor at that time was granted a vision of a beautiful white hind while he was riding over Mendip in deep distress at the pestilence that was striking his people.

XI
The Nuclear Age

Brockley church, to the north-east of the A370 as it runs from Congresbury to Bristol, is set in a time-warp of Somerset history. Three main buildings, of which the church is one, and a collection of farm sheds stand away from the main road on the further edge of a stretch of pasture that was once wide parkland. The late seventeenth century court beside the church is now an old people's home; a much-restored Tudor farmhouse stands behind it, reached by a farm road going over a cattle-grid into which the owner, who has lived there since the early 1950s, has kindly inserted a small wooden ladder for the benefit of any hedgehog, foolish enough to fall through the grating. It was she, who pointed out to me the small group of trees commemorating royal events, planted by the side of the road leading from court to farm.

The church itself, restored in the 1820s by the Piggot family, who then lived at Brockley Hall by the main road, is now cared for by the Redundant Churches Foundation. It is a model of early nineteenth-century church architecture, complete with a box family pew and, naturally, several monuments to the Piggot family. In the churchyard, among clusters of autumn cyclamen, there is a grave adorned with skull and crossbones, and reputed to be that of a pirate.

Late twentieth-century business has, temporarily at least, left this place alone. It is one of the few small sections of the county which, having little to offer the tourist, has been left to its dreams. Elsewhere such ancient clusters of buildings have either been destroyed to make way for road building or other improvements or they have been tidied up as museum exhibits. In many cases that has been beneficial. Up to the 1960s, before the listing of buildings of particular historical interest, many great houses such as Brockley Court were simply wantonly destroyed. One such loss, and it is a serious one, was John Billingsley's house in the woods near Oakhill.

As the eighteenth-century author of the Board of Agriculture's review of farming in Somerset and as a founder of the Bath and West Show, he would have been amazed at the enormous herds of black and white Friesians, which in Somerset as elsewhere, have replaced the more modest numbers of shorthorns and red Devons grazing pastures defined by ancient boundary hedges, many of which have now been grubbed out. At least on the Somerset levels, the rhynes, or wet fences, have had to be left alone. Billingsley would also have known the county as a place of elms, many of which formed part of the old hedges. They disappeared during the elm blight of the 1970s, and newcomers, like myself, who arrived here in the 1980s, find it hard to envisage that lost landscape.

We are now more familiar with the open views of the levels, appearing like an Alice in Wonderland chessboard when surveyed from the top of Glastonbury Tor, treeless except for the willows by the water. The arguments about the responsibility for drainage however continue in the same old way. The first big change came in 1974 when land drainage became a national responsibility; the second with privatisation of the water supply, when the control of the river and sea defences were given to separate authorities, the former being controlled by the National Rivers Authority. The vast importance of the latter can be judged from the events of December 1981, when a particularly strong high tide, combined with adverse weather conditions, caused the flood waters to reach as far inland as the M5. In response to that disaster a massive sea wall was constructed from Huntspill to Burnham, changing the character of the sea front dramatically. It proved strong enough to withstand the onslaught of the storms in January 1990, which so severely eroded the sand dunes, further along the coast by Berrow and Brean.

Earlier, inland flooding of the River Brue caused such immense problems to the town of Bruton and the surrounding area that a flood scheme had to be put in operation, although in Somerset generally, river control does not apply to the head waters. The three great Bruton floods occurred in 1962, 1979 and in 1982, when the waters rose above the church wall. Now a 130-year flood alleviation scheme, like that operating in the Thames Valley, has been instigated. Three million pounds of Wessex Water's money was spent on building a barrier of Mendip limestone, beneath which the river flows as it enters Bruton.

In one respect, among the upland pastures, the landscape shows signs of reverting to an earlier pattern. Here, in Somerset, as elsewhere, fields of pale blue flax are added to the patchwork of the landscape, bringing a welcome relief from the harsh, jarring yellow of the rape. Flax has always been a Somerset crop, and as well as being rendered into linseed oil, it is now used, I am told, in the manufacture of linoleum, which is enjoying a renewed popularity. You can see something of the industries based on earlier uses of flax in the cloth trade in the Museum of South Somerset in Yeovil.

The other 'new' crop to appear on the Somerset landscape of recent years is represented by the conifers which cover so much of the uplands of Mendip and the Quantocks. On the whole, the Forestry Commission has done its best in recent decades to marry its planting to the contours of the landscape and to add broad leaf planting to its scheme for commercial crops. No such considerations will operate when the national forests are sold up to private concerns, and even now the Commission's economies mean that the trees are no longer cared for at a local level. Until the 1980s, the foresters lived close to their trees and knew the woodlands intimately: now the forests in the west of Somerset are managed from Exeter; those on Mendip, from Marlborough. Even so, it is much better that the Commission, with its generous attitude to public access, should control these lands than that they should be sold off to private and frequently, foreign owners.

An alteration to the Somerset landscape, and one that was even more controversial although more local than conifer planting, occured in the mid-sixties when the nuclear energy plant was set up in the north of Cannington, at Hinckley Point, on the Bristol channel. Despite the glossy leaflet welcoming visitors to the power station and showing laughing children in the meadows around it, Hinckley Point and its proposed addition is viewed with serious local misgiving. Aware of this, the authority informs intending visitors of its green intentions, reminding them that the power station occupies a Site of Special Scientific Interest, and that a wealth of birds and butterflies can be found in the neighbouring maple woods. Nature trails have been developed around the station, but I imagine that the Authority will not encourage walkers, although they cannot forbid them, to take the public footpath between the reactors and the foreshore. Those who venture there will find a scene of death and desolation, the hot water from the cooling system which is pumped out there having killed such fish as were not originally drawn into the pipes; while behind the high, barbed-wire fence, the reactor, so spruce and white on its other side, shows a vista of rusty decay. By 1992, the old station (Hinckley A) was declared to be in such a badly deteriorating condition that planning permission was sought for a third power station on the site.

A less potentially lethal but even more devastating mark on the landscape is made by the limestone quarries in the east of the county, on the Mendip Hills between Shepton Mallet and Frome. This area is being rapidly destroyed by the greatest concentration of quarrying in Europe. To measure the extent of the destruction in one small locality, it is only necessary to think of Asham Wood which has lost a third of its 340 acres to the quarries. At least four of the quarries operating in this area have penetrated beneath the water table, possibly with dire consequences. However, the need for roadstone in the south of England is such that the harmful destruction of the landscape seems to be an insignificant matter. If the Somerset quarry owners get their way and receive permission to go down to sea level, so flattening the hills for ever, they will run out of stone in less than twenty years if the current rate of consumption continues. Few people seem to look that far ahead or ask if present convenience is worth future desolation.

The trouble is that, unlike its coal, Somerset stone is cheap to get out of the ground. The main cost comes in transportation. This has two disadvantages. In the first place, rail-heads solely servicing individual quarries take up even more of the countryside; and in the second, the cost of transportation makes it uneconomic to re-use the aggregate and so reduce the need for ever more intensive quarrying. As an instance of the scale of limestone being taken out of Somerset one afternoon in July 1994, I counted fifty-six rail-containers carrying stone from one quarry alone snaking through Reading station, while I was waiting for my train.

It has been suggested that as a temporary measure, the coal batches (Somerset's term for slag heaps) from the disused coal mines could be a source of material for the roads, but the idea has never been put into practice. Meanwhile, ever more elaborate road schemes are constantly being put into operation. One of the currently most controversial of these, designed to 'improve' the A303 on the edge of the Blackdowns between Ilminster and Marsh on the Devon border, has had the effect of totally deleting an area of medieval field systems only a few years after it had been officially designated as an Area of Outstanding Natural Beauty. As Mary-Rose Mangles, a Somerset councillor, declared when the plan was being debated, 'the whole scheme will mean even more tons of Mendip limestone being quarried out of the hills'. Indeed, as Tom Elkin, a former warden of a part of Mendip, itself designated as an A.O.N.B., once observed, 'The time will come when those who want to see Mendip will have to go and look at the roads of Essex.' The new A303 proposal will, however, ensure a shorter journey for those seeking traces of the hills.

At the beginning of the century, the quarries did provide work for many people. Admittedly the work was hard, the conditions poor and the quarrymen had to provide their own tools, yet at least there was an opportunity for employment. Now, Whatley quarry, which covers over 300 acres and is perpetually seeking to expand, can be run by a dozen people.

Unemployment in the county is part of the national pattern;

so sadly are the young, homeless beggars sleeping, unbeliev-
ably, in the shop doorways of the comfortable, Trollopian city
of Wells. This particular phenomenon is brought about partly
by the proximity of Wells to Glastonbury, for decades the
mecca of the 'New Age' and a magnet for the dissatisfied and
dispossessed.

Another national problem is the general conservation of the
landscape and the preservation of wild life, matters that have
become the concern of such bodies as English Nature and the
various county Trusts. Among Somerset's own particular
problems is the conservation of the remaining wet lands which
have not been drained and the restoration of areas devastated
by peat-taking. English Nature is currently co-operating with
the Somerset Trust for Nature Conservation to redeem three
and a half thousand acres of exhausted peat workings by
constructing a landscape of reed beds and open water, which
should be a haven for wildlife. It will be know as Avalon
Marshes.

That new reserve will complement the one on the wet lands
of Catcott Heath, on the western edge of the peat moors,
which was purchased by the Somerset Trust in 1972. This
seventeen-acre patch is special in that it forms one of the few
remaining stretches of bog land in the area not to have been
destroyed by peat cutting.

A look through the list of the other reserves managed by the
Trust gives one an idea of the extremely varied nature of the
county. In contrast to the wet lands, for example, the 180-acre
Langfield Heath reserve to the north of Wellington is the
largest area of lowland heathland in the county and one that
has always remained common land, never having been
reclaimed for agriculture. Several of the reserves include
stretches of ancient woodland; among these are Boon's Copse
and Buller's Copse to the south-east of Taunton, both part of
the original Forest of Neroche. Part of the Cheddar woods
includes another patch of ancient woodland, once part of the
Royal Hunting Forest of Mendip. There the Trust now looks
after such matters of historical interest as a defunct ochre
mine and the deep gulleys worn down by horses during

World War I, dragging heavy trees down the hill. Of more immediate concern and of more relevance to the Trust's primary function is the national reserve for the preservation and study of doormice that has been set up amongst these trees.

On Mendip, the Trust owns Chancellor's Farm, where the fields have never been subject to any artificial fertilisers. The result is that the meadows, whose hay is never cut before the middle of July, produce a diverse array of wild flowers. The limestone grasslands of Chancellor's Farm are being well cared for, for it is not enough just to leave a place alone. On the Blackdown Hills, on the south-western edge of the county, the wild flower meadows are threatened by invasive scrub because of a lack of controlled grazing. On the Quantock Hills, the massive spread of bracken is another threat to the open grassland areas, fifty per cent of which could well be lost by the beginning of the next century.

From 1977, the headquarters of the Somerset Trust has been at Fyne Court, which replaced the Quantock manor house at Broomfield when it was destroyed by fire in 1894. The Trust is restoring the vegetation of the Court's parkland to its natural state as a wooded coombe and it has converted the turreted folly, once used as kennels, into a bat sanctuary.

English Nature preserves several Somerset sites for the nation. On Mendip, the authority owns the ashwoods above the village of Rodney Stoke as well as a slope of grassland, which was once an intensely cultivated strawberry field, providing fruit for Covent Garden. Somerset landscapes, preserved by the National Trust include the upper part of Cheddar Gorge, the woods of Wells Tor, and, to the west, the headland of Bossington, round the old coastguard station on the eastern side of Porlock Bay.

Inland from Porlock, the National Trust owns fourteen farms on the Holnicote estate, previously belonging to the Acland family. All of these farms now have conservation clauses in their tenancy agreements. The Trust also owns 170 cottages in the area and these are kept for local people rather than being let out during the holiday season. The estate includes the Horner oakwoods, registered as a Site of Special Scientific Interest and boasting at least 165 lichens, which flourish in this pure air. The strips of Douglas Fir making up the coniferous woodlands of the estate were first planted in 1919 by Sir Francis Acland, one of the first commissioners of the Forestry Commission.

There are two major problems with vegetation on Exmoor and the Quantocks. The first relates to the perpetual menace of uncontrollable rhododendron, which virtually kills all the land it covers; the second is the decline of the heather moorland. It has been estimated that sixty per cent of Exmoor's heather has been lost since 1950, the result of the increased number of cattle grazed on the moor. The current scheme is to limit the grazing by keeping cattle in the stockyards for longer periods during the winter months.

All this preserved land provides a natural haven for wildlife. Bird watchers, particularly, are able to appreciate the many varieties of duck and other waders attracted to Somerset's wet lands on the moors and levels and on the mud-flats around the maritime reserve to the west of Bridgwater Bay, where the low-lying headland culminates in Stert Point. The furthest marshlands of that area, beyond the village of Stert, provide a welcome contrast to the cooling towers of Hinckley Point along the coast to the west and the acres of mute battery sheds around Cox's farm, which form a reproach to this ancient common land.

One wild creature, namely the Exmoor pony, is peculiar to this county. It is the present policy of the Exmoor National Park to leave these herds of dun-coloured, 'mealy-mouthed' creatures as far as possible in their natural state, controlled only by a regular worming, for the sake of the sheep with which they share the moorland grazing. These animals, which are close descendants of the tiny prehistoric horse, only grow up to twelve hands. They are said to have migrated from Russia to south-west England soon after the last Ice Age. Some of them are tamed and sold world-wide, having been selected as foals at the annual round up of the herds, which takes place each October at Warren Farm.

Only those dealers professionally interested in the breed are invited to attend the Warren Farm horse sale; however, anyone walking across the wilder reaches of the moor may well come across a herd of these ponies. If you want to make sure of seeing them, it is best to go on one of the walks organised by the National Park guides.

More static aspects of by-gone Somerset are brought to life in the various local museums, or in the central collection in the castle at Taunton. In addition, some farms such as that at Thorney Moor on the levels near Muchelney are open to visitors and demonstrate the changing patterns of agriculture in the county.

Occasionally, an historic installation will be restored for present-day use. Such is the case of the wooden lighthouse, set up on Burnham sands in 1832 and designed to guide ships in Bridgwater Bay, who would line it up with a second larger inshore light. This little lighthouse, recently restored and put on to fully automatic working, is now used purely for local traffic. Those pilots must rely on it alone, for the inshore light is no longer operational, but that white-painted tower has also been preserved and the alignment between the two is quite clear in daylight as you look across the bay from Stert Point.

The old canals have not been restored to useful life, but stretches of them are now being used for pleasure boating and plans are going ahead to create a 100-mile circuit in the county based on a renewed stretch of the Bridgwater and Taunton canal. Several of the lost railways have also been restored by steam train enthusiasts. In the east there is a stretch of line across Mendip from Cranmore, and part of this is used for conveying stone from the quarries. In the west there is an extensive restoration for holiday traffic from Watchett to Minehead and Taunton. In some places, notably in Cheddar, short stretches of disused line have been preserved as walkways; at Shepton Mallet and Pensford there are massive disused viaducts, whose upkeep is now becoming a problem for the authorities. Throughout the county, the landscape is marked by embankments and tracks of the railways, which changed the face of Somerset in the nineteenth century.

As the twentieth century draws to a close, road building is making an even more indelible signature. I have described how the M5 ate up Edithmead in the north of the county, and how the widening of the A303 has totally altered the Ilminster/ Ilchester area. As ever larger container lorries are allowed on the roads, the need to divert traffic from Somerset's towns and villages, including the medieval city of Wells, has become acute. As I write, a great swathe of ring road is being cut across the moors so as to keep the heavy traffic out of the centre of Glastonbury. One must reckon it to be the lesser of two evils, although it is sad to see tons of roadstone killing off the moors, and a pity to lose the old 'tin bridge', a familiar landmark which once spanned the lost Somerset and Dorset railway. In this as in so many other aspects of life, the challenge in Somerset, as elsewhere, is to preserve the past without restricting the future. The tragedy is that with modern tech-nology, once the landscape is altered to suit an immediate need or gain an immediate profit, the change is irreversible.

XII
Bath

Set in the valley of the River Avon, between the hills of Lansdown (where Somerset properly begins) and Combe Down verging on Mendip to the south, Bath has alway been a proudly independent city throughout all the fluctuations of its fortunes. Yet from its earliest beginnings the course of its history has been inter-woven with that of Somerset, a connection which continued even during the decades in which the city was part of the temporary county of Avon. Long before the Romans discovered the hot water springs for themselves and made the place one of their most opulent baths in western Europe, lead was being brought here from Celtic mines on Mendip, and Celtic forts guarded the course of the Avon through this fertile valley. Many of these fortified enclosures, such as Little Down Camp at Lansdown have their attendant barrows, while to the south, at Bathampton, near the site of the University, there are clear traces of Celtic fields.

The mythology of Bath is purely Celtic. Bladud, the legendary founder of the city, whose stone head overlooks the baths, was said to be the son of Lud and the father of Lear, and thus well entrenched in the matter of Britain. The folk-tale has it that Bladud was banished from his father's court on account of a highly infectious 'leprosy' (a term then used for any skin complaint). Shunned by society, the young prince was forced to become a swineherd, presumably attending the pigs rooting for beech nuts in the thick belt of trees which still crown the cliffs to the south of the city. These animals were not immune from the infection that Bladud had picked up, but he noticed that their sores were cured when the animals wallowed in the warm mud of the valley bottom.

What was good for pigs, Bladud discovered, was good for man too. So, in the place where he was cured, he founded a city.

By the time the Romans came to settle the South-West, the springs of Bath erupting from the underground waters of the Mendip hills were well known to the Celts, who dedicated them to their goddess Sul. At that time, the area we are talking about was on a much lower level than the present city, so that when the Romans built their elaborate baths, temples and accompanying villas it was on land which seldom rose much higher than the level of the present public gardens by the river, which you now approach by descending flights of stone steps. This means that such traces as we have of the Roman building lie well beneath the stones of the medieval city, which was mostly lost to the elegance and grandeur of the eighteenth-century architecture.

The first great Roman thermal bath was completed in the first century AD and dedicated to Minerva, the goddess of wisdom, in conjunction with the Celtic goddess Sul. This bath, which also served as a temple, is now preserved and inter-preted for visitors in the heart of the city, near the medieval abbey. Fragments of the Roman temple came to light in 1790, but it was not until the 1880s that the Great Bath was discovered and restored, to the extent that although the pedestals around the bathing pool are Roman, the columns which they support are, in fact, Victorian. However, there are more than enough signs of Roman civilisation in the stones of Bath to make us appreciate something of the splendour of Aqua Sulis. Indeed it was Pevsner's view that the Roman remains at Bath not only equalled those of Hadrian's Wall, but 'may be said to rival in some sense even the great imperial structure of Rome itself'. Even if this claim seems exaggerated, a visit to the Roman baths at Bath is one sure way towards an appreciation of Roman civilisation at its height in Britain.

There is no doubt that these baths, patronised by the wealthy citizens of the Empire, were also visited by local Romano-British citizens afflicted by the rheumatic pains brought on by the damp conditions of dwellings on the low-lying Somerset moors. We can be certain that Somerset men brought lead from Mendip to line the great Roman bath and that coal, from the twisted seams around the present-day Radstock, kept the perpetual fire burning before the joint altar of the two goddesses.

By the second and third centuries, great Roman mansions were established around the baths and traces of them have been found beneath the sites of medieval buildings. For over two hundred years antiquarians have retrieved Roman remains in Bath. In 1727 a statuette of Minerva was dug up in Stall Street to the south of the site of the main bath.

The main Roman cemetery was situated, as always, outside the confines of the city, and in the usual manner lay beside a main highway, in this case it was the one that lies to the east, beneath the present Walcot Street, off the London Road. From the cemetery inscriptions, we learn that the Roman city of Bath had a brief Christian history. The epitaphs are not always complimentary: a follower of the Arian heresy, which emphasised the humanity of Christ above his divinity, was described as 'a dog of Arius'. Another inscription tells us of a sectarian assault on the pagan temple. The tables were turned when piratical invaders under the command of Niall of the Nine Hostages set sail across the Irish Sea, entered the Bristol Channel, and ransacked the Roman settlements on the Avon.

When the Romans left Britain, the fortunes of Bath faded completely. It is generally believed that the Anglo-Saxon poem, *The Ruin*, is a lament for the ghostly state of the vanished city: 'Bright were the castle-dwellings, many the bath houses . . . many a mead-hall full of the joys of men, till Fate, the mighty overturned that . . . the city fell to earth. The multitudes who might have built it anew lay dead on the earth.'*

Yet the Saxons did eventually build Bath anew, when they took possession of the city after the Celts were defeated at the Battle of Dyrham (some ten miles to the north) in 577. However any connection between Saxon Bath and Wessex is tenuous, for it seems that the city was for long under the control of Mercia and the Midlands. Links with Wessex were

* Translated by R.K. Gordon. *Anglo-Saxon Poetry* (Everyman/Dent) 1926.

to be established in 973 when Dunstan officiated at the coronation of Eadgar as King of all England. The ceremony took place in Bath Abbey, which had grown out of the Saxon monastery founded in 676 by the king, Osric. The Bishop of Bath and Wells still officiates at every coronation.

By the beginning of the tenth century, Bath was one of the garrisoned Burghs, fortified against the Danes. The remains of the Roman walls were used for this purpose, and within them a regular street pattern was laid out, which survived until the Middle Ages and which can still be traced today. This does not mean that the subsequent history of the city ran smoothly. On the death of William the Conqueror, the much hated William Rufus gained possession of Bath and its Abbey. This aroused the wrath of the barons, among whom was the French bishop, Geoffrey of Coutance, whose lands included about a tenth of the county of Somerset. As a gesture of their enmity to the king these barons systematically destroyed the Royal Borough of Bath. The Abbey was mercifully saved by John de Villula of Tours, whom Lanfranc, the Archbishop of Canterbury, consecrated Bishop of Bath in 1088. He built so vast a cathedral here that, the present Abbey only occupies the site of its nave.

Bishop John de Villula also extended the scope of the monastery building and in addition to that he took advantage of Henry I's licence on the enclosure of hunting parks to create a monastically controlled space to the south-east of the city. This well-sited stretch of land, now largely owned by the National Trust, was to have an important secular role in Bath's later history.

At the collegiate school which Villula set up, the young Aethelhard, who was to become generally and widely known as Adelard of Bath, received his early education. He was to go on to teach throughout Europe and even further afield, and has been widely acclaimed as the first translator of Euclid.

Throughout the Middle Ages, the prosperity of both the priory and the city of Bath depended on the wool trade. As its importance as a market town grew, the old walls were rebuilt yet again. You can see a partial reconstruction of them at Upper Borough Walls to the north of the Abbey. On the west bank of the Avon, to the south of Pulteney Bridge, you can also discern the remains of the medieval East Gate.

By far the most popular vestige of medieval Bath, however, is Sally Lunn's house to the south of the Abbey. Now a coffee house serving Sally Lunn tea-cakes to a recipe introduced into Bath by that Huguenot refugee who once lived here, it was built in 1480 on the site of the priory kitchen, which in its turn stood above the buried remains of a Roman mansion.

At that time, as it had been for several centuries previously, the Avon was crossed at the site of the present main road bridge to the west of the railway station. This is still the main road link between the city and the county of Somerset, and we can imagine its use by the wool merchants as well as by farmers bringing produce into the city and people from Bath setting out across it on pilgrimage to Glastonbury.

The present Abbey, which provides the main ecclesiastical link between Bath and the rest of Somerset, was begun in 1499 under the direction of Oliver King, Bishop of both Bath and Wells; and it was designed by Robert and William Vertue, master masons to Henry VII. Built in the Perpendicular style, it is most justly famous for the glory of the fan vaulting which William Vertue designed. Although only the stonework of the choir and chancel is original, the vaulting in the nave, restored between 1864 and 1871 under the direction of Sir George Gilbert Scott, retains the splendour of Bishop King's vision.

It was, in fact, a dream of angels that inspired the fifteenth-century bishop to rebuild the abbey church. That dream is translated into stone on the west front. There amidst the angels, laboriously struggling up a Jacob's ladder to the turrets, is one whose pride perhaps has caused him to be forever falling between heaven and earth. The Gloucestershire poet, U. A. Fanthorpe, has caught the meaning of this medieval stonework for the twentieth-century tourists who find:

> This moment is as much a dream
> As Jacob's nightmare on the Abbey wall,
> Above with straining angels, who with wing
> Correctly folded, desperately crawl
> Along their monstrous ladder.

Until the Reformation, the Abbey held most of the land in and around the city, and, even more significantly it also controlled the springs which fed the healing baths. With the Dissolution, which coincided with the decline of the wool trade in the South-West, this stable prosperity crumbled and Bath went into one of those periods of stagnation and decay which have punctuated her history.

For a century or so time seems to have almost stood still. John Speed's map of Bath, drawn up in 1610, shows that the city was then largely contained within the medieval walls. Even after the turbulence of the Civil War in which Bath served both as garrison and hospital, first for the Royalists and then for the Parliamentarians – and even after the destruction and chaos caused by the fearful battle of Lansdown in 1643 – the city remained little changed. Gilmore's plan of Bath drawn up in 1694 still shows a medieval town.

A little earlier in the seventeenth century, Celia Fiennes came here on her ride through the West Country. She had little good to say of the city, considering that 'the baths in my opinion makes this town unpleasant, they are thicke and hot by their steam and by its own situation, so low encompassed with high hills and woods'. Other contemporary accounts of Bath are even less favourable, for at that time the medicinal baths themselves were sordid and disorderly. The bathers had to expect that cats, dogs and pigs (dead and alive) would be among the filth that was hurled at them by jeering crowds. When Samuel Pepys made his diary entry about a visit to the Cross Bath at four o'clock in the morning, he was probably being unusually restrained when he wrote, 'It cannot be clean to go so many bodies in the same water.' That particular bath must have been cleared of people, commoners anyway, when James II's wife, Mary, bathed here as a cure for infertility. It worked; she conceived almost immediately thereafter and that bath got its name from the cross (now disappeared) which was erected to mark the event.

Although the city was in such a vile condition at the end of the seventeenth century, the healing springs still drew the crowds who came to gamble as well as to bathe. Today, people like U. A. Fanthorpe's tourists come in their coachloads to the city, not to take the waters but to get a glimpse of its eighteenth-century elegance. Yet had it not been for the work and enterprise of three men, Bath might well have remained a decaying and tawdry Las Vegas of the English south-west, despite the visit that Queen Anne made here in 1703.

The first of these three to arrive at the city was one Richard Nash, an unlikely character from Swansea who had left Oxford University without a degree and thereafter dropped out of both the army and the law. However, while he was a student at the Middle Temple in 1695, he was elected to present a pageant before William III. This was so successful that the King offered him a knighthood, an honour that he refused. Perhaps he had already set his sights on a more prestigious title, for generations still know him as Beau Nash.

It is not surprising that shortly after Queen Anne's visit to the city, Nash, drawn by the gambling, decided to make Bath his home. It is a matter for admiration, however, that almost immediately he took the city to his heart and determined to turn it into a worthy focus of elegant society. By 1706 he had raised £18,000 by public subscription for the much-needed repair of the roads both within and around the city. At the same time he organised a band of music so successfully that he had virtual control over the Assembly Rooms, the social centre of Bath.

In her splendid book on Bath, Edith Sitwell quoted Oliver Goldsmith's estimation of this man: 'Whenever people of fashion came, needy adventurers were generally found in waiting. With such Bath swarmed: and among this class Beau Nash was certainly to be numbered in the beginning, only with this difference, that he wanted the corrupt heart too commonly attending a life of expedients, for he was generous, humane and honourable even though by profession a gamester.'

Goldsmith also translated two epitaphs inspired by Nash's death in February 1762. One, by a Dr King, drew attention to the Beau's custom of always wearing a white hat: 'A symbol of the candour of his mind'; the other was by Goldsmith's acquaintance Dr Oliver, the inventor of the Bath Oliver biscuit. Here Nash was commended for holding decency and decorum sacred and for the gentle manner in which he corrected mistakes in dress and decorum. He particularly abhorred the practice that some ladies adopted of wearing white lace aprons to the Assembly Rooms, and no matter how expensive the garment or how well connected the lady, he insisted that the offending garment be removed.

Nash's portrait shows a heavy-jowelled, small-mouthed, wide-eyed visage, far removed from the romantic fantasy he must have had of himself when he travelled through the city in a post-chaise drawn by six grey horses and attended by outriders and footmen. By 1738 he was organising another royal occasion, and, as the lynch pin of the fashionable world, welcomed the unfortunate Frederick, Prince of Wales to Bath. The event was commemorated by the obelisk which still stands in Queen Square and for which Alexander Pope, with the greatest reluctance, wrote an inscription.

Beau Nash's great contemporary in Bath was the wealthy and philanthropic Ralph Allen, a Cornish man born in 1694. His grandmother kept the post office in Columb and it was while he was staying with her, as a very young man, and helping her with her official duties that he was noticed by a Post Office Inspector. The official was so impressed by the general demeanour and ability of young Ralph that a position was procured at Bath for the lad. Once in Bath, Allen went from strength to strength. He pursued his career in the Post Office with ingenuity and imagination, devising a system of cross-posting throughout England and Wales whereby the mail did not automatically have to go through London as had previously been the case. Although it happened nearly eighty years after his death in 1764, it was due to his pioneering work that Bath had the honour of being the first city in which letters franked with a postage stamp were mailed. That historic event took place on 2 May 1840 and was commemorated a hundred and fifty years later when Bath's refurbished postal museum in Broad Street was officially opened.

Ralph Allen moved in the highest society in Bath. As well as generally impressing the city's leading citizens with his business acumen and abilities, he made a particular impression on General Wade, who had come to live in Bath, by detecting a Jacobite plot. In this case the bond was so strong that Allen married the General's natural daughter. Although he was only mayor of the city for one year (1742), Allen was generally known as The Man of Bath, and was able to exercise considerable influence when he backed Pitt as parliamentary candidate for the city. Yet he appears always to have been a modest man, a complete contrast to Beau Nash. His friend, Alexander Pope, summed up his character in his epilogue to the satires of Horace:

> Let humble Allen with an awkward shame
> Do good by stealth and blush to find it fame.

Allen's fame is literally written in stone, for many of the eighteenth-century buildings that we admire in Bath today are of the stone cut from his quarries on Combe Down to the south of the city. Ever ingenious, he devised a way of bringing the great golden slabs of limestone by canal to the building sites. He naturally used the same stone when he came to design his own great mansion in 1734. For a site he chose the old monastery lands of Prior Park, enclosed by Bishop de Villula. The house is a school now, but the extensive grounds are owned by the National Trust, which gives the public access to landscaping largely devised by Pope. In 1755, when his mansion was complete, Allen set a Palladian bridge, resembling the one at Wilton, in his grounds. There are said to be only four such bridges in the world. This one, with its delicate balustrades and narrow roof, is particularly enchanting.

Despite his reputation for modesty, Allen always had a taste for the theatrical, and as far back as 1726, when he was still quite new to the city, he caused an immense folly to be put up on the skyline of the hills to the south-east of the city. This took the form of the curtain wall of a medieval castle, and indeed it is generally known as Sham castle. It stands still, as dominating and impressive as ever, but should you climb up to it you will find free-standing wall in the middle of a cow pasture.

None of the plans that Ralph Allen devised both for his own dwellings and generally throughout Bath, would have been possible without the skill, imagination and fine taste of the architect John Wood, who as a young man of twenty-two designed his own house (now number 3, Old Lilliput Lane, next door to Sally Lunn's) in 1727. Both Wood (who probably came from Yorkshire) and his son were to enjoy Ralph Allen's patronage throughout their work in Bath. It is mostly that work which visitors come to see today.

John Wood the elder designed Queen Square and made his own home there, at what are now numbers 14 and 15. He also was to have a house at number 41 Gay Street, which runs into the Circus that he designed. Standing on the hill to the north of the city, the circus was John Wood's most ambitious concept. Sadly, he did not live to see its completion, which was undertaken by his son.

It is to John Wood the younger that we owe the grandeur and elegance of the Royal Crescent, Bath's most famous street. Number One, a house furnished as Jane Austen might have known it, is now open to the public from Tuesday to Saturday throughout the year. A visit to it might well be combined with one to the Georgian Banqueting Room in Bath's Guildhall. Built in the late eighteenth century and flanked by Victorian wings, this building is not unduly impressive from the street, but once inside, the majestic proportions of the hall set off by Corinthian columns and adorned with stupendous chandeliers enable you to envisage Bath high society at its most sumptuous in a way that no other place, not even the Pump Room (by the Roman Baths) or the Assembly Rooms (now part of the Museum of Costume), is able to do. Concerts are sometimes held in the Guildhall and it is worth making a special effort to attend.

There was always, of course, another side to Bath, as to any great city, and to his credit John Wood the younger was almost alone among the architects of his time in caring for the whole of society and not just for the rich elite. In a paper, re-issued in London in 1806, and now kept in the Royal Institute of British Architects headquarters in London, he expressed his concern that the 'habitations of that useful and necessary rank of men, the LABOURERS, were become for the most part offensive both in decency and humanity'. After spending time visiting these artisan dwellings, he put the case even more strongly, for he found them, 'shattered, dirty, miserable hovels scarcely affording shelter for the beasts of the forests'.

The wretched hovels that John Wood visited on Combe Down and off Wellsway, south of the Avon, where the poorest people lived, have long crumbled away; and few, if any, of the visitors who come to Bath to let their imagination take part in the city's heyday, spare a thought for how the majority of the permanent residents had to live. Where John Wood's treatise was acted upon, fine, solid terrace cottages, boasting the new innovation of a privy to each strip of garden, were put up, mostly in the eastern part of the city, where the fine free stone was more readily available.

The people who lived in those terrace cottages had much to thank John Wood the younger for; but Bath is primarily a city for the rich, and his name will always be synonymous with the Royal Crescent. In fact, there is only one of the grander, eighteenth-century buildings of Bath that was not designed and executed by one John Wood or the other. The notable exception is the famous Pulteney Bridge, spanning the Avon at the city centre. It was designed in 1770 by Robert Adam at the request of the wealthy Sir William Pulteney, who had married a Bath heiress and, by judicious handling of her fortune, earned himself a reputation as the richest man in England. His bridge is the only one of its kind in England, still retaining narrow shops – booths almost – on either side. On the eastern side of the Avon, Great Pulteney Street, completed in 1790, culminates in the former Sydney Hotel, one of the last buildings to mark Bath's eighteenth-century splendour. It has now become the Holburne of Menstrie Museum, which specialises in displays of calligraphy, ceramics and textiles as well as housing a permanent exhibition of paintings, porcelain and glass. It stands in the Sydney Gardens, where Jane Austen was sent by her Mama to go and look for a husband.

When they were first laid out, these gardens were described

as 'the most spacious and beautiful public gardens in the kingdom'. They remain a delightful oasis, with a free informality which contrasts happily with the regimented municipal flower beds set out on the west banks of the Avon. To appreciate how the latter contrast with Georgian formality, you will need to visit the Georgian gardens laid out near the Circus in 1770. They are open from May to October and set out to a plan located by the Bath Archaeological Society. The flower beds are filled with plants known to have been popular in eighteenth-century town gardens.

The spiritual welfare of the dwellers in the Circus and the other elegant parts of the city was the concern of Selina, Countess of Huntingdon, who was determined that John Wesley's message should reach the rich as well as the poor. A difficult, tense and ego-driven evangelist, with a physical presence which in her portrait by John Russell, reminded Edith Sitwell of 'a fillet of boiled plaice', she managed to retain a following, although Wesley himself succeeded in keeping his distance. Her chapel, opened on 6 October 1765, stands on the west side of the Paragon near the Buildings of Bath Museum and the rooms housing an enchanting national collection of naive art.

The Countess probably had little time for Bath's more astringent critics and satirists of her time. The *Oxford Book of Eighteenth-Century Verse* includes an anonymous poem 'On the Diseases of Bath' which echoes Pepys's earlier reflections:

> If to the Pump Room in the morn we go,
> To drink the waters and remove some woe,
> Idle the project we too late explore;
> To find, to move one plague, we've dared a score.

The most notable, and it seems generally popular, critic of Bath society was a little, crippled milliner, the daughter of a dissenting minister. Despite her disfiguring disability, her intelligence and sharp wit brought her invitations to the country houses of her rich patrons. Moreover, they appear to have enjoyed her verses, even when they did not know that she was the author, for her *Description of Bath*, published anonymously in 1733 when she was forty-six, was still being re-issued after her death and had gone into eight editions by 1767.

Her fellow-writer, Jane Austen, cast several wry glances at Bath society in her novels, but when she lived in the city, between 1801 and 1805, the glory of Bath was starting to fade. The failure of the Bath banks in the 1790s, together with the national recession caused by the Napoleonic wars, put an end to the great building schemes, although the decline was not so severe as the city had experienced in the previous fluctuations of its fortunes. The eleven-year-old Princess Victoria came here in 1830 to open the park, beneath the Royal Crescent, that still carries her name; and shortly afterwards, Dickens made his home here while he wrote *The Pickwick Papers*. These events both indicated a slight upturn in Bath's prosperity more significantly marked by the restoration of the Abbey, begun in 1833; but it was not until the 1890s that the Guildhall was extended. One of the more charming pieces of Victoriana in the city is a figure of Rebecca at the well, put up beneath the north wall of the Abbey in 1861 by the Bath Temperance Society and bearing a message, doubly significant for a spa town: 'Water is Best'.

One Victorian building, the Beckford tower on the heights of Lansdown, is not strictly within our area, but it is worthy of inclusion here, because its belvedere offers quite the finest view of the city as a whole. This tower was built to the design of Henry Edmund Goodridge between 1825 and 1827. It originally housed the art treasures collected by William Beckford of Fonthill in Wiltshire. After his death, his daughter gave the surrounding land for a consecrated graveyard in order that her father might be buried here. So the tower, which is open to the public on weekend afternoons, has something of the feel of a mausoleum.

The twentieth century opened with an optimistic flourish, marked in Bath by the building of the Empire Hotel, set back from the Avon on the corner of the Grand Parade and the Orange Grove. Started in 1901, it was built in three distinct styles, castle, mansion and cottage, representing the different dwellings of Victoria's people.

There were no notable new buildings until after World War II, in which Bath had its full share of destruction by air raids, although it has been argued that the city was more severely damaged architecturally by the planners of the 1950s and 1960s than by the German bombs. Certainly the thrusting, over-conspicuous, green-roofed housing by the London Road to the north-east, and the mercifully out-of-sight, starkly unimaginative university building on the hills to the south support that view. In the 1970s there was even a scheme to rip up Walcot Street, which once housed the Victorian poor and which has long been something of an artists' colony.

Suceeding generations have been more sensitive to historic buildings, but their preservation presents fresh problems. Bath attracts thousands, probably millions, of tourists each year. Whether they conscientiously, book in hand, follow Pevsner's perambulations, listen to the chirpy (and very informative) guides on the tour buses, or simply walk and stare, these worthy people are the cause of an unease, best expressed by Bath's contemporary novelist, Isabel Colegate. In *The Summer of the Royal Visit* (1991), her narrator is of the opinion that 'The threat to our city now is the threat of tourism, which by turning it into a toy deprives it of its dignity'. That is a global modern dilemma. It will take people of the calibre of Ralph Allen and both of the John Woods to solve it for Bath.

XIII
Bristol

At the top of the steeply wooded cliffs that tower above the southern banks of the Avon, as it flows beneath the Clifton Suspension Bridge from Bristol docks to Avonmouth, there are two spectacularly sited Iron Age forts. One, almost destroyed by quarrying, is now bisected by the road that runs up to the bridge. In its prime it must have been of supreme importance. Triple earthen walls and two ditches enclose an area of some seven acres; and from the nature of the rubble, archaeologists have proved that the inner wall had tie-beams running through the stone and that, at some time, the timber was set alight. Perhaps that was done deliberately as a way of strengthening the walls, like those of the vitrified forts of eastern Scotland.

Such speculations can be intriguing, but in order to fully appreciate the hill forts that once guarded the Avon, you should go a little further west and walk through the woods to Stoneleigh camp. This is a two-banked fort, a lesser construction than its neighbour, but impressive enough, especially when you climb up on its high outer wall and look down over the treetops at the river in its steep and muddy bed. Stoneleigh faces another hill fort across the water – Boundary Walls – where people walk their dogs on Clifton Downs.

The river that these three forts once guarded has been the focus of Bristol's history throughout the centuries. Difficult as it is to navigate on account of its phenomenal tides, it has formed the basis of the city's trade from the time the Romans sent their galleys out from Sea Mills, well inland from present day Avonmouth. A Roman pier has been discovered at Sea Mills and we can speculate that it was from here that the legionaries were ferried across the Severn estuary for service in the camps at Caerleon, Caerws and Usk. Other than that, unlike Bath, there are very few records of Roman occupation in Bristol. A villa was excavated on the northern shore of the Avon between Sea Mills and the Bristol Channel in 1947; and at the end of the nineteenth century another was discovered on the western outskirts of Keynsham.

Because a river was so crucial, for so many centuries, to the siting and growth of Bristol, it is not strange that when the Saxons settled here they called their town Bristow, the settlement by the bridge. That name still appears on documents, such as William Smith's plan of the city, until the late sixteenth century. Bristolians are still famous for the way they add an 'l' to the end of any word ending in a vowel sound, and that is how the city acquired the name we now know it by.

The Saxon bridge was located more or less on the same site as the present Bristol Bridge, a stretch of the Avon which was the heart of the city until the early part of the twentieth century, when ships were moored at Broad Quay, a few streets away, to the west. That water has been filled in now and the traffic races towards the shopping centre of Broadmead past a stretch of municipal amenity horticulture. In the time of the Saxons, that bridge over the Avon formed the link between two, often contentious kingdoms: the Mercians and the West Saxons. In various forms the division persisted. Although Bristol was made a county borough with its own shire officials as long ago as 1373, there was always a general assumption that the part that lay on the north bank of the river was a part of Gloucestershire and that on the south bank part of Somerset, so forming the most northerly part of the county.

The heart of the Saxon settlement was on the hill to the north of Bristol Bridge, now flanked to the west by the church of St Nicholas, at the foot of the High Street.

Until recently the church, no longer used for its original purpose, housed a museum of Bristol's history; it now serves as the city's tourist information centre. On the further side of the green hill where Bristol Castle stood are the 'curtain walls' of a largely pedestrianised shopping centre. It is fitting that the heart of commercial Bristol should be here, for it was the Saxons who first established this place by the western river as a trading post. In doing so, they increased its wealth to such an extent, that by the time Domesday Book was compiled, Bristol was rated as rich and important as Norwich, Lincoln and York. Now the only tangible reminder of Saxon Bristol is the relief sculpture of the harrowing of hell in the south transept of the Cathedral.

Until 1542, Bristol Cathedral was the church of the Augustinian abbey founded in 1140. The magnificent Norman arch, which dates from that time, has recently been given its due prominence. Until recently, a road ran alongside the Cathedral making it almost impossible to appreciate the true majesty of the building. The city council must be congratulated on the unusual and admirable feat of actually doing away with that road and all its attendant traffic, and on creating this green space in the city's heartland.

The other Norman legacy to Bristol was the castle, destroyed on Cromwell's orders in 1656 and excavated in the late 1980s. Standing, as we have seen, on the site of the Saxon settlement, it was an important stronghold throughout the Middle Ages. The outline of its history and an explanation of its stones are set out around the excavated site, which retains its dignity despite the Disneyesque battlements which join the Norman and medieval ruins to the Galleries shopping mall.

As Bristol trade flourished during the later Middle Ages, it was always to Somerset's advantage, for the southern side of the Avon provided the easier berthing for the merchant ships. In the early thirteenth century, Henry III, who owned manors in the northern part of the city, determined to right this imbalance by channelling the waters of Bristol's other river, the Frome, which ran into the Avon just below Bristol Bridge. Broad Quay stood by a branch of that diverted river, which now runs underground.

This had the gradual effect of draining the marshes of the Avon valley, although the memory of them was and still is recalled by the names of certain sections of the city, such as Marsh Street across the flower beds from Broad Quay. The original Bristol Quay, now Welsh Back, is a street running behind the warehouses on the north side of the Avon to the west of Bristol Bridge.

It was on the site between Marsh Street and Broad Quay that the new harbour was completed in 1247. It was to last for nearly seven hundred years. At the same time, the new parish of St Stephen was created, although it was nearly two hundred years before work was started on the church. Meanwhile, on the Somerset side of the Avon, the church, which Queen Elizabeth I was to call 'the fairest, goodliest and most famous parish church in England', was nearing completion. Although the present building of St Mary Redcliffe is said to date from 1294, it shows evidence of some much earlier workmanship in the breath-taking magnificence of the north porch.

Throughout the fourteenth century, Bristol continued to build up its fortunes on the wool trade. The cloth-workers' guilds were concentrated on the Somerset side of the Avon, near the lost Temple church, whose name, like that of Temple Meads Station and the north Somerset village of Templecloud, recalls the time when the Knights Templar of the twelfth century were established in Bristol. No doubt but that they drew much of their wealth from the Bristol cloth merchants.

Evidence of the wealth from that trade is apparent in many of the city churches, such as the nave of St Mark's on College Green, a tiny church which has now become the Lord Mayor's chapel. Like most other medieval churches it has largely been swamped by later additions and Victorian restorations. The secular buildings, which give evidence of Bristol's medieval splendour, include the gateway, at the northern end of Broad Street, through which Henry VII was to pass in 1486 and Elizabeth I some eighty years later. It stands by the fourteenth-century church of St John Baptist, whose tower tops that gateway, and which is itself built into a remaining stretch of the town wall. The gate is adorned with the two figures of Brennus and Belinus, the legendary founders of Bristol.

Inside the church there is a monument to Thomas Rowley and his wife. Rowley was a fifteenth-century Bristolian, associated with the building of St Mary Redcliffe, and immortalised two hundred years later by Bristol's boy poet, Thomas Chatterton, who claimed to have found manuscript verses by him. Rowley was a friend of William Canynge, member of a wealthy merchant family, which had settled in Bedminster, on the Somerset side of Bristol, in the mid-fourteenth century. Although his ancestors were clothiers, the fifteenth-century William Canynge was a ship-owner, dealing, of course, in cloth, but also trading as an importer of wine, dried fruit and hides from southern Spain and Portugal.

One of his nine ships, a vessel of five hundred tons, was named *Mary Redcliffe* for the church with which he will always be associated. During his lifetime he had an effigy made of himself. You can see it in the south transept of the church today, beside that of his ancestor, another William Canynge, who is accompanied by his dog, to whom the sculptor has given a big bone. Beside the fifteenth-century William Canynge lies his wife Joan, who died in 1467. In the following year William, who had been five times Mayor of Bristol and twice elected to represent the city at Westminster, was enabled, as a widower, to be ordained priest. A second effigy, this time in alabaster and presumably worked after his death in 1474, is also in St Mary Redcliffe, although it may have been moved there from the church in Westbury-on-Trym, then in the county of Gloucestershire, where the former merchant was dean of a small college.

In the years immediately following William Canynge's death, Bristol's growth in importance as the port associated with the transatlantic explorations flourished. Many voyagers set out from the city in search of the Isle of Brasylle, thought to be the source of a valuable dye, a woad known as Brazilleto, fragments of which had been carried to the west coast of Britain by the gulf stream.

John Cabot, *alias* the Venetian adventurer Giovanni Caboto, is said to have met Bristol merchants in Spain in 1493. Two years later, he came to the city to discuss the funding of transatlantic navigations. In March 1496, Henry VII gave his blessing to an expedition that would head to the west, keeping all the time on the latitude of Bristol, that is well to the north of the West Indies and Central America. In the late spring of 1497, with one unsuccessful voyage behind him, John Cabot, with a crew of eighteen, sailed to Newfoundland. As I write, the final touches are being made to the replica of his ship, the *Matthew*, in which that expedition was made. This second *Matthew* is due to set out on her maiden voyage in May 1996, as the culminating event of an International Festival of the Sea to be held in Bristol's dockland. Victorian Bristolians had their own way of honouring the city's hero, and did it by erecting a tower on the top of Brandon Hill, a place from which you can get the most extensive view of the southern part of the city as it stretches into Somerset. If you want to see how Somerset melts into the southern part of Bristol, then you must go up to Dundry Hill. In 1484, well before John Cabot made his historic voyage, the Merchant Venturers of Bristol erected a church tower there, ninety-seven and a half feet high. It was done essentially to serve as a landmark for sailors.

It was from Dundry quarry, owned by the Bishops of Bath and Wells throughout the Middle Ages, that most of the building stone for Bristol was drawn. The line of communication from that steep southern site to the city was so vital that Bishop Thomas Beckington granted forty days indulgence to anybody who contributed to the repair of the dangerous road linking the two places.

Queen Elizabeth's visit to Bristol in 1574 cost the citizens over £1,000 a very great sum at that time. She stayed in a magnificent house, built four years previously on land owned by Sir John Young and standing on the site of the present Colston Hall. Some ten years after her visit, Sir John built himself two lodges higher up the hill. One of these, Red Lodge, on what is now Lower Park Row, is managed by the city's museum and art gallery and so is open to the public. It is certainly worth visiting, for although the exterior of the building has been considerably altered, the interior remains true to its Tudor origins and is fashioned with elaborate carvings and fluted columns.

The other secular Elizabethan building to seek out in Bristol is St Bartholomew's Hospital to the north of the Colston Hall. It was the site of a row of almshouses in the early thirteenth century which became modified to house Bristol Grammar

School in 1590. Under the name of the Queen Elizabeth Hospital it was modelled in practice and ethos on Christ's Hospital in London. An archway of the original school remains. It leads to a courtyard which still retains four Tudor doorways.

Close by, there is a curiously steep alleyway, fortunately 'stepped' in 1669 and now known as Christmas Steps. That public benefit was bestowed by a wealthy wine merchant, Jonathan Blackwell, who not only reconstructed the narrow passageway but also provided it with street lighting as well as seats where a half-way pause could be made. That he could afford to be so public-spirited is some measure of Bristol's growing prosperity throughout the seventeenth century despite the turmoil of the Civil War.

This is not to suggest that Bristol was unaffected by that war, for indeed the city suffered considerably during the course of it. Although Bristol declared for Parliament in 1642, it was soon overcome by Prince Rupert, who kept a Royal garrison there, and one so large that it had outposts as far to the south as Nunney, near Frome. The moated castle there was captured by the New Model Army for Parliament in August 1645. You can still see where the cannon breached the wall of the four square, moated fortification. At the beginning of August in that same year, Bath surrendered to Parliament, and the Royalist fort at Portishead surrendered before the month was over. This left Bristol in a fearsome state of siege. The city was to capitulate on 11 September to Sir Thomas Fairfax, who had been assisted by some two or three thousand Parliamentary supporters from north Somerset.

Today, a visitor to Bristol can see at least one significant sign of those tumultuous times, as well as the excavated remains of the castle, demolished during the Commonwealth. Around the Cabot tower on Brandon Hill, a landscaped rock garden has been created over the earthworks of a Civil War fort, which includes a nearly-complete gun platform. The whole site, I am told, is one of the best sources for Civil War archaeology in the whole of England.

There are plenty of signs of Bristol's wealth during the

seventeenth century, part of which grew out of the dubious trade with the West Indies, smirched by the terrible horrors of the shipment of slaves. This has also left its mark on the city, in the form of the large houses of the slave traders. The trade was to continue, with some vigour, for nearly two hundred years, and it is a relief to turn from contemplating that source of wealth and consider the start of Bristol's glass industry. Examples of this famous blue glass from the seventeenth century are on display in the museum on Park Street.

Throughout the reign of Charles II, the port of Bristol was heavily engaged in naval shipbuilding. This caused Samuel Pepys to make a visit to the shipyards while he was staying in Bath during the summer of 1668. He noted in his diary for 13 July of that year, that the city's High Cross, which then stood on the Cathedral Green and which has since been removed to Stourhead in Wiltshire, was comparable to the one at Cheapside.

By 1673, King Street, so called in honour of Charles II, was completed. It is still one of the finest streets in the city, standing between what was then the truncated inlet of the Frome and the Avon flowing under Bristol Bridge. If you approach this street from the west you will be confronted by the Merchant Venturers' Almshouses for retired seamen, rebuilt at the end of the seventeenth century. They still serve their original function. You can, however take coffee in a slightly later almshouse, no longer used for its original purpose. The preserved building of 1701 fronts on to Merchant Street and forms an unexpected and welcome contrast to the chain stores of the Broadmead shopping area.

At the other end of King Street from the earlier, pink-washed almshouses, you can drink something a bit stronger at the Llandoger Trow, a pub made up of three timber-framed houses and called for the special sturdy sailing barges that once plied the Bristol Channel between Somerset and South Wales. It is reputed that this inn was the setting which Robert Louis Stevenson chose for the kidnapping of David Balfour by the evil Ebenezer, when he came to write *Kidnapped*. Stevenson actually stayed here while writing *Treasure Island*, and in his walks round the neighbouring area he must have come across 'The Hole in the Wall' on the corner of Redcliffe Way. This inn still retains the spyglass, which once gave the customers early warning of the press gang men. The boast is that Stevenson used the inn as a model for Long John Silver's hostelry, 'The Spyglass'.

At the end of the century, Queen Square, to the south of King Street was being laid out. It was named in honour of Queen Anne, who visited the city in 1702. It had previously been known simply as the square on the marsh. When it was completed, twenty years after 'great Anna's' visit, it must have been a pleasing sight, dominated by the new Customs House on the north side, flanked by uniform three-storey red brick houses and graced by an equestrian statue of King William, which still remains. Many of the original Queen Square houses were to be destroyed in the riots of 1831, indeed, only about a third of them survived that uproar. However, since the abolition of traffic along the road running diagonally across the square, some of the early charm has been restored. Even in its heyday, however, there were serious disadvantages to living in Queen Square. The marshes were never properly drained and the stench from the tidal Avon which swept round it, drove those who could afford to do so to take houses in the fashionable heights of Clifton, whence that river's gorge was simply picturesque.

Both Coleridge and Southey (who was born in Bristol in 1774) knew Queen Square in its early elegance, when they came from their lodgings in College Street to use the library in King Street, still standing by the Merchant Venturers' Almshouses. Indeed, there are many eighteenth-century buildings in King Street, including the Bunch of Grapes public house. The most famous and delightful of all, however, is the Theatre Royal opened in 1766, and so the oldest theatre in the country to have been used continuously for its original purpose. Sarah Siddons, who they say still haunts the theatre, as well as Garrick, Kean, Irving and Ellen Terry, all trod its boards.

It was during the eighteenth century, in which Bristol

overtook Norwich as the second city of England, that the Bristol-born merchant, Edward Colston, who had settled by the Thames at Mortlake, decided to use most of his wealth (accrued through his participation in the slave trade) to benefit his native city. In 1706 he bought Sir John Young's Great House (where Queen Elizabeth had stayed) and turned it into a school for fifty poor boys, appointing the Merchant Venturers to be its governors. Thomas Chatterton was to be a pupil there. He had been born posthumously in November 1752 in Pyle Street by St Mary Redcliffe, where his father had been headmaster of a small charity school. His family had been sextons at the church for generations.

From the time he was twelve, and he was to die before his eighteenth birthday, Chatterton was fascinated by the character of Canynge's friend, Thomas Rowley, and nearly all his work is based on so-called Rowley manuscripts, which the boy must almost have come to believe were genuine. In his own voice, Chatterton published an account of the opening of the refurbished Bristol Bridge for foot passengers in September 1768. Wheeled traffic was not able to go over it for a further two months. The three-arched bridge had to be widened by the middle of the next century, but otherwise the bridge that Chatterton hymned, is as we see it now. The cost of its reconstruction from the medieval original was immense and had to be recouped by toll charges. These tolls were due to cease in 1792, so when they continued into the following year, there were massive riots and demonstrations.

On the evening of 18 September 1793, some ten thousand people assembled on the bridge, forcibly turning out the toll keepers and sawing the toll gates to pieces. When new gates were put up towards the end of the month another mob of several thousand set fire to them.

Despite these disturbances, Bristol was in the process of imitating Bath as a fashionable watering place, and indeed succeeding fairly well. Hotwell, where springs of water from Mendip's underground channels bubbled up through Avon mud, was the site of the Bristol spa. It lies on the north side of the river, below Clifton and to the east of the Suspension

Bridge. The Hotwell season fell between April and October and for several years at the end of the eighteenth century, Bristol habitués would move to Bath for the winter season. There do not seem to be many records of a reverse trend. Hotwell's days of glory have all but vanished now and the place is dominated by the multi-directional road bridge across which traffic swirls on its way to Avonmouth and the M5. Although Bristol's social life could never compete with the elegance of Bath, the Thursday Balls held in the Assembly Rooms, which were to be destroyed by the building of the railway, were conducted with the formal protocol that Beau Nash had laid down for the neighbouring city.

The Bath architect, John Wood the elder, has left a more enduring mark on the city in the form of the Exchange in Corn Street. It is a colonnaded building containing a square, open court and standing well back from the street. In front of it are the four brass 'nails', stumpy pillars on which business transactions were confirmed during the previous centuries: a process which bequeathed the phrase 'to pay on the nail' to our language. The eleven bays of John Wood's Palladian design are a substantial reminder of Bristol's standing as a trading centre that had to be seriously reckoned with.

The native Bristol architects of the eighteenth century were drawn from the Paty family, Thomas (1718–1789), and his sons John and William.

Many of the buildings in Park Street as well as the houses along the roads which run off it, still bear traces of this family's designs. You can look more closely at William Paty's work by visiting number 7 Great George Street as it is now in the care of the Bristol Museum and Art Gallery. This house was originally built between 1788 and 1791 for John Pinney, a sugar merchant who retired from his West Indian plantation in 1783 to found the Bristol firm of Pinney and Tobin.

His house still bears some traces of his occupation, particularly in the form of a cold-water plunge in what was to become the house-keeper's room. William and Dorothy Wordsworth came to stay here in 1795 and we have Dorothy's word for it that her brother was 'very much delighted with the whole family, particularly the father, Mr Pinney'.

John Pinney's third son, Charles, who was born in this house, was to be the unfortunate mayor of Bristol at the time of the riots in 1831 which were set off by the delays in passing the Reform Bill. On 29 October of that year, Sir Charles Wetherell, a noted opponent of Reform, came to Bristol to open the assizes. It was the signal for an outbreak of destructive demonstrations by a populace which had no other way to make its voice heard. In the course of the uproar, the Bishop's Palace was burnt down, but the cathedral was mercifully saved. As we have seen, the main rioting took place in Queen Square with the total destruction of the Customs House.

The Mansion House also suffered. It was set alight and the contents were looted, the rioters getting happily drunk on the contents of the cellar. Some of the furniture was saved by the intervention of Isambard Kingdom Brunel, the great railway engineer and founder of the line from London to the West Country, the G.W.R, popularly known as 'God's Wonderful Railway'. At the time of the riots he was in Clifton, recovering from an accident sustained during work in the Thames Tunnel; but being a strong supporter of law and order and, one suspects, never liking to be far away from the action, he was not slow in getting down to Queen Square. However, it was left to the wretched Charles Pinney, a strong supporter of Reform, to read the Riot Act and call in the troops.

Quite apart from his intervention in Queen Square on that fatal autumn day, Brunel left a most enduring signature on nineteenth-century Bristol. The three prime examples of his work to be seen in the city today are the Suspension Bridge over the Avon Gorge, the original Temple Meads Station and the SS *Great Britain*.

It was as far back as 1753 that a Bristol wine merchant, William Vick, put together the funds to build a bridge across the Avon gorge. Thomas Telford proposed the original design, which Brunel modified. Work had actually started on the Clifton side of the bridge, when the Riots as well as severe financial difficulties, brought the work to a halt. In 1836, two years after Telford's death, the project was taken in hand again. This time a start was made on the Somerset side. It was not long before Vick's coffers were totally empty and it was not until five years after Brunel's own death in 1859, that there was enough money for the bridge to be completed. That was not altogether a matter for rejoicing. There were several protests at the desecration of the majesty of the gorge.

Temple Meads Station seems to have been more universally popular. The original Great Western, or London and Bristol, railway station lies to the north of the Gothic façade of the present station. Built in an imposing Perpendicular style, the original station now houses the National Exhibition of the British Empire and Commonwealth, a use which Brunel would surely delight in. Other minor railways ran out of Bristol. The line to Portishead Docks opened in 1860. It is still in spasmodic use and runs beside the river, just above the high-tide line, along the Somerset side of the Gorge, with the remnants of the Iron Age forts high above it. In 1873, Bristol was connected by rail to the Somerset coal mines. The spectacular vestige of that railway being the dramatic sixteen-arch viaduct high above the village of Pensford. Then, in 1886, the Severn Tunnel was opened and at last Somerset had a direct land link with Wales.

Brunel concerned himself with shipbuilding as well as with railways and bridge building. His first venture, *The Great Western*, was launched in 1837. An even more ambitious project followed that: a ship designed for the transatlantic run. Old sailors say that it is unlucky to change a ship's name, and this one was changed twice. The great vessel was known on the drawing board as the *Mammoth*. That was altered to the more biblical *Leviathan*, and by the time she was ceremoniously floated by Prince Albert in 1843, she had become the *Great Britain*. When she was finally completed two years later, she was the largest vessel in her world. A year later, the bad luck struck and she was grounded off northern Ireland.

The cost of refloating the *Great Britain* bankrupted the company that owned her and she was sold to various owners in the southern hemisphere, being used mainly to take immigrants to Australia and to sail round Cape Horn to California. On one of the latter voyages, a storm drove her to seek refuge in the Falkland Islands, where she lay derelict in Port Stanley, functioning as a warehouse for half a century. Then, in 1970, she was reclaimed, ignominiously loaded on to a pontoon and brought home to Bristol. Restoration work is constantly going on, but much has been completed and visitors are most welcome aboard her in the Great Western dock off Gas Ferry Road.

Among the nineteenth-century buildings in Bristol which are worth visiting for purely twentieth-century purposes, I would make priorities of the Arnolfini gallery at the end of the Narrow Quay and the fish market by St Nicholas' church. The gallery gets its name from Van Eyck's painting of the Arnolfini marriage, a picture much admired by Jeremy Rees, who founded the Bristol gallery in 1961. The Arnolfini was originally built as a tea warehouse in 1830. It is now used for displays of contemporary art, and among its most exciting exhibits of the last decade was the great circle of hand-prints of Avon mud executed by the Bristol-based minimalist, Richard Long, whose work arises out of an immediate contact with earth and rock. That particular example of his work is now displayed in London's Royal Festival Hall.

The fish market was purpose-built in 1874, when its cast-iron gates, topped by a fish motif, were put in place. When it was built, the covered market, which faces it across a narrow passageway, had been in existence for over a century. Originally that market dealt solely in fruit and vegetables, but now it does a flourishing trade in all sorts of merchandise; whereas the fish market remains loyal to its original function.

From 1867 to 1871, work was going on to provide the city with a worthy building for its museum and library. A little higher up Park Street from the present Museum and Art Gallery, the building that housed its Victorian predecessor was to serve as the University student refectory until the 1990s. It is a most impressive structure, modelled on the Doges' Palace in Venice and boasting a great portico supported by eight massive pillars.

The University of Bristol grew out of the incorporation of the Bristol Medical School into the College of Science and Literature in 1876. It was not, however, until 1925 that the 215-foot high Gothic tower, the most inescapable mark of the University building, was completed. It was financed by the Wills family, which owned the tobacco firm that for decades was one of the city's greatest employers. It was backing from Wills that enabled the University College of Bristol to obtain full university status in 1909. It was to number Sir Winston Churchill among its chancellors.

At the beginning of World War II, Bristol was thought to be a safe zone for the reception of evacuees, among whom were the staff of the B.B.C. headquarters. This all changed during 1940, when the city was attacked by German bombers from north-west France. Like many other badly bombed cities, Bristol was faced with the immediate post-war necessity of rebuilding large areas of the city centre, and, like many another, she sadly misused that opportunity. On the more positive side, however, the city did excellent work in rehousing people who, during the 1930s, had been living in appalling slum conditions. The city fathers of the 1950s should also take pride in the new Council House, curving round the west end of the Cathedral green. It was officially opened by the Queen in 1956. To my mind, it forms a pleasing if not particularly architecturally significant backdrop to the medieval, Georgian and modern buildings around it.

Now that Avon is to disappear as an administrative county, Bristol will fully regain its proud and ancient borough status and its less clearly defined links with Gloucestershire to the north and Somerset to the south. In this brief look at the marks of time on this truly multi-faceted city, I have concentrated almost entirely on the Somerset side, while being aware that Bristol is an organic whole and that no clear-cut divisions can properly be made.

I would, however, like to conclude where I began, on the Somerset side of the Avon gorge, and visit Bristol's largest pleasure park. It lies around the seventeenth-century Ashton Court, whose impressive south front has been attributed to

Inigo Jones. The court was owned by the Smyths, a family of Bristol merchants from 1545 until the latter part of the twentieth century. It now hosts a great range of activities, catering for the cultural and sporting life of Bristolians and their Somerset neighbours. It is from this parkland that the intrepid, with some pounds to spare, can take a balloon ride and look down over the basket's side at both Bristol and the hills and moors of Somerset.

Bibliography

Chapter I

Alcock, L. *By South Cadbury, is that Camelot: Excavations at Cadbury Castle 1966–1970* (Thames & Hudson) 1972

Bulleid, Arthur *The Lake Villages of Somerset* Sixth edition (Glastonbury Antiquarian Society) 1968

Coles, J.M. and Orme, B.J. *Prehistory of the Somerset Levels* (Somerset Levels Project) 1980

Eardley-Wilmot, Hazel *Ancient Exmoor* (Exmoor Press) 1983

Grinsell, L.V. *The Archaeology of Exmoor* (David and Charles) 1970 *Stanton Drew Stone Circles; Somerset* (Department of the Environment) 1976

Chapter II

Brampton, Keith and Fowler P.J. (eds) *The Roman West Country* (David & Charles) 1976

Leach, Peter and Dunning, Robert *Ilchester* (Somerset County Council) 1990

Leach, Peter *Shepton Mallet: Romano-Britons and early Christians in Somerset* (Birmingham University Field Archaeology Unit) 1991

Margary Ivan D. *Roman Roads in Britain* Revised edition (John Baker) 1967

Chapter III

Dunning, R.W. *Arthur: The King in the West* (Alan Sutton) 1988

Pearce, Susan M. *The Kingdom of Dumnonia* (Lodenek Press, Padstow) 1978

Porter, H.M. *The Celtic Church in Somerset* (Morgan Books, Bath) 1971

Chapter IV

Anglo-Saxon Chronicle Translated by G.N. Garmonsway (Dent, Everyman) 1972

Blair, Peter Hunter *An Introduction to Anglo-Saxon England* Second edition (Cambridge University Press) 1977

Costen, Michael *The Origins of Somerset* (Manchester University Press) 1992

Darby, H.C. *Domesday England* (Cambridge University Press) 1977

Pearce, Susan M. *The Kingdom of Dumnonia* (Lodenek Press, Padstow) 1978

Porter, H.M. *The Saxon Conquest of Somerset* (James Brodie) 1967

Robinson, J. Armitage *The Saxon Bishops of Wells* British Academy Supplement Paper IV 1918

Stenton, Sir Frank *Anglo-Saxon England* (Oxford University Press) 1971

Chapter V

Aston Michael (ed) *The Medieval Landscape of Somerset* (Somerset County Council) 1988

Dunning, Robert *Somerset in Domesday* (Somerset County Council) 1986

Williams, Robin and Romey *The Somerset Levels* (Ex Libris Press) 1992

Ziegler, Philip *The Black Death* (Collins) 1969

Chapter VI

Moss, Arthur *Moss on Somerset* (Cannington Press) 1991

Chapter VII

Wigfield, W. McD. *The Monmouth Rebels* (Alan Sutton) 1985

Wroughton, John *A Community at War: The Civil War in Bath and North Somerset, 1642–50* (Lansdown Press) 1992

Wyndham, Violet *The Protestant Duke* (Weidenfeld & Nicolson) 1976

Chapter VIII

Beresford, John (ed) *Diary of a Country Parson* 1924

Hobhouse, Edmund M.D. (ed) *Diary of a West Country Physician A.D. 1684–1726* (Simpkin Marshall) 1934

Mitchell, Brigitte and Penrose, Hubert (eds) *Letters from Bath 1766–1767. Reverend John Penrose* (Alan Sutton) 1983

Chapter X

Derrick, Freda *Country Craftsmen* (Abbey Barn, Glastonbury)

Fraser, Maxwell *Companion into Somerset* (Methuen) 1947

Thomas, Edward *In Pursuit of Spring* (Thomas Nelson) 1914

Wade G.W. and Wade J.H. *Rambles in Somerset* (Methuen) 1912

Wyatt Phyllis *A Somerset Childhood* (Dovecote Press, Dorset) 1989

Young, Kathleen *The Green Velvet Dress* (Tallis Press) 1989

Chapter XI

There are no current books dealing purely with the problems facing the Somerset landscape, although there are many articles in various journals. So I would suggest that anyone interested in pursuing any of these matters further should write to: The Somerset Trust for Nature Conservation, Fyne Court, Broomfield, Bridgwater, Somerset TA5 2EQ for a list of recent publications and papers.

Chapter XII

Haddon, John *Portrait of Bath* (Robert Hale) 1982
Mitchell, Brigitte and Penrose, Hubert (eds) *Letters from Bath 1766–1767. Reverend John Penrose* (Alan Sutton) 1983
Hardy, Paul and Lowndes, William *Bath: Profile of a City* (Redcliffe, Bath) 1984
Pound, Christopher *The City and its Landscape* (Millstream Books, 7 Orange Grove, Bath) 1986
Sitwell, Edith *Bath* (Faber & Faber) 1932

Chapter XIII

Ison, Walter *The Georgian Buildings of Bristol* (Kingsmead Press) 1978
Among the many excellent books on Bristol, published by the Redcliffe Press Ltd., 49 Park Street, Bristol BS1 5NT, I would particularly recommend:
Belsey, James & Harrison, David *Images of Bristol 1850–1910*
Bettey, J.H. *Bristol Observed*
Buchanan and Williams *Brunel's Bristol*
Crick, Clare *Victorian Buildings in Bristol*
Little, Bryan *John Cabot*
Little, Bryan *The Story of Bristol*

The author and publisher would like to thank Elma Mitchell and U. A. Fanthorpe, and their publisher, Peterloo Poets, for permission to quote from their work.

Index

Abbots Way 25
Aethelard 59, 174
Alabaster mines 105
Alderman's Barrow 14
Aldhelm, St 57, 58
Alfoxton 127
Alfred 51, 60, 62–64, 66, 69
Alfred's Tower 117
Allen, Ralph 119, 178–180, 184
Aller 60, 61
Ammerdown 118, 122
Arthur *x*, 2, 21, 22, 47–50, 53–55, 144
Ashton Court 199
Ashwick 113, 122, 123
Athelney 60, 63, 64, 86, 91, 146
Athill, Robert 154
Aubrey, John 12
Austen, Jane 180, 181, 183
Avon, River 3, 171, 185
Axe, River 3, 32, 42, 43, 87, 155

Babcary 116
Babington 115
Balch, H. E. 155
Baltonsborough 63
Banwell 31, 142
Barle, River 20
Barlynch 78
Barrington Court 96, 108, 152
Basket making 146
Batcombe 92
Bath *xi*, 30, 35, 36, 38, 39, 43, 55, 68, 94,
    113, 119, 124, 128, 171ff.
Beacon Hill 33, 34
Beckford Tower 183
Beckington 107
Berrow 100
Billingsley, John 119, 122–124, 162
Binegar 90, 95, 147, 148
Bishop's Lydiard 93, 116
Black Death 83–85, 89
Blackdown 30, 43, 156
Blackdown Hills 1, 66, 110, 165, 167
Blackmore, R. D. 78, 143
Blagdon 154
Blake, Robert Admiral *xii*, 104, 105
Bleadon 132
Bleadney 9, 87
Bondfield, Margaret 152

Bossington 167
Bradford-on-Tone 78, 81, 82
Brean Down *xi*, 44, 89, 128, 132, 156
Brendon Hills *ix*, 4, 14, 62, 133, 144
Brent Knoll 18, 93
Bridgwater *ix*, *xii*, 91, 94, 98, 102, 109, 125, 127
Brigid, St 49
Bristol *xiii*, 49, 84, 104, 105, 107, 112, 119,
    139, 185ff.
Brockley 161, 162
Brompton, Ralph 90
Brue, River 2, 74, 84, 162, 163
Brunel, Isambard Kingdom 132, 140, 196,
    197
Buckland St Mary 56
Bulleid, Arthur 22, 23, 26, 159
Burnham 153, 169
Burrington Combe 43
Burrow Mump 146
Bury Castle 19

Cabot, John 189, 190
Camerton 31, 33
Canals 124, 130, 131, 169
Cannards Grave 34
Cannington 60, 95, 102
Canynge, William 189
Caractacus Stone 47, 48
Carantoc, St 50
Carhampton 50
Castle Cary 104, 116, 126
Catcott 100
Catsgore 40
Chancellor's Farm 167
Chantry 134, 154
Chard 55, 85, 103, 129, 136, 139
Chardstock 74, 75, 85
Charterhouse 29–33, 135, 152
Chatterton, Thomas 194
Cheddar 47, 64, 66, 73, 74, 120, 124, 169
Cheddar Gorge 43, 64, 125, 167
Cheddar Woods 166, 167
Chedzoy 106
Cheese 124, 138
Chew Magna 81
Chew, River 3, 75
Chew Valley Lake 154
Chewton Mendip 3, 67, 90, 92, 103, 118
Cider 125

Civil War 103–106, 109
Clatworthy Castle 19
Cleeve Abbey *xi*, *xii*, 50, 76, 77, 94, 96
Clevedon 16, 127, 144
Clifton 185
Cloth Trade 90, 99, 105, 120, 135, 174, 188
Coal Mines 4, 39, 112, 113, 118, 119, 132, 133, 148–152, 165, 173, 197
Coleford 112, 113
Colegate, Isabel 184
Coleridge, Samuel Taylor *xii*, *xiii*, 19, 50, 111, 126–128, 193
Collinson, John 70, 114, 115, 117–120, 124, 125
Colston, Edward 194
Colt Hoare, Sir Richard 31
Combe Down 119, 171, 179, 181
Combe Florey 143
Combe St Nicholas 65
Combe Sydenham *xii*, 96, 117
Combwich *xii*, 27, 35, 59, 60, 98, 100
Compton Dando 39, 43
Compton Martin 79
Congar, St 51
Congresbury 16, 17, 51, 54
Cook, Arthur J. 150
Cothelstone 159
Cow Castle 20, 21
Crewkerne 68, 95
Croscombe 90, 100
Crowcombe 93
Culbone *xiii*, 14, 46, 47, 127
Curry Rivel 101, 125

Dairy Farming 124, 138
Dead Woman's ditch 19, 20
Decuman, St 50
Derrick Freda 155, 156
de Villula, Bishop, John 174, 179
Dickens, Charles 143, 183
Dissolution 94, 176
Dodington 73
Dolebury 17, 31, 65
Domesday Book 67, 68, 71–73, 157
Doulting 58
Downside Abbey 142
Dowsborough Camp 18, 20
Drainage 86–88, 100, 121, 122, 137, 138, 147, 162, 187, 193
Dundry 190
Dunkerton 149
Dunkery Beacon 10
Dunstan, St 63–65, 67, 174
Dunster 20, 50
Dursden Drove 88

Eardley-Wilmot, Hazel 13, 62
East Coker *xiii*, 41, 113, 157, 158
East Quantoxhead 91, 102
Ebbor Gorge 7, 88, 118, 123
Edithmead 154, 155
Eliot, T. S. *xiii*, 157, 158

Elworthy barrows 19
Emborough 118, 124, 148
Enclosures 89–91, 100, 122, 123
Evercreech 74, 93, 148
Exe Head 41, 138
Exe, River 3
Exmoor *ix*, *xi* 1, 2, 4, 11, 13, 14, 20, 46, 47, 73, 74, 88, 99, 109, 135, 138, 141, 168, 169

Fanthorpe, U. A. 175, 177
Farleigh Hungerford 76, 103, 104
Farringdon Gurney 119
Fielding, Henry 126
Fiennes, Celia 176
Fives 115, 116
Flax 163
Forches Corner 56, 57
Fosse Way 4, 33–38, 40, 44
Fox, George 110
Fraser, Maxwell 155
Frome 109, 113, 151
Fyne Court 143, 167

Gerard, Thomas 52, 58, 73, 74, 79, 97, 99, 100, 105
Gildas 52–54
Giso, Bishop 67
Glastonbury *x*, 22, 23, 48, 49, 53, 54, 56, 57, 62, 64, 65, 67, 72, 74, 82, 83, 86, 91, 92, 94, 121–123, 159, 166, 170

Ham Hill 4, 15, 110
Harold (Godwinson) 69, 70
Haselbury Plucknett, 79, 138
Hatch Beauchamp 95
Hautville's Quoit 11, 81
Hawkridge 73
Hestercombe 152
High Ham 64, 93
Hillfarence 78
Hinckley Point 60, 164, 168
Hinton Charterhouse 77, 90, 94, 157
Hinton St George 110
Holcombe 65, 89, 159
Holnicote 167
Hone, Dom Ethelbert 159
Hornblotton 141
Horner 168
Hugh, St 77, 78
Huntingdon, Countess of 113, 182

Ilchester 35–38, 40, 45, 85, 86, 94, 108, 110
Ilminster 65, 129
Indract, St 49, 50
Ine *x*, 49, 56–59, 63
Iron-works 133, 134

Jefferies, Richard 144
Jeffreys, Judge *xii*, 98, 107, 108
Jekyll, Gertrude 152
Jocelyn, Bishop 83, 85

John, King 74, 83

Keyne, St 52
Keynsham 52, 186
Kidder, Bishop 121
Kilmersdon 80, 115, 118, 141, 161
Kilve 158
King, Alice 143, 144
King, Bishop Oliver *xi*, 94, 175
Knight Frederic 138, 139

Lace 136, 152
Lake villages 22, 23
Lamyatt Beacon 44, 45
Langfield Heath 166
Langford Budville 101
Langport 66, 88, 92, 104
Lansdown 171, 176
Larkbarrow 139
Lawrence, Berta 146
Lead mining 28–31, 33, 51, 77, 90, 105,
  118, 134, 135, 148, 152, 171
Leland, John 50, 92, 110
Livestock, 95, 123, 139, 162
Locke, John 108
Long Ashton 114
Long, Richard 198
Low Ham 40, 41
Luccombe 72, 104, 105
Lullington 80
Lutyens, Edward 152
Lytes Cary 97, 98, 117

Maes Knoll 81
Measbury 24, 33
Marston Bigot 117
Martock *ix*, 115, 116, 120
Meare 87
Mells *ix*, 9, 10, 103, 117, 133, 134, 142,
  153, 158
Mendip Hills *ix*, 2–4, 7, 8, 11, 28–30, 42,
  64, 66, 73, 74, 110, 112, 125, 165, 172
Middlezoy 8
Midsomer Norton 113, 119
Milborne Port 68
Minehead 99, 145, 154
Milverton 67, 72, 93
Mitchell, Elma 27
Mole's Chamber 27
Moorlynch 78, 107
Montacute *xi*, 16, 70, 71, 75, 79, 86, 94, 96,
  97, 136, 139
Monmouth, Duke of *xii*, 98, 106, 108–110
Morris, Claver 123, 124, 126
Muchelney, Abbey 65, 67, 71, 77, 86, 94,
  100, 156

Nash, Richard 177, 178
Neroche, Forest of 73–75, 141, 166
Nether Stowey *xii*, 91, 98, 127, 128
Nettlecombe 62, 80, 81
Newbolt, Henry 158

Ninehead 130
North Petherton *ix*, 62, 73, 74, 91, 113
Norton Fitzwarren 21
Norton St Philip 95, 108, 157
Nunney 134, 191

Oakhill 112
Oare 78, 143
Oath 62
Old Cleeve 140
Orchard Portman 140
Orchardleigh 142, 158
Othery 62
Otterford 82
Outmoor 91
Over Stowey 142

Pagan Hill 44
Paper making 106, 119
Parret, River 2, 87, 100, 132
Peasedown St John 66
Peat 147, 166
Pen Hill 156
Penn, William 111
Penselwood, 55, 117
Pensford, 112, 169
Pepys, Samuel 176, 192
Petroc, St 50
Phelips, Edward 96, 97
Pilton 74
Pinkworthy 138
Pinney, Charles 196
Pitminster *xi*, 59, 94, 95
Pitney 40
Polden Hills *ix*, 106, 107
Pope, Alexander *xiii*, 125, 179
Porlock 6, 13, 46, 47, 61, 69, 70, 86, 95
Poundisford *xi*, 96, 142
Priston 67, 72

Quakers 110
Quarries 4, 9, 16, 42, 119, 134, 147, 148,
  164, 165, 190
Quantocks 73, 126, 167, 168

Rabbits 89
Rackley 87
Radstock 119, 132, 149–151
Railways 131, 169
Raleigh's Cross 133
Ralph of Shrewsbury, Bishop 83, 85
Ramspits 88
Richmont Castle 75
Rodney Stoke 93, 100, 153, 167
Rowberrow 65, 118, 135
Rowley, Thomas 188, 194
Royal Crescent 180

Sampford Arundel 72, 78
Sea Mills 29, 185, 186
Sedgemoor 100, 106, 107, 122
Selwood Forest 73, 74

Selwood, Abbot John 92
Selworthy 70
Setta Barrow 27
Sham Castle 179
Shapwick 106
Sharp, Cecil J. 159, 160
Sharpham Park 126
Sheep 123, 124, 139
Shepton Mallet ix, 35–37, 44–46, 103, 109, 121, 126, 157, 169
Shipham 31, 68, 135
Silk 135, 136
Simonsbath 20, 109, 139
Skinner, John Revd 8, 10, 134
Somerton 59, 74, 118
South Cadbury x, 21, 22, 38, 54, 68
South Petherton 68, 82, 95, 116
Southey, Robert xiii, 193
Stanton Drew xi, 11, 12
Staple Fitzpaine 141
Star 31
Steep Holm 52, 53, 61, 70, 105, 128
Stert Point 168, 169
Stevenson, Robert Louis 192, 193
Stogumber 80
Stoke Bottom 119
Stoke Pero 141
Stoke St Gregory 146
Stoke sub Hamdon 116
Ston Easton 118
Stoneleigh Camp 185
Stoney Littleton 8–10
Storgursey 59, 79, 80
Street 53, 140
Sweet Track 24–26

Taunton ix, xi, 58, 78, 91, 92, 94, 96, 99, 102–104, 107–111, 114, 115, 120, 127
Tennyson, Alfred 144
Thomas, Edward 158, 159
Timberscombe 50
Timsbury 119
Tolland 109
Tom's Hill 139
Tone, River 87
Tongue, Ruth 160
Toplady, Augustus Revd 113
Treborough 14, 134
Triscombe 103
Trudoxhill 111
Turner, William Dean 97

Turnpike Trusts 129, 130

Uphill 29, 31, 32, 44, 49

Walton-in-Gordano 114
Warren Farm 89, 168, 169
Watchet 50, 61, 62, 68, 70, 99, 106, 119, 126
Wedmore 61, 66, 68, 87
Wellington 120, 153
Wells ix–xi, 50, 57, 63, 67, 82, 83, 85, 91, 94, 97, 103, 105, 107–109, 116, 121, 122, 129, 130, 138, 159, 166, 170
Wells, H. G. 158
Wemberham 42
Wesley, John 111–113, 119
West Camel 65
Westbury-sub-Mendip xi, 7, 74, 89
Westhay 23, 26, 88, 147
Weston-super-Mare xi, 145
Westonzoyland xii, 106–108, 122, 137
Whatley, 41, 154, 165
Whiting, Abbot 94
Whitelackington 107, 108
Whitestaunton 66
Wick Barrow 59
Williton 61, 115
Willows 146
Wimblestone 32
Wincanton xii, 102, 103
Winsford 78, 88, 148
Witham 77, 78, 84
Wiveliscombe 85
Wood, John ix, 180, 195
Wood, John, the Younger 180, 181
Woodforde, Parson 116, 120, 125, 126
Woodspring 94
Wookey Hole xiii, 3, 7, 29, 42, 66, 125, 155
Woolavington 123
Wordsworth, Dorothy xiii, 127, 195
Wordsworth, William xiii, 126, 128, 195
Worlebury 17
Wrington 116
Writhlington 149, 152
Wulfric, St 79
Wyatt, Phyllis 154

Yeovil 85, 86, 99, 108, 120, 137
Young, Kathleen 11, 156, 157
Young, Thomas 128